Starr —
HE makes [?] [?]
things New // Yves.
All y[?] All

Eph. 3:16-20

Michelle [?] Mead

THE SKY IS *Always* BLUE

The Story Behind "Remember ME"® Jewelry

MICHELLE MEADE

Hayward, WI 54843

Hayward, WI 54843

The Sky Is Always Blue
by Michelle Meade

Printed in the United States of America.

International Standard Book Number 978-0-9801128-0-1

Cover illustration by Michele Colaner

Layout and design by Ambassador Productions, Gainesville, FL

Poetry copyright 2007 by Michelle Meade

Contents

MY PRECIOUS FAMILY

Left to right: *Kaylin, Gabriel, Paul, Michelle, Elianna, Joshua and Isabella.*

Dedication

I DEDICATE THIS BOOK to my precious family. Paul, I thank God for you; your heart has chosen to stay all these eighteen and a half years in spite of me. You'll always be my blue-eyed boy and "my sweetest thing."

To my beloved children, Joshua, Kaylin, Elianna, Isabella, and Gabriel. You are the soul delight of my mother's heart. You have already imparted into me more treasure than I could reciprocate in many lifetimes. I am an exceedingly rich woman to be rewarded with such an undeserved legacy. Thank you for your unconditional love, and for putting up with all my "computer-hogging" these past two years.

When I grow up I want to be just like the five of you.

Remain in His Love.

With all my heart,
Mom

THE SZYMANSKI FAMILY

Upper Row, Left to Right: *Chris, Paul, Michelle, Matthew, Stan, and Joe.* Seated, Left to Right: *Mike, Ria, Mom, Dad, and Gigi.*

Acknowledgments

WITH THE FULLNESS OF MY HEART, I thank my amazing parents and siblings for your love and support.

I thank God for every one of my friends who has loved and encouraged me faithfully throughout my journey. You are precious to me.

Maria, your loving determination to make a home in my heart has changed my life forever—I'm eternally grateful for your friendship.

Michele, my sweet friend, can I ever adequately thank you for the painting that graces the cover of this book? Every time I look at that window of hope, my heart lurches towards His; *the sky IS always blue.*

Above all,
Of course, I *Remember You* …
You are my Love … my Everything …
I am nothing without You.

With *all* my heart,
Your girl

Introduction

TO THE CASUAL OBSERVER, I appear to be a thirty-something wife, mother of five, daughter, sister, and friend. I *am* all those things, but perhaps most telling of all, I'm an *"Overcomer."* To really know who I am and what you'll discover in my story, pause for a moment, find a mirror, and peer deeply into your own eyes. There you'll find me.

The color of our skin may differ, our cultures may be worlds apart, and we may disagree on political issues and even have opposing religious beliefs. Beyond every barrier that appears to separate us, we share a common strand that ties our hearts together and is reflected in your eyes. *You and I both have pain.*

I know not a soul who rejoices in suffering, but the truth be told, it's woven into the very fabric of who we are. Character, faith, values, strength, and endurance are all created on the loom of life, and oh how it hurts to have our threads twisted and spun. Oftentimes we have no sense of the design until the project is completed, so we must learn to trust the One who already knows what the final product will be, and allow Him to apply the proper pressure to push us through His skillful hands.

My journey of Trust has been arduous and frankly not so "pretty" to tell. My deeply troubled soul lay awake countless nights, pleading with my mind to cooperate with my heart. I fought through gruesome bloody wars in the confines of my unquiet mind. At the height of these sufferings, the horror became intolerable and I was overwhelmed by insanity. However, it was here—right in the middle of the madness—that His Love penetrated the blackness, breaking forth the dawn of new life within. Perpetually stumbling, I landed safely in His arms and fell deeply in love. Our love relationship was not developed in a church or on a holy mountaintop, but in the wreckage of my tattered soul.

My story of divine rescue is compelling evidence that God is real. The collisions of my humanity with His divinity, my weakness with His strength, my inability with His provision, and my despair with His eternal hope formed the foundation for "Remember ME"® Jewelry, Inc. He said to bind my testimony around my neck, that I might always "Remember" His Love and Faithfulness as it is uniquely expressed through Symbols and Poetry. These treasures from Heaven were lifelines scribbled onto scrap pieces of tear-stained paper in the middle of the night, providing the nourishment I needed for that moment. These were not merely doctrinal truths, but living Hope tattooed on my soul by the finger of God.

I would not trade these past fifteen years of suffering for all the world's treasure, for in this place I have come to *know* by personal experience the boundless expanse of God's extravagant Love ... not merely acquiring intellectual knowledge about God, but *knowing* Him in all the special, intimate ways one *knows* a cherished friend. True freedom is found *in the knowing*. It's the reason that I wrote this book.

May every shackle be loosed, every bondage obliterated, and every fear be suffocated by the *knowledge of His unfathomable Love.*

It's All in the Knowing

VOWS ARE EXCHANGED, TRUE LOVE IS FOUND
BUT THE SEED OF THIS LOVE LAY ATOP OF THE GROUND
THE TILLING, THE SOFTENING, THE BREAKING MUST BE
FOR THE LIFE OF THE LOVE IS FOUND IN THE SEED
ENDURING THE SEASONS OF STORMS IN THE NIGHT
NEW MERCIES AWAKEN THE DAWN WITH HIS LIGHT
KINDLING THE FLAMES, PRESERVING THE CORE
THIS SEED HAS A CHANCE TO BECOME SO MUCH MORE

BUT THE SOIL OF THE HEART NEEDS LOOSENING STILL
REMOVING THE ROCKS, RELEASING THE WILL
PREPARING THE GROUND TO FULLY RECEIVE
THE FULLNESS OF LOVE THAT DIES WITH THE SEED
HIDDEN IN DARKNESS, A CHANGE TAKING PLACE
NOURISHED WITH PATIENCE, FORGIVENESS, AND GRACE
NOW A LOVE THAT IS ROOTED, GROUNDED, AND SURE
REGARDS WITH AFFECTION THE COST TO ENDURE

THE WILDERNESS DROUGHTS, THROUGH THE WINDS AND THE RAINS
THE PLANTING PRESERVED, AND THE BEAUTY REMAINS
THIS VINE AND BRANCH, NOW SO INTERTWINED
ONE EXULTING THE OTHER, BY HIS DESIGN
WHERE CAN THE SECRET TO THIS LOVE BE FOUND?
JUST LOOK AT THE ROOTS FROM THE SEEDS IN THE GROUND
DEEPER AND DEEPER, THESE ROOTS KEEP ON GROWING
LIVING IN LOVE—"IS ALL IN THE KNOWING"

ALL MY LOVE,
M. MEADE

CHAPTER 1

"Lover"

you think this and that
will mask the pain
you search to be made whole
but nothing else will fill the void
'cept the Lover of your soul

"O my Love, you have stolen my heart ..."

JUST SAY THE WORD "PAIN" and most of us automatically rush to the cabinet for a bottle of relief. We have become people who will do anything to avoid it, use anything to numb it, and blame everyone else for its cause, rather than look within.

As long as I can remember, I have run from pain. Literally and figuratively I have picked up my feet, my thoughts, and my hopes, and have traveled as far and fast from the source of any suffering as I could run. It never occurred to me that avoidance was not a helpful solution. Often, I ran around the same "mountain" for years.

I know what you're thinking: I'm a perfect candidate for Dr. Phil. Read a few chapters more and you'll see how right you are.

Where to begin? I have no recollections of my childhood prior to fifth grade. I only know what my parents and older siblings repeat as we look through old photos and reminisce. My favorite baby photo is of my smiling mother holding me closely to her cheek ... in fact, so closely that you can't really tell just how chunky I was. Unfortunately, the next picture reveals me in all of my rolls of glory; it's still up for debate whether I was hiding a basketball inside my jumper or if that really was the massive bulge of flesh it appeared to be. I obviously had issues with food from the womb.

The next photos reveal a happy-faced toddler, clutching a ragged, black velvet, stuffed cat. I am told that the cat was permanently stuck to my body like an additional appendage. I was a cutie with dimples, large brown eyes, and tousled waves of long brown hair. Oh, I *was* cute. But just look at my mullet in the next picture! This butchery was so atrocious that my mother should have been jailed for misuse of scissors. When gazing at this fiasco, all you can do is feel sorry for both mother and child.

My mom assured me, "Everybody loved you, Michelle. Absolutely everybody. You were adored, kissed, and doted on by everyone. You were so very loved."

I don't doubt it; I just wish I could remember some of it, any of it.

My father is an imposing figure standing six feet two. To this day, he is a no-nonsense kind of cowboy, explaining in no uncertain terms exactly what he thinks. Every man, woman, child, and dog runs for cover when he raises his voice. But this tough fella has always had a soft spot for his bambinos, especially his three girls. In difficult moments in my adult life, my dad would motion for me to come over and would ask me, "You need some lovin'?" I would nod yes and fall into his large lap as he gave me his classic daddy squeeze, complete with sound effects for good measure and humor. These father-daughter moments of comfort were re-enactments of a childhood experience that he described to me on numerous occasions.

Every time the story is retold, it is still as savory and sweet as the first bite of dessert.

And then there are the memories I do recall. We moved when I was just about to enter fifth grade from the house of my birth in Canton, Ohio to Deerfield, Ohio. We lived there exactly one year, which was sufficient punishment for all (except for my sister Maria who fell in love with her future husband, which was the only redeeming aspect of that move).

Mom holding me.

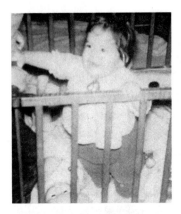

Clockwise from upper left: *Me as an infant Sumo wrestler. The happy toddler with her sister Maria and beloved black cat. Me with a mullet.*

I keenly recall my brother Matt chasing, maiming, and then killing a huge rat in ninja fashion with my mother's broom. We were not allowed to flush the toilets until the end of the day with a bucket of rainwater. This sent my niece Heidi into potty-training regression when she visited "grandma's house," because she was deathly afraid. Who wouldn't be? I was ten years old; yet I still winced at the dark, rusty, brown, polluted water mixed with waste.

My ten-year-old life consisted of spying on my teenage sister and her boyfriend Steve in order to gather juicy information to tattle. It was more than romantic curiosity; I took great pleasure and satisfaction in sneaking up and getting her into trouble. What bothered me most was her happiness. No one should have been allowed to be happy there.

Besides the toilet situation and occasional rats, we had other problems associated with poverty. More times than my mom cares to recall, she had no idea what she'd answer to the daily barrage of the repeated question, "What's for dinner?" Both parents have properly reminded us, "You never went to bed hungry. The Lord always provided. Someway, somehow, but *always*."

True, but unfortunately He didn't provide regular sandwich bread for our school lunches. This proved to be upsetting for my older brother, who would conceal his peanut butter and honey hot dog buns. It was too embarrassing to stomach. He wasn't the only one who suffered the judgment of new classmates who had grown up together, knew each other well, scorned the "new kids," and enjoyed the affluence of regular sandwich bread. I felt friendless, which made school a nightmare for me, too. To everyone's delight (except for Maria, of course), we moved back to Canton for the following school year into our old, familiar, comforting, "normal" house.

I remember very little except that I was generally pretty miserable. I can't imagine what could have been so upsetting for an eleven-year-old whose toughest job was to be home before the streetlights came on after a full day of play with neighborhood kids. I was just so sad. I have no idea why I was inclined toward melancholy when I should have been happily watching Scooby-Doo.

My mom wore out the knees of her slacks, praying for me during my turbulent teenage years. I was a sassy, know-it-all teenager with troublesome depression and mood swings. I got drunk, but not frequently because I was mindful to make sure that my list of "goods" outweighed my list of "bads." I was an honor roll student and a good athlete. I usually avoided rowdy parties, managed to stay out of major trouble with boys, and generally chose to do "right" things. Well, except for a couple occasions, like the time I convinced my friend Kellie to take her parents' car and joyride around Canton when we were only fourteen. Fortunately, no one was hurt. However, the trust our parents once had in our ability to make intelligent, responsible decisions was as demolished as the crashed stone facing of Kellie's house.

I also encouraged another friend to steal her mother's work key, so a band of us could sneak into a huge indoor public pool facility at night and skinny dip. As our mixed group recklessly flaunted bare bodies around the pool, we all lost a bit of innocence that night. But again, I felt that we were being good by not "crossing the line" and engaging in any physical acts. Those poor pubescent boys were no doubt tortured by the parade of lovely teenage curves as they passed by with the warning to look, but not touch. You never saw a more ridiculous sight as half-dressed kids scrambled and dodged through bleachers to escape the pursuing security guard. Amazingly, we managed to elude him and found safety back at my friend's house. With the rush of victory, we high-fived one another in a teenage-rebellion mission accomplished.

In spite of those few lapses in judgment, I thought I was a pretty good kid. Of course, I compared myself to those who got drunk repeatedly, smoked pot, or slept around (or to those who indulged in all three, which was not uncommon). However, despite good grades, good behavior, and the appearance of having it all together, there was nothing I could do to feel good about my life and myself.

I was told frequently that I was attractive; I was strong and lean from sports and exercise. Yet somewhere between my mind and the mirror, there was a profound disconnection, an awful misinterpretation. In an effort to achieve a tight, svelte body, I ate only one meal (if two baby carrots constitute a meal), limited my intake of water, and exercised two hours a day without fail. But, despite all my efforts to be beautiful, I was never satisfied. Mirrors were fierce enemies to be avoided.

My older sister Geri (affectionately nick-named Gigi) suspected depression to be a serious issue with me, but I was already a master at masking my problems. Although Gigi might have suspected the trouble that lay beneath my facade, I had myself completely fooled; I was totally blindsided by my first breakdown. In retrospect I don't know why I was surprised. I set myself up perfectly for collapse. I had created the textbook recipe for disaster: depleting nutritional stores through bouts of binging and starving, and then pushing myself to meet unrealistic expectations. Worse, I made sure that I was alone. I allowed fear and insecurity to keep everybody away—particularly those I knew genuinely cared about me.

Ironically, my schoolwork (at which I excelled) triggered my unraveling. I studied extra hours to achieve the high grades that came more naturally to most of my brothers and sisters. And then one unsuspecting day *it* happened. I missed an "A" by a few percentage points in my high academics chemistry class.

It was as if something inside me broke loose. Instead of coming to terms with the disappointment of having done less than my best, I found myself crying uncontrollably and running from the lab in the middle of class. Slumped down against a wall in the girls' restroom, I wanted to die ... literally end my life over a grade. I remember feeling detached, like I was watching this happen to someone else.

In the midst of all of this inner turmoil, my parents decided to move across Ohio again during the summer prior to my senior year in high school. Such a wrenching move would unhinge even an emotionally healthy high school junior, but I was far from emotionally healthy. This move was horrific. Living in "Loserville" was the proverbial straw that broke the back of my discontent. I truly loathed every minute of it ... and I do mean every minute of every hour. "Happy" was not a word in my vocabulary, and quite frankly, I resented anyone who felt the right to use it. In addition to the fun to be had by all (sarcasm fully intended), a troubled family member made an inappropriate sexual advance that *completely* freaked me out.

I talked to the God of my childhood when I experienced duress of soul, but all my prayers were completely one-sided. I didn't expect Him to listen to my whining, let alone reply. My relationship with God was very uncertain, although I felt I had right to a vicarious relationship with Him through my mother because she was very devout. We siblings had a scary joke among us: When we couldn't find mom in one of her prayer closets, we surmised she had been "raptured," and *we* had been left behind.

I grew up in "The Church," but tragically never made any real connection. I knew every Bible story frontward and backward, but completely missed His Heart interwoven throughout each one. Maybe that's because I was downright terrified of God. Terrified. My religious thinking was all centered on my performance. If I continued to keep my list of "goods" substantially higher than those "bads" of my base nature, then God would approve of me. If not, I might as well consider myself smote. Continual striving and subsequent failure were rich soil with which the roots of shame, rejection, and insecurity could twist deeply and turn firmly into my heart.

Interestingly enough, my escape from purgatory (aka Loserville, Ohio) came in the form of Oral Roberts University, a Christian college in Tulsa, Oklahoma. When my brother Matt suggested that I graduate from high school early and come on out and "hang" with him for his last semester, it took all of two seconds to decide. Perhaps I could find the same peace and perspective that Matt had found there.

For the first time in my life, I experienced a rush of expectancy and hope. I was ahead of the education game and truly enjoyed my brother's offbeat company. He introduced me to his comrades: Milton, Wordsworth, and Keating, and we memorized their poetry "for fun." The beauty of literature and the order of law made a perfect marriage, and I declared a major in English with law school to follow. Matt and I spent all our time together, allowing lighthearted silliness to mitigate the seriousness of study. The familiar heaviness lifted just enough to discover another feeling that had lain dormant for so long.

The sky was blue. This was a simple, yet heavenly realization for a soul who had dwelt so much in darkness. The eating disorders and excessive exercise were no longer compulsions. I was completely distracted from my obsession with my appearance by a newfound devotion to intellectual pursuits. In fact, I began eating and eating and eating, gaining fifteen pounds of comfort. The food did both my body and soul good. I was far less anxious and far more carefree. I was slowly experiencing small victories in my life, and it felt wonderful. I tried to ignore the dread that surfaced occasionally to suggest happiness and contentment were only temporary residents.

Boyfriends had always been the Velcro fix for my insecurity. Male attention was flattering, but no boy could capture my heart. I wouldn't allow it. The whole scenario of opening myself up to potential rejection was as appealing as a long gaze into the mirror. With my eyes affixed firmly upon scholarly pursuits, I intended to keep boys on the unlit back burner. Meeting Paul Meade changed all that.

Every spring day after classes, Matt and I studied in the baseball stands while teams practiced on the field below us. As the days passed, try as I might not to notice, I found myself studying the shortstop much more closely than the books that lay open on my lap. I couldn't resist watching his fluid movement as he gracefully fielded ground balls. My eyes smiled when I watched him play, even though I wouldn't allow my face to reflect any interest. He had a way about him that made me want to take a closer look off the field.

I observed him in the cafeteria and here and there on campus. He wasn't a typical puffed-up jock, which was enormously refreshing. His understated self-assurance, boyish good looks, and the bluest eyes I had ever seen drew me out of my shell.

I received a single red rose delivered to my dorm room on Valentine's Day. The note was a messy, handwritten scrawl that simply read, *"Been thinking of you."* I dismissed all the curious squeaks of interest from all the girls on my floor, wondering who my secret admirer could be. My roommate Jennifer went straight to her connections and fished out clues, discovering it was indeed a ballplayer. A thrill ran through me when I discovered that the rose was from Paul. The ballplayer, who had caught my eye while fielding those grounders, was thinking of me.

I was reluctant when a number of friends went out on a group date to dinner and a movie. By now everyone knew Paul had sent me the rose. And although they were well intentioned, I found their relentless efforts to "fix us up"—engineering seating arrangements and making embarrassing comments—obnoxious. After that date, I didn't want to think about Paul Meade anymore. I don't know if my typical withdrawal was happening prematurely to save time and energy or if I already sensed that there was much more at stake. I decided that the library might be a better study hall than the baseball stadium, but my determination was short-lived; day after day I found myself wandering to the bleachers instead. Despite my every attempt, I could not deny this unfamiliar longing.

Then he called. We talked the night away, but it felt as if only moments had past. Time stood still, and I found it difficult to catch my breath. After only two dates, we were inseparable. How quickly I traded my noble scholastic intentions for a blue-eyed ballplayer named Paul Meade. Fast and furious, we fell deeply in love. It was the first *real* love for us both, and our sexual chemistry was explosive. No matter how close we got, it was not close enough. We spent a lot of time parking in his old Cutlass Supreme, while Bono serenaded us with "Sweetest Thing."

At one point, I encountered a moment of reason and restraint as I reflected on the speed and intensity of our growing relationship. I pondered the conceivable scenarios of where this seriousness might lead. All were frightening prospects. I broke it off. It was a pitiful sight: The two of us, standing on the stairs of the campus LRC, looking as if we were both about to receive lethal injections. The separation lasted an anguishing forty-eight hours; for once, "happy" was a word in my world.

In 1989, a sequence of bad administrative choices at ORU led to the demotion of the university's Division I athletic status to the National Association of Intercollegiate Athletics. Paul decided that he had to transfer to the University of Texas if he had any hope of catching the attention of pro baseball scouts and having a career in the game after graduation. Suddenly our cozy little world was shaken. Paul's impending transfer meant one of two things for us as a couple: either this would be end of our life together or I would go with him and this would be the beginning.

Under a shade tree one hot June day, we tossed up the idea to get married as if we were casually deciding dinner. "The Proposal" was less than romantic, but we were too stupid to care about such formalities. In order to stay together, we made a rash decision to get married in the upcoming month. We both had no idea what difficulties lay ahead. We were so young and oh so naïve. I immediately forgot all my reservations and ambitions, and placed my heart completely into the care of a boy only nineteen years old himself. Our physical attraction for each other was so intensely magnetic that I don't know

The happy couple.

how the earth managed to still spin on its axis, or how the stars didn't fling themselves down from the sky from polar disruption.

My much wiser, eldest sister Gigi tried to dissuade me from that which she observed would be a huge mistake. She wasn't opposed to marriage as much as she was opposed to the timing. We were rushing into a lifetime commitment.

Gigi logically pointed out that we could make sensible alternate arrangements. Tulsa, Oklahoma to Austin, Texas was a drivable distance for long weekends. A semester apart would have been a true test of our love. And if need be, I certainly could transfer to UT the following year. She made perfect sense to someone who might listen to reason, but my mind was made up.

The real issue was sex ... and now! For some reason, I considered premarital sex as one of those sins that would weigh heavily on my "bad" list and stand as an irreversible mark on my "spiritual record."

What an absurd game to abstain from intercourse on moral and religious grounds prior to marriage while indulging in everything else. Religion had twisted my thinking. I paid such close attention to the letter of the law that I missed the point altogether.

The wedding was on. It was the shortest engagement in history—only three and a half weeks from announcement to ceremony. Gossip of a pregnancy swirled and surrounded us, but for the first time in my life, I didn't care what anyone thought. I was so confident we were making the right decision. He was my prince. I was his princess. We were all that mattered.

We tied the knot July 15, 1989. The day began with the groom and party taking batting practice at a local ball field while the bride and company went to the local YMCA to shower and dress. The ceremony was as much a blur as the glamorous reception held atop a grain and feed. The fragrant aroma of the cows below couldn't put a damper on my delight. Paul was mine and soon we would finally celebrate our love fully.

Little did I know, "finally" would not happen that night, or the night after that, or the night after that. I tried desperately to push away the panic and despair that washed in like a flood, but it was as futile as trying to lift a semi truck, using only the strength of my petite body. I lay there, rehearsing the conversations I had had with Gigi, wondering if she had been right, if I had misinterpreted love. Were Paul and I merely two teenagers with revved up hormones that suddenly came to a halt at the most inopportune time? Worst, what if it was *me*? What if he had suddenly realized what my mirror knew all along?

"You just made the biggest mistake of your life" taunted me that very first night and continued for many, many years to come.

Of course, I could not explain away the frustration of failure with an extremely long day, too much wine, and two inexperienced virgins. There was no honeymoon fantasy to give us time to ease into our new relationship. We drove from the wedding immediately into a life dominated by the demands of baseball.

The whole experience was the most biting reality check of my life. I could never confess the inner turmoil and inexpressible disappointment, even to myself. Paul and I appeared to be the happiest couple on earth when we met my family, waiting to see us off after our first night together. Somehow I determined to make it work, and convinced myself that it would get better with time. *Smile on, girl. Game on, girl.*

Paul's life quickly overshadowed mine. I soon became the loving, supportive trophy wife who loyally attended her husband's baseball games and worked to help make ends meet rather than attend school myself. Despite my every effort to try to shake the blues that steadily crept in, and the endless miles

I ran to forget them, depression quickly grew into despair as I watched my princess status dissipate right before my eyes.

Baseball and studies were now the focuses of Paul's world. This shocking reality was a bitter pill to swallow for a nineteen-year old girl who left family, friends, and every dream behind to follow this man as he pursued his dreams with a single-mindedness that seemed to shut me out. Attempts to capture his attention were as futile as they were endless. When rational discussions failed, I initiated routine dramas with all the ranting and biting criticism of a desperate woman. Besides throwing tantrums, I often threw whatever object was nearest, aimed at his head. Once, intending to make a point that would not soon be forgotten, I hurled our eighteen-inch black and white TV across the room. I wanted to see explosions from both the television and Paul. Instead, much to my dismay, Paul quietly picked the television up, plugged it back in, and resumed watching ESPN. I was furious! Indifference wounded and infuriated me more than anything else. *Love me or hate me ... but do not just merely tolerate me, Paul Meade.*

Of course, all my dramatic attempts to get Paul's attention and win his affection only succeeded in driving him further away. I felt trapped, and the desperation deepened. Divorce was regarded a greater offense than pre-marital sex on my "bad" list. (Perhaps that little bit of insight should have been considered during my pre-wedding non-deliberations). But, were there no loopholes in God's Law for stupid young kids who didn't know what they were doing? Was there no way to rectify mistakes?

"Until death do us part ..." echoed in my mind.

Though I didn't feel I had the moral or religious right to break my vows legally, I felt I should sever them emotionally in order to protect what was left of my heart and my sanity. I planned to return to school, throw myself into academics, and pursue my own dreams, convinced that this would lessen the ache. As I went to register for classes, there was a hopeful spring in my step for the first time in a long time. I allowed myself to think that maybe things would turn out okay after all.

I was wrong. Just prior to the start of fall semester, I got the crippling news that I was pregnant. Every dream shattered, every hope deferred, every song unsung.

If marriage to Paul had felt like a trap, being pregnant immediately threw the bolt on the lock on the door. There was no way out now. The only thing worse than divorce on my list of "bad" offenses was abortion. I was no less desperate than those who walk through the doors of Planned Parenthood with a problem and leave with a solution; I was just enormously afraid of God and the consequences. I would keep this child.

The longest ten months of my life ended as cruelly as they began. My trusted obstetrician went on vacation; I was three weeks overdue and fifty pounds overweight when an inexperienced, inept intern turned the birth of my son into savage brutality. It took two and half hours and five hundred stitches to close up the aftermath. I waited for the mythical joy of new motherhood to bubble up as I held the precious bundle, for truly he was the most beautiful thing my eyes had ever beheld. But, there was no bubbling, just a quiet ache of stolen youth and lost opportunity. Holding this miracle of life could not swallow the death that encompassed my soul.

The stitches from the delivery ultimately healed, although my heart kept tearing at the seams. I instinctively mothered Joshua with all the rigors and devotion expected of me, but my heart was not in it. Though I truly loved him deeply, I was drawing from an empty well.

Paul had an amazing baseball season that year and was drafted by the Cleveland Indians organization in the ninth round. No amount of running could free me from what lay ahead.

CHAPTER 2

"Found"

you were lost . . . wandered away
into the luring night
without (W)e you chose to stay
alone and out of sight
anguishing in pain to find
I knew what I must do
leave my other 99
to run and rescue you.

THE CRAZY LIFE of a minor league ballplayer became a family affair as Paul, Joshua, and I traveled the country. I accepted living as nomads out of suitcases, having no furniture, sleeping on egg crates, and surviving on poverty-level income. I could not accept a life of loneliness and indifference.

Motherhood was my only saving grace. It was impossible to do anything but smile ear-to-ear when I took this boy into my arms and studied his small face. Joshua was perfection. He never cried. Ever. I heard precious suckling sounds when he was hungry, and he could sit in a wet diaper all day and still coo gently. There was simply nothing that could disturb his peace ... well, except his completely clueless, first-time mom.

Josh and I were temporarily staying with my in-laws in Iowa while Paul went to "Rookie Ball" in Kinston, North Carolina. Stress and chaos had taken a heavy toll on me. My mind was a bit disorganized, and I sometimes forgot to do things I should have. Paul's younger brother Tony and I took Josh to the grocery store with us, and I completely forgot to clasp the baby car seat buckle. We gleefully swung Joshua back and forth when suddenly the car seat popped into a locked position and my three-month-old baby went flying through the air, landing face first on the pavement fifteen feet ahead!

I cannot describe my terrified alarm.

"I just killed my baby!" I thought as I rushed to his aid.

Utter silence for ten excruciating seconds confirmed my fears.

Shock finally gave way to emotion, and he wailed loudly. Miraculously, he only suffered a few minor scrapes and bruises.

The bruises hadn't even healed when I did my next *really* stupid thing. Trying desperately to lose the thirty additional pregnancy pounds, I was dieting, running, and of course, tanning to conceal the cellulite. One hot June morning, I took Josh to a local pool and spent the entire day under the summer sun. Josh was his perfect self, sleeping and lying contentedly in his car seat while I soaked up the rays. I protected my lil' love with an umbrella I placed over him to keep him sufficiently shaded. I thought all was well. I couldn't have been more wrong. The good news was that you could no longer see the scrapes and bruises from our mishap the week before. The bad news is that they were hidden beneath the deepest shade of red I had ever seen in my life! I didn't realize the sun reflected off the pavement and directly onto Josh.

In spite of my missteps as a new mother, I loved this child fiercely. Josh and I were inseparable from the day he was born. He was a voracious eater and thoroughly enjoyed the affection and intimacy associated with nursing. He slept in our bed tucked beneath my arm, cuddled closely to my chest. His constant presence lessened the pangs of loneliness. There were times when I looked into his hopeful eyes and felt as if everything would be all right. He was pure joy. He was everything I was not: content, peaceful, happy, and full of life. He was *almost* enough.

Despite the joy that Joshua brought, the longing ache for approval and love from Paul and God felt deferred indefinitely; although it was present, it was not evident to *my* eyes. I couldn't shake the repeated thoughts of darkness that hung over my life as damp folds of shroud. I was in a tunnel, convinced that any perception of light at the end was only an illusion. Every time I tried to "do the right thing" to please God, I was left reeling from my repeated failures.

And my marriage? With each passing day, the hopes of a genuine relationship slipped further and further out of reach. Rookie ball was not going as well as Paul had hoped. Consuming pressures of performing on the field left him depleted. He brought his discouragement home to a wife who couldn't comfort him and a newborn son who needed him to be strong.

This princess felt reduced to a nuisance that her wounded prince was forced to appease. When he needed me most, I

Paul and Joshua on the baseball field before a game.

needed him more. I spun 'round and 'round though every ridiculous effort to salvage what remained; yet I only managed to deepen the divide. Both God and Paul were aloof and far, far away. Striving for their love left me empty.

Webster was thinking of me when he defined "alone" as lonely, solitary, deserted, abandoned, forsaken, desolate, detached, friendless, isolated, and unconnected. I could hardly wait to put all *that* on my resume.

Because of our "gypsy" lifestyle, by the time I met a neighbor or started making a friend or found a church, it was time to relocate to another team. Opening my front door to the familiar face of our postal carrier was the highlight of my day and often my only adult connection. Little did he know that his cheery smile and daily inquiry, "Hey, Mrs. Meade! How are you? How's the little guy?" carried me through many a day.

Sometimes Paul was gone for weeks and being alone became increasingly insufferable. The most difficult times were at night when Joshy was sleeping. The distractions of the day were silent in the darkness, and there was nothing to quell the constant obsession to end the misery.

It was all about to come to a head on a steamy night in Columbus, Georgia. Paul returned from one of his two-week road trips, and we had a huge blowout argument with blaming and defending flying from both directions. There was never any closure when we battled, so the wounds stayed open and raw, and despair deepened with every angry word. The pain was unbearable. With every fiber of my being, I wanted everything to be all right. I wanted to see the sun again. I knew I had settled on just "existing," but existing was more like dying than living.

I was dying inside.

Dying.

I will never forget that night. Physically and emotionally exhausted from the argument, I lay in bed in the sweltering darkness beside my husband, the father of my son, this stranger. My sweaty nightshirt clung to my frame the way despair clung to my soul. Paul's familiar breathing, as he drifted into fitful sleep, magnified. With each exhale I became increasingly agitated. Which was worse—this slow painful death that could drag out hideously for years or putting an end to it quickly and painlessly once and for all? There in the hot darkness, the "father of lies," "the enemy of my soul," taunted me and tempted me until I finally conceded.

I slowly, silently lifted the damp sheet and slid out of bed. I mechanically stepped one foot in front of the other toward the bathroom as if I were programmed ahead of time to walk through a sequence of scenes not written by my own hand. As I reached for a bottle of pain pills, I suddenly realized the enormity of what I was about to do. I collapsed to my knees on the cool floor. Clutching the answer tightly to my chest, I sobbed a cry so deep that I could feel my insides pulling apart with every choked heave. I pushed aside images of my son, my mother, and the few others I loved. I knew there would be severe aftershocks of dismay from all who thought they knew me. I never told anyone about the darkness that surrounded me. Only the most astute observer could have seen the pain behind the shadows of my almond brown eyes.

Out of the blackness, deep within, I heard a startling voice of protest, devoid of anger and full of tenderness.

"Michelle."

Could it be true? The prospect was absurd to me. I was always crying out; never did I expect a reply. Was it possible? I hushed myself to listen.

"I have a good plan for your life. Trust Me. Look to Me for satisfaction and fulfillment. I AM the One who loves you."

Hot, bitter tears fell afresh. I shook my head in anger and wished He had said nothing at all after whispering my name.

What mocking sarcasm! How could God declare His Love while refusing to rescue me from drowning in a sea of despair?

My anger was stilled by His voice once again, and this time He reached for the only warm part of my heart sacredly reserved for my boy and joy.

"My love, remember Joshua."

Joshua.
The only twinkle in my eye.
Joshua.
The only reason to get out of bed each day.
Joshua.
The only source of joy in my life.
Joshua.
Would I abandon him?

Abandon? I never even considered that before. Could I dare plant roots of insecurity in the heart of my young son by my own bitter hand? Would I leave fear and rejection as his inheritance?

Could I possibly?

Thoughts of our lazy days together flashed before my eyes: doing whatever his heart's desire was for the moment—

Joshua—my little boy, my biggest joy.

23

throwing four thousand whiffle balls toward his tiny body as he squealed and laughed with delight, or feeding the ducks, or reading his favorite books aloud for the millionth time. My world was his world, and his entire little world lay crumpled on the floor.

The answer was painfully clear: our world must go on.

There had to have been some heavenly satisfaction that evening. Though I would not allow His love to break through my cold, hard heart, the selfish truth of my intentions and the devastating effects it would have upon my child pierced the pain. I did not consider myself rescued at the moment, but I was grateful that He preserved the tender innocence and trusting heart of this little boy, my joy, Joshua.

I quietly emerged from beneath the vanity where I had crawled to curl around my sorrow and spend my final minutes, and carefully returned the pills to their resting place. I padded back to bed beside Paul and closed my eyes to sleep, wanting to quickly put this night in the dungeons of my memory; instead I lay there wondering if I heard correctly...

Didn't He say, *My love?* I felt silly asking myself that rhetorical question, but I was stunned.

Impossible.

Those are the two most beautiful words I had ever heard.

"My love ..."

It was a powerful statement of belonging.

Could I possibly matter to the heart of God?

Is there really any way the God of the Universe actually ran to answer my desperate cry?

If so, why?

I knew it could not have been because of my worthiness, for my list of "bads" soared off the charts by considering the "unthinkable." So why would He care?

It was apparent to me that the value of saving me was to spare Joshua's life from irreversible damage. For as his mother,

I loved him deeply, more deeply than any other person ever could. Besides, he is just absolutely *precious*.

Who wouldn't starve themselves from food and live heartily off his munchable cheeks? Who could deny his pleas when he'd belt out "AGAI-I-IN!" after spinning 'round and 'round until he fell into a heap of laughter? Who could resist melting into a puddle on the pavement when he stared up at the night sky, innocently asking, "Moon, come play with me?"

Oh, there was limitless evidence that Joshua was precious. However, I was an altogether different story. My life represented frustrated failure and ungrateful discontent. I knew I was a mess, but felt helpless to change. I couldn't understand why He desired to save my life, let alone call me *His love*?

It had to be a figment of my imagination. I hoped sleep would terminate the ludicrous thought.

As I restlessly tossed and turned, Psalm 139 surfaced above the rubble of pain and rolled over and over in my mind. I had used it to earn myself an "A" for a paper I wrote in high school. I could recite from memory each poetic verse, yet the meaning merely ricocheted off the iron bars of my wounded heart.

LORD, you have examined my heart and know everything about me. You know when I sit down or stand up. You know my every thought when far away. You chart the path ahead of me and tell me where to stop and rest. Every moment you know where I am. You know what I am going to say even before I say it, LORD. You both precede and follow me. You place your hand of blessing on my head. Such knowledge is too wonderful for me, too great for me to know! I can never escape from your spirit! I can never get away from your presence! If I go up to heaven, you are there; if I go down to the place of the dead, you are there. If I ride the wings of the morning, if I dwell by the farthest oceans, even there your hand will guide me, and your strength will support me. I could ask the darkness to hide me and the light around me to become night? —but even in darkness I cannot hide from you. To you the night shines as bright as day. Darkness and light are both alike to you. You made all the delicate, inner parts of my body and knit me together in my mother's womb. Thank you for making me so wonderfully complex! Your workmanship is marvelous—and how well I know it. You watched me as I was being formed in utter seclusion, as I was woven together in the dark of the womb. You saw me before I was born. Every day of my life was recorded in your book. Every moment was laid out before a single day had passed. How precious are your thoughts about me, O God! They are innumerable! I can't even count them; they outnumber the grains of sand! And when I wake up in the morning, you are still with me! (Psalm 139:1-18, NLT)

"Just as Joshua is precious and irreplaceable to you, My love, you are precious and irreplaceable to ME."

Although I could not accept this revelation of love, oddly enough, on that hot steamy night in Columbus, Georgia, I closed my eyes for the first time with a hopeful question surfacing in my thoughts: *What if it's true?*

CHAPTER 3

"Abba's Heart"

I just want to hear your voice

I miss you don't you know

you used to climb upon My knee

but that was long ago

"Remember ME" again

My Love's always the same

here I'll wait, don't hesitate

I'm calling out your name

I WAS EVIDENTLY NOT A VERY GOOD STUDENT of life, making the same mistakes repeatedly, stubbornly turning from one thing to the next to try to numb the pain. The bitterness and prolonged despair ultimately forged a determined, hardened heart. Divorce was my answer. I would divorce Paul, and at the same time divorce myself from pain and re-enter life with vigor, pursuing the dreams that lay precariously on life support. A "you go, girl" sort of finger-snapping sass brought forth the courage necessary to sever the marriage. I had made up my mind; it was my only hope for a life worth living.

My decision to divorce was made just prior to my brother Matt's wedding in the fall of 1992. I dreaded having to attend his wedding for several reasons. I would have to face my family with my decision and their disapproval. My own bitter failure would stand in the starkest contrast to the beauty and purity of true love between a bride and groom filled with hope for the future. Moreover, I hated the thought of traveling from Tulsa to Washington, DC and back in the confined quarters of a mini van with those who loved me, who might truly get a real gaze into my eyes. I could not bear for them to see my damaged soul.

My brother Matt was the personification of my dream. He was currently practicing law and preparing to embark on the next promise of good as he wed the woman he had prayed for. He was everything I wanted to be. I should have been happy for him, but my misery consumed me. Stares, comments, and whispers suggested that everybody else knew what I was trying so hard to conceal.

"What's wrong with Shelly? She is so thin! Is she sick? What's the matter with her? Why does she look so unhappy?"

I was one hundred pounds, twenty-seven pounds less than I had weighted at my own wedding only a few years earlier. My gaunt, sunken cheekbones made a dramatic frame for the

My brother Chris, Josh, and me at Matt's wedding.

shallow eyes that darted back and forth. I managed to skirt any real confrontation with the truth until the torturous twenty-hour drive back to Tulsa.

I can still hear little Joshua saying, "Mama, look! Kaus a comin'! Mama! Kaus a comin'."

Despite my repeated attempts, I could not stop the tears from spilling quietly down my cheeks as I stared out the window and watched the endless row of cars whisking past us on the opposite side of the highway. How I longed to be in any one of them, going absolutely anywhere but back to Oklahoma. I kept my gaze fixed in the opposite direction of my sister Maria, hoping she wouldn't notice the tears. She was the closet to me of my six brothers and two sisters. She invited me down to visit her and Steve in Texas several times, and we were starting to develop a friendship that transcended the sibling relationship. She had forgiven me for my bratty younger sister years when I tattled and stained all her clothes. She was worthy of my confidence, but I was afraid of the fallout.

Unfortunately for me, Maria not only saw the tears, she anticipated them. She was relentless with her pointed questions as she continued to pursue. Finally her persistence paid off, and I cracked. I shared the pain that had lain in secrecy and wept openly on her shoulder for hours. It felt good to unleash all the garbage that ate at my soul. I nearly finished a sigh of relief when she pulled out both barrels aimed directly at my heart.

"If you divorce Paul, it won't change a thing. Not one thing. It won't change the fact that I love you, God loves you, and the rest of your family loves you. But I have to tell you that divorce is *not* your answer because Paul is *not* your problem, as much as you think he is. *You*, Michelle, are your problem, and you cannot run away from yourself."

I was just about to angrily respond, but she sucked in another breath and continued, "Hunny, you cannot continue to run away from the pain, and if you try, you'll only find hurt after hurt until you finally discover no other arms but *His* can fill what you are longing for."

She retold God's love story of the ages. She explained that Grace was a gift and that I didn't need to "earn" God's approval. She concluded her exhortation and tried to find my eyes, which were still staring blindly out the window. They were dry now and full of anger.

How dare she? How dare she take my treasured pain, exposed to none, and stomp on my vulnerable heart with a simple answer to complex problems? How dare she absolve Paul and point the finger back at me? How dare she imply that anyone could possibly know my suffering? How dare she shatter my beliefs and hopes of a new beginning?

I felt betrayed by her and upset with myself for daring to trust someone with my heart. That'll teach me. Voices raised so loud, the van shook.

To avoid any further discussion, I acquiesced and nodded in agreement. But my true intention was to tell Paul that I would not be joining him at spring training this year. This was it. No more merry-go-round for me. I felt as if three and a half years suggested a solid effort by any reasonable standard. I couldn't imagine compiling any more heartache onto the fragments of my soul.

My first obstacle was facing the challenge of a potential custody battle. Paul was an excellent father, and he would have grounds to question my emotional stability. He loved his son and would fight for him. Rightly so. I also would have to overcome incredible odds to raise Joshua alone and put myself through school without any outside help. Realities of where I would go and what I would do to support Josh and me were not matching up with my idealistic escape plan.

Would the freedom from the chains of a bad marriage be enough to suppress the pain of potentially losing my son and watching him raised by someone else? I consoled myself with the thought that no court would award Paul custody while playing ball, but I also knew his family would offer every assistance to afford him the option. Though the questions and apprehensions were continuing to mount, I felt I had exhausted every other option.

Unlike the usual ranting, raving, and furniture throwing, this time I calmly and soberly announced I would not join him at spring training. At first he thought that my declaration was another one of my desperate attempts to get his attention, but when he looked into my eyes and saw the cold, withdrawn determination, his lips trembled. I felt he feared losing Josh more than losing me, and that only fanned my quiet fury. His icy indifference and continual rejection were nothing short of emotional abuse, and now it was payback time. I was intent on hurting him as much as he had hurt me.

Paul quickly jumped to his own defense because Lord knows I would not. My machine gun was locked and loaded to shoot down every one of his responses. I verbally sliced and diced all of his defenses into tiny, little shreds while simultaneously delivering comprehensive lists of wrongs. First, he did his favorite avoidance technique by joking around to make light of the situation. Within moments he realized I was resolute.

He was reduced to tearfully pleading, "I suck. I admit it. I promise that things will be different. I'll be different. Please don't walk away, Michelle. Don't throw everything away."

Being a man of mental discipline who trained and restrained his emotions, it was peculiar to see him raise his voice, let alone cry. I was shocked and frankly amused. What a troubling indication of sickness this was—sickness in our marriage, sickness in my heart—to think this was some sort of victory having finally aroused a heart-felt response from him.

"Paul, you say the same thing every time we get to this point, but *nothing* ever changes. There is nothing more I can do or say to convince you of my love or to cause you to love me in return."

"Michelle, I know I haven't been the husband I should have been. I admit it. I'm asking you for the chance to be," he pled.

His tearful pleas and promises were too little too late. In spite of his heartfelt arguments to give him another chance, my answer remained the same. Then anger reared its ugly head as he posed question after question that I could not answer concerning my immediate plans.

"Where are you going to go? Just how do you think you're going to support yourself, Michelle? I bet you'll find someone to cater to you."

I maturely retorted, "Guess what? It is no longer any of your damn business!"

"Josh is my business regardless of what you choose to do, Michelle. Don't you *ever* forget that!" he challenged.

I knew he was right, but I didn't want to give him that right. I wanted to refuse him the way he refused me. I wanted to withhold his heart's desire the way he withheld mine. I wanted to be free from this entangled fiasco, but I began to realize there was going to be no easy way out. Taking Josh from his dad would be detrimental; I just hoped I could be enough of a parent to compensate for his loss.

Sobbing with my head in my hands, I struggled against Paul as he pulled me close to him and forcibly turned my face to his until I had no choice but to look into his smoldering blue eyes still filled with tears. He held my gaze for only a few seconds, but it was all that was needed. It was impossible to continue to pretend I was the only victim in this whole mess. His eyes reflected the same pain and disillusion as mine. I shut my eyes and wrenched my face from his hands, knowing that if I looked one more second, my resolve would shatter. I twisted free from his grip to retreat to the bedroom, but he followed close behind and grabbed me, roughly parting my lips with his own. At first I refused because I knew in my heart that making love was just a band-aid over a bloody gash. But, absolutely starving for attention and affection, I simply could not resist.

Afterward, however, as I lay in bed, listening to his familiar breathing, tears steadily fell in rhythm to my beating heart. What now?

I dared to think past the usual negatives and pondered a few "what ifs." What if God really does love *me*? What if there could be something better? What if I have been missing the obvious? What if Maria was right? I was able to answer most questions with an angry, justifiable refute, but at least the debate was progressing in the right direction. It was hope enough to get me to Winter Haven, Florida for another spring training.

Back in the throes of yet another trying baseball season, I was confronted with the same demons of the past, and my butt was getting authoritatively kicked. A new fixation was now added to into the ridiculous mix. I found myself obsessing about every tiny physical symptom, imagining my impending death. A migraine = a brain tumor; menstrual cramps = ovarian cancer; and a muscle twitch = Lou Gehrig's disease. I knew, rationally, it was absurd, but my mind simply refused to dismiss the symptoms and go on. Instead, the worst-case scenarios played over and over in my head.

In addition, I was continually beaten down by depression. I wailed in unison with Eddie Money the chords of self-pity, "I wanna go back, go back and do it all over, but I can't go back I know. I wanna go back, go back 'cuz I'm feeling so much older, but I can't go back I know..."

I know it is absurd to try to live in the past, but that is all one can do if the present is unbearable and the future inconceivable. I would occasionally crack open my Bible and sometimes would read through a devotional ironically given to me by Paul's former baseball coach. The devotional was designed for people in recovery from addictions, and it walked through the Serenity Prayer for 365 days:

> Lord, grant me the wisdom to accept the things
> I cannot change,
> to change the things I can,
> and the wisdom to know the difference.

I read it and sometimes found comfort, but usually I was drawn to whatever would sympathize with my miseries. It's odd how comforting our own pain can become. I continually watched romantic movies, soap operas, and anything else on television that fed my discontent. What a foolish damsel in distress I was. However, nothing compared to the day I read *The Bridges of Madison County*.

I was Francesca! That was me! But where was my dashing photographer, Robert Kincaid? My heart throbbed through every wretched page. If ever there was a romantic fantasy to seduce and bewitch, *this was it.* I'm sure that book singly drove the death nail into many a marriage. I couldn't shake its haunting suggestion for years.

I counted down the days of the baseball season day-by-painful-day on the calendar. Paul traveled weeks at a time, leaving me to fester privately. Enduring the loneliness and solitude was like listening to the drip of a leaking faucet. How I wanted to fix *or* irreparably break that faucet so that it gushed! Instead I continued to listen to its anguishing drops.

Drip.

Drip.

Drip.

Drip.

I sabotaged every intention of a hopeful New Year's Eve by watching "Pretty Woman" late that afternoon. This produced a volatile mix of bitterness and regret when combined with my present misery. Paul didn't know what hit him when I grabbed my coat and his mother's car keys, and announced that I was "outta there." I drove to the nearest convenience store, flashed my ID, and purchased some alcohol and a pack of cigarettes.

Empowered by my "forbidden purchases," I went to an abandoned parking lot and drank, smoked, and talked myself into a stupor. When the alcohol had dulled all reason, I stomped on the accelerator of the Honda Prelude, careening around the icy pavement as fast as I could, forcing the sports car into thrilling spinouts and figure eights. For hours, I was no longer in a parking lot minutes from Paul's parents' home; I was in a reality TV show of my own. With a cigarette dangling from the side of my mouth, I explained to an enthralled (and appropriately sympathetic and shocked) studio audience what an ass my husband was, what a nightmare our baseball lifestyle was, and what a mess I was. The lively, intelligent, and bitterly sarcastic conversation entertained until I was too drunk to make sense. My vocabulary was eventually reduced to strings of four letter words slurred into the dark winter sky and mingled with tears.

Miraculously I made it back to Paul's parents house in tact. In the entryway, I met Paul's brother Tony, preparing to leave for Colorado. At the sight of his skis, I began laughing uncontrollably. They were the funniest things I had ever seen, so long and skinny and aerodynamically shaped, just like ... skis. He looked perplexed as I continued to roll on the couch in a fit of hysteria. Paul walked out of the kitchen holding Josh and glanced at me with such disgust it nearly sobered me instantly. I followed them downstairs and tried to grab Josh so I could snuggle him, fall asleep, and forget the evening. Paul pulled away, refusing to let me near either of them.

"You make me sick," he said angrily.

"Yeah, well ... I make *myself* sick, so we're in complete agreement. Now let me hold my son!" I said, reaching for Josh once more.

"Michelle, I'm not letting you near Josh like this. Go and clean up. When you're sober, I'll let you have him," he said firmly, holding me back at arm's length.

"Let go of my arm and give me my son, now!" I demanded.

Paul's grip tightened as he repeated his last statement once again slower and more emphatically than before. He enunciated each syllable crisply. I broke loose from his grip and spun through the room, rampaging and throwing things as I screamed in protest at Paul's refusal. Paul went to the bedroom and locked the door to keep his hysterical, drunken, cigarette-smoke-reeking, infuriated wife away from his son.

I couldn't put up much of fight after punching the door a few times because I was forced to retreat to the bathroom to spend the remainder of the night embracing the toilet bowl, violently purging every ounce of liquid from my body. The journal entry of New Year's Day, 1993 expressed my misery succinctly:

Somber beginnings. A six-pack of White Grenache and a pack of 100 Lights numb reality. Humiliation and vile purges frame the night and the memory. There is no escape.

The following day was about as awful as it gets. I stood, crying in the shower until the hot water tank refused to indulge me anymore. I felt paralyzed by shame over my inability to conquer the consuming depression. In spite of my best efforts, despair was now escaping the confines of my private pity-parties, invading every moment of the day. I knew I needed God and all of heaven to fix the colossal mess sitting motionless in a ball on the floor.

Needing to be forgiven, needing to be comforted, and needing to be contained by some form of hope, I wept quietly. I felt much too undeserving to dare to expect any of these needs to be met, but much to my dismay, He found me once again.

"Michelle, all who put their hope in Me will not be put to shame."

I felt as if divine arms were holding me as peace washed over my distress and calmed the inner storm.

CHAPTER 4

"Trust in ME"

do not doubt, do not fear

for your God, I AM) is here

Trust in ME, on My Name call

I'll keep your foot so you won't fall

I'll strengthen, help, and hold your hand

Trust in ME and you shall stand

I know the way, wait and see

it shall unfold as you Trust In ME.

I WAS SO GOOD AT "talking the talk" (being fake). I knew all the appropriate things to say at just the right time. I would sit in church and look around and wonder how many other people had pasted smiles on their faces when they were really dying inside. I sensed that I was not the only one.

Lauren and Dawn were two of the few girlfriends with whom I still kept in touch from my Oral Roberts University days, and we three planned to meet for lunch at Grady's Grill one cool January day. Upon arriving at the restaurant, I went to the restroom to re-wash my hands (touching public door knobs with my bare hands was daunting), and then proceeded to our table to see both girls visibly upset.

"Michelle, are you all right?!?" they both exclaimed.

"I'm fine," I said, confused by their alarm.

"Isn't that your car on fire?" Lauren continued.

"I don't know what you guys are talking about …" My words trailed off when I heard the sirens and turned to watch a fire truck pull in and proceed to put out the flames in our tiny Dodge Omni. Apparently, loose brake wires caused the fire from a U-Haul that was not properly connected. I walked out, quietly assessed the car damage, shrugged my shoulders, and walked back toward the restaurant. Reluctantly they followed, but it was obvious they were both much more troubled about what had just happened than I.

"Michelle, you could have been seriously hurt … and what about your car?" Lauren said, a bit distressed.

"Yeah, but I'm fine and the car …who knows? We'll figure something out," I continued, unaffected by the apparently traumatic event. We returned to lunch.

The looks on their faces grew only more concerned as our conversation continued, and I recounted my personal reality show in the parking lot in my mother-in-law's Honda. I mimed the cigarette hanging out of the corner of my mouth. I described the brilliant and thrilling driving maneuvers on ice. And finally, although I could barely speak through my own laughter, I ran through a quick recap of witty observations with which I had regaled my unseen studio audience. It was a re-run worthy of network television. They must have interpreted my funny re-enactment of the New Year's Eve "extravaganza" as a cry for help because both strongly suggested I go to counseling before it "gets out of hand."

A counselor?

What's next? A shrink?

I don't think so.

I revealed too much information about my so-called life, and as we parted from lunch, I felt completely embarrassed by the error. I didn't give a lot of credence to their suggestion until I realized it might be beneficial for me to get a "professional opinion" that my life sucked. That way I could justify any course of action I deemed necessary to survive, including divorce.

Within a few weeks, after a few discrete inquiries, I got the name of a counselor that came highly recommended by several people. And although it took a few tentative attempts at dialing the phone and overcoming my own aversion, I made an appointment.

I felt humiliated walking into the counselor's office. I was certain that all eyes were on the giant pink "loser" sticker on my forehead. When it was my turn, the counselor greeted me warmly, shepherded me into a plush, comfortable, silent office, and asked me to sit down. I sat there looking at my shoes for what seemed like thirty minutes.

Finally he asked, "So why are you here, Michelle?"

"My friends think I need some help," I replied.

"What do you think?" he asked.

"I don't know," I said, wishing I hadn't considered this pathetic option.

"Do you want to tell me about it?"

"Do you want to throw up? Just kidding ..." My voice trailed off and I shifted around in my seat to waste a couple of the remaining one thousand, one hundred, and sixty painful seconds left of the session.

"Why not tell me some of the reasons your friends thought you needed help," he suggested.

"Symptoms, I guess ..." I started, but paused, trying to posture my statements to sound casual and incredulous. "I guess my friends were concerned by my lack of response when my car caught on fire and some other comments I made ..." I stopped short of completing my sentence when I realized it would open up issues I did not wish to dive into.

"What comments?" he questioned.

"Stupid! Stupid! Stupid!" I silently chided myself.

"Joking comments about a drunken New Year's Eve rampage didn't sound as funny to them as it did to me, I guess. They thought I needed some help, so here I am." I cringed. I couldn't have felt more pathetic.

"Do you drink regularly?" he questioned.

"No! It was just a stupid attempt to numb my misery, I guess."

"What exactly does your misery refer to?" he asked.

"Everything really, but my marriage most specifically," I said quickly, only to wait tortuously for the next question.

"Do you want to talk about it?" he suggested more than inquired.

"Oh, I don't know ..." I admitted, hoping he'd divert his questioning elsewhere.

"What does "everything" include?" he asked.

"My life consists of a continual string of disappointments. Worst of all is my relationship, or more accurately, lack of relationship with my husband," I said.

"What bothers you most in all of this?" he questioned.

"Being invisible," I said quietly, almost in a whisper.

"What do you mean by that?"

"I only exist in his world when he chooses to acknowledge me, which is very seldom," I soberly admitted.

"How long has it been this way?"

"Since I said 'I do,'" I said, trying to keep the bitterness restrained.

"What happened?"

"I don't know. I mean I thought I knew. Hundreds of times I thought I figured out why he didn't love me anymore and attempted to fix it, but each time I only made things worse. You have any problems I can fix?"

My nervous attempts at humor were failing miserably.

"So he has actually told you he doesn't love you anymore?"

"Not exactly," I responded.

"Then how do you know?"

"I know," I said defensively, slowly enunciating both words as if to punctuate my statement with authority.

"How?"

A frustrated sigh gave me a few seconds to think about how I could possibly describe the heartache, hopelessness, and sense of entrapment that come with being bound by a loveless marriage.

I continued, "I feel as I am living out a life sentence without any chance of parole, all because I said 'I do.'"

The words came out icy cold and emotionless.

I looked down and began again, "I used to think he was incapable of love. I mean, incapable of showing love. But then I had our son, and I never saw more tenderness, compassion, and affection pour from one human to another. This display of love toward our son crushed me because it became clear that it was matter of choice and not capability."

"Does that make you resent your son?" he questioned.

"No. It just became an indictment of our marriage, against Paul. Joshua is worthy of his love and affection. I clearly am not." Saying those words aloud caused the pain to fall down my cheeks against my will.

"Could the two of you consider some marriage counseling?" he suggested hopefully.

Quickly wiping my eyes, I said, "No, I don't think so."

I knew Paul would resist the idea, and frankly the thought of us berating one another in front of a third person was unthinkably humiliating.

"I'm glad you're here though, Michelle," he said, continuing carefully. "Our time is going by fast and I want to ask you a few questions to determine if you need additional treatment."

I shifted around in my seat like a kid getting a haircut. "Additional treatment?" I echoed.

"Yes, perhaps from a physician or psychiatrist."

I could feel the "loser" sticker burning on my forehead again. The questions started coming faster than I could think how to answer.

"Do you have crying spells?"

"Sometimes."

"How often?"

"Depends on the week, I guess."

"How would you rate your depression? Mild with occasional blues? Moderate with regular down times? Or severe with a continual heaviness that affects your daily life?"

Silence.

"Oh, I don't know. Depends, I guess," I lied.

His gentle mannerisms and kind eyes indicated that he sincerely cared. There was a long silence as he looked at me in a way that almost made me want to be vulnerable and open up. I was guessing he already knew I was severely depressed by his need to question me further. This way, he could point to a list of affirmatives to support his supposition. I played along in order to get through the session.

"Do you lack enthusiasm for things you used to like?"

"Yes."

"Do you feel hopeless?"

"Generally."

"Have you experienced loss of appetite or sleeplessness?"

"Yes."

"Have you had thoughts of hurting yourself or others?"

Ouch. Aren't the seconds up yet? "Do you have a bathroom?" I asked quickly as I squirmed in my seat once again.

"Michelle, we're about done. If it can wait …"

"No!" I nervously blurted out.

"No, you haven't thought of hurting yourself, or no, it can't wait?" he asked, genuinely confused by my abruptness.

"Ah … both," I lied again. I couldn't admit *that* or the desperate pleas for help that my soul cried daily. I simply couldn't.

Upon my return he concluded, "Michelle, based on our short session today, I highly recommend you go see Doctor …" He scribbled down a name and continued, "He sees several of my regular counseling patients and prescribes medications as needed. In your case, I believe an anti-depressant would prove to be a significant help to you. He could determine that."

I remained silent as he explained, "I also recommend that you continue to see me or another qualified counselor several times a month." He looked up again and with his kind eyes continued, "Michelle, you will see light again …"

I grabbed the note, quickly mumbled, "Thank you," and walked out. I balled the paper and shoved it into my jeans pocket while shaking my head "no" to the receptionist's question, "Would you like to make a second appointment, Michelle?"

I justified my refusal because of our upcoming relocation, but truthfully, denial remained my automatic response. If I didn't delve into the pain, maybe it wasn't as deep as I feared. I frantically searched the parking lot for my car, and in the safety of solitude, I sobbed with my head in my hands. Quiet heaves echoed the familiar sound throughout the car as if being lulled. I quieted momentarily. Silently my gaze followed the gentle back and forth movement of the leaves as they danced effortlessly with the wind. The trance-like state was broken when a crying toddler resisted his mom across the parking lot.

"I have to go home," I thought as I nervously remembered that Josh and Paul were waiting for me. Licking my finger, I roughly scoured the running black mascara and eyeliner off my face. Peering at the pathetic reflection was enough to set me off and frustrated sarcasm surfaced as I began raving aloud.

"What a waste of time and money! Maria said all I need is God, and this guy thinks I need a shrink and some drugs. Maybe there is a place for psychos like me where you worship and pass around the narcotics all at the same time ..."

I wasn't about to go on medication. I had concluded that mental illness was merely a medical excuse for personal weakness. There is no diagnostic proof; therefore symptoms alone define the disorder. On any given day with trying circumstances, anyone could "feel" clinically depressed. I had some character flaws that needed to be addressed; my antidote was to buck up, get a positive attitude, and be grateful. But every time I fell, I loathed myself more than the time before. Driving home, I began one of my one-sided "conversations" with God.

"What do You want me to do here? I AMMMMMM TRYYYYYYYING! Just give me anything ... a clue. Something. Tell me what to do because I feel as if I can't go on like this ..." I kept pleading until I neared the familiar turn into our drive. I parked the car, and sat quietly for a few moments to pull myself together before I greeted Josh and Paul. Reentering my life meant the curtain was going up ... the show must go on.

However, in the stillness I heard His voice deep within.

"Trust Me, Michelle, with all your heart. Rely on Me and I will give you life."

"You said that before, ya know," I mumbled in frustration. I was longing for a quick fix and this sounded way too much like a process.

I sighed in resignation.

How could I trust God with my heart? I couldn't imagine letting anybody take a look at my heart, let alone God. It needed a serious cleaning before it could be presented to anybody, especially Him. But maybe He could show me how to fix myself?

I reasoned that "seeing the light again" was a matter of seeking help from either a shrink with a side of drugs or God. In the weeks to follow, I began to consider God. I blew the dust off my Bible and started looking for answers the best way I knew how. I randomly opened it up to see if a verse applied, but usually the genealogy of unpronounceable names left me bored. Then I'd flip, flip, flip, read a little here and there, flip some more, read a little, and flip some more. But one book kept me.

I loved the Psalms. Reading David's heart somehow opened mine. He unabashedly admitted he was afraid, angry, and uncertain all throughout his poetic cries to God, which made me feel kindred toward him. He seemed so real to me, unlike most other "Christians" I knew. I could picture him discovering God as he lay in the fields, tending his sheep, staring up at the skies in wonder. I was awestruck to realize God remained faithful to David even when David wasn't faithful to God, that God delighted in David's praise, even crazy-underwear-dancing-praise, and finally, to read that David was a man after God's own heart.

That moved me.

I wondered what made David so special? I discovered that David was chosen by God to be a conquering king not because of his ability or stature, but because of his heart. In fact, David was the least of all his brothers sent before Samuel to be chosen and anointed as king. He was a mere shepherd boy and would have been completely overlooked had not God's eye been set on him. This was the beginning of a life-altering discovery: God uses ordinary, flawed people to do extraordinary things. This new revelation started to impart hope that just *maybe* He could do something with *even* me.

———*mm*———

My newfound hunger for God actually proved to be a marvelous distraction from my miseries. Paul and I coasted along, and it looked as if the skies were clearing when we got the news of his winter ball assignment in none other than Maui, Hawaii! Maybe baseball wasn't so bad after all. Oh, yeah! Tropical paradise, endless beaches, sun, surf! Aloha, baby!

Unfortunately, tropical paradise was difficult for me to see from inside the toilet bowl. It was so unfair that I felt perfectly fine until the plane touched ground on Maui, and then I was hit with a plague. I was never so sick in my entire life. When the prolonged sickness increased as the days and weeks passed, I became very concerned as thoughts of chronic illnesses consumed me.

Paul mentioned my situation to one of the team trainers, hoping that he could recommend a good physician. He told Paul that a physician came in around once a week to hang out with the team. He assured Paul that it would be no problem for this doc to talk with me. I felt uncomfortable about it, but beggars can't be choosers, and I was desperate to know what could be causing this prolonged illness.

"Maybe a simple consultation might answer a few questions," I assured myself.

My husband was already out on the field when Josh was scooped from my arms, and I was ushered into a dirty trailer filled with baseball paraphernalia. The next thing I knew, the "doctor" cleared off a bench, asked me to lie down, and proceeded to feel around, asking questions.

"Does this hurt? How about here?" I closed my eyes as he poked around.

I imagined myself elsewhere to calm my increasing anxieties, but the damp stench of humidity and sweaty equipment refused the daydream. I stiffened as the edges of my panties were pulled down and he began pressing around my pelvic area.

"Yes! That hurts!" I said as he applied pressure, more out of panic that he'd continue lower if I didn't say anything than a response to actual pain. He paused for a moment and I sighed in relief. The worst was over and now I could get the heck out of there.

My eyes popped wide open when I heard the slapping sound of rubber gloves being pulled over hands and wrists. Before I could protest, he quickly spread my knees and gave me a pelvic exam! No explanation, no warning, no nothing.

I felt completely violated. He was so matter of fact. It was all I could do not to throw up all over him.

"Well, I think you have an entopic pregnancy," he said flatly.

I didn't hear anything else he said after that because I was in shock. On the cold bleacher seats, I held Joshua as close to me as possible, burying my face in his jacket, trembling through the entire game. I tried to console myself: "At least he used gloves."

When the game was over, there was the usual fanfare that included signing autographs. It was an eternal ride home with a car packed full of sweaty players. By the time we were through our own front door, I had completely shut down. I managed to mention to Paul that I might be pregnant, but I don't recall ever sharing with Paul that whole scene in the baseball trailer. I never wanted to see that guy again, let alone confront him.

Shortly thereafter, we saw a doctor in a real doctor's office where the nurse informed us that the test results confirmed pregnancy. However, this doctor said that everything looked fine and that I had nothing to worry about. As an afterthought, he said, "The constant nausea and vomiting are *merely* severe morning sickness and will likely subside after twelve weeks."

Merely. I oughtaaa...

I spent the next few weeks crawling around our loft apartment, never too far from the toilet or a trashcan. I bawled like a baby until my sweet mama hopped on a plane and came to my rescue. Just hearing her voice was calming; to have her there was heaven.

I have loved the sun my whole life, ruining my skin with a golden tan for as long as I can remember. But now the Hawaiian sun, the holy grail of sun-seekers from all over the world, had to be shut out. The few renegade rays that made their way through the blinds in the morning made me ... you guessed it ... absolutely nauseous. I was in Maui—paradise beyond description, but needed to lie down indoors in complete darkness. Incapacitated, Mom took my place in the sun.

Her sunny disposition and determined faith were contagious. When Mom said it was going to be all right, I believed her. She made her signature healthy concoctions and figured out what combinations of food were tolerable for my stomach. In a matter of weeks, I felt I would survive after all.

Since having my own child, I grew to respect my mother in a whole new way. I also began to understand and appreciate things about her that in my younger years, I would have either ignored or despised. This was especially true of her faith. She has always been the cornerstone of our family; one-by-one we all came to recognize the power of the ceaseless prayers that upheld us. Though very vocal about her beliefs, my mom was very private about the pain that drove her into the arms of her God. She never complained. In fact, there was a positive confession on her lips at all times. From watching my mom all those years, I drew strength in the midst of my own struggles as I attempted my own walk with God.

How foolish were my first steps toward a real relationship with God. I began using the Bible like a source code, finding just the right Scriptures for the corresponding ailment. Unintentionally, I started to see God as my personal "pharmacist," willing to barter. I thought that if I could offer Him just the right "prescription"—the exact formula of Scriptures, prayers, and (most crucial of all) the proper amount of personal faith, He would hand-deliver the answer I was looking for. The amazing thing was that He never scorned my efforts. He patiently moved me forward despite my selfishness.

The way my pregnancy was going, I knew that when my mom left, it wasn't wise for me to stay any longer than necessary in Paradise Lost. I spent a month in Arizona with my parents instead, and it was a nice respite from baseball life.

I probably should take a minute to explain my continual love-hate relationship with baseball, because it was the very center of our world. I loved the game, loved it. I loved the way the clay infield looked perfectly groomed before the first pitch. I loved the manicured diamond of green that beckoned balls to land in its lushes. I loved the smells of the stadium as hotdogs and peanuts filled every inhalation. I loved the statistical nature of the game; you could fail seven out of ten times at the plate and still be a winner. I loved the surge of nervous energy every time Paul was on the mound or up to bat. During those nearly nine years of baseball-driven life, I cheered my guts out, cried my heart out, and sat through more rain delays and extra innings than I care to recall.

The hate side of this relationship with the game was deep and dark. The life of a minor league ballplayer was not glamorous for a family man. While other players partied, slept with endless women, and shacked two to four players to an apartment to pocket money, Paul, Josh and I scraped pennies to make rent and buy food. The financial strain, however, was secondary to the emotional stress that rose and fell by the day. You never knew where you were going to play, when you would have to pack up and relocate to another team, or whether or not tonight would be your final at bat. And *never* did you have a real place to call home.

Then there was the egotistical "it's all about me and my daily performance" nature of the game that wore on me like grinding teeth. It was another reason I felt invisible. Nothing in my daily world mattered in comparison to shifting batting averages and win-loss records. Thankfully, unlike nearly every other married man on the teams we played, I never worried about Paul being unfaithful. But there was a continuous pit in my stomach when I looked into the trusting eyes of the unwitting wives. It was a sad reality of the game.

A month in Arizona without a ballgame was a refreshing change of pace. For once, it was "all about me" and my pregnant self. After Paul joined us there, we drove to Iowa, where we would spend another consecutive off-season living with his mom and stepdad Tom. I have nothing but love for the both of them; they couldn't have been more supportive. Paul's dad was the same way. The three of them gave everything in their collective power to enable us to survive the harsh demands of minor league baseball. So I could scarcely complain about our living arrangements, but it was not easy being pregnant and miserable with no private place to host my pity parties.

My moods swung like a crazy pendulum and Paul paid the price right along with me, never knowing what he'd find when he came home. Normally I was quiet and solemn, but approachable. Now, during this troublesome pregnancy, he'd often find a hostile, combative, desperately unhappy wife keeping him up with nightly arguments he could never win. There were a lot of tears shed during those intermediate months. My pursuit of God was temporarily sidelined by the all-consuming misery of being *me.*

CHAPTER 5

"I Know"

This symbol represents the compassion of God.
He captures each tear that drips down your face,
and tenderly places them into His bottle.
When you cry, you are not alone.
When you think no one could possibly understand
the pain you feel... He knows.
He is right there beside you, collecting those
precious drops.
a weary mind, tears you sow
down your cheek the pain it flows
tattered, on your knees you go
He'll hold your face and say, "I Know."

THE DAYS AND MONTHS have a way of passing in the same manner for the best of times and the worst of times; there is no respect to circumstances. The sun rose regardless of whether or not I wanted it to. Another demanding season of ball with a rocky marriage and a new baby on the way were incomprehensible, so I deferred to the modus operandi: simply go through the motions.

Paul went off to spring training, and I hoped against hope we'd be assigned to the AA Canton/Akron Indians in the place I was born and raised. Some of my family still resided there, and Canton was the closest thing to "home." I held my breath until we landed safely on the AA roster, and I knew that I was going home.

It was a comfort to have my big sister Gigi in Canton. She has always been "the main load bearing wall" in the structure of our family. With an enormous amount of responsibility as the eldest sister, she helped raise and care for the household of children. Her positive influence seeped into the negative areas of my life. She was a fitness trainer, incredibly beautiful and lean; there wasn't an un-sculpted muscle on her body. Yet, unlike me, she refused to let her focus be dominated by outward appearance; she kept spiritually fit above all. She also possessed an incredible marriage, and walked in her role as "wife" with such grace. She was wise, strong, and constant in the face of storms, and I felt better just being near her. I also knew I could rely on her to be there for me at the birth if Paul was on an away trip when the time came.

I began having contractions less than ten minutes apart when I called Paul in Connecticut to ask if there was any way he could make it back. The Indians were kind enough to fly him home, and he landed just as they broke my water. Quite unlike Joshua's arrival, I was completely medicated from head to toe and in the hands of a competent physician when Kaylin Briana Meade made her safe, but fiery-red, screaming-mad entrance into the world!

How could a baby this beautiful be this miserable? Wailing, screaming, and projectile vomiting were the hallmarks of our first months together. All of that with a weepy, agitated, sleep-deprived version of my normal self and you have an idea of what this sweet mother and child portrait must have looked like. Together, we were a total mess.

Thank God for Josh. His sweet disposition helped make up for his sister's lack. He awoke, went potty, dressed and fed himself, and then lovingly woke me up later with songs. That was typical Josh; he *ran* at seven months, talked in complete sentences with three-syllable words by the time he was a year old, potty trained *himself* at fifteen months, ate everything you put in front of him, was lovey-dovey, and couldn't have been happier! I had a divine firstborn child, which was an unfortunate comparison for baby number two.

Kaylin and me just before the storm.

With the stress of the ball season, managing an unhappy baby, and the heaviness of the postpartum blues, I felt as if I were dragging fifty-pound weights on each shoulder. Nursing wasn't going well either and every feeding proved to be an exercise in frustration. Could things possibly get any worse? I comforted myself with the thought that they could not. How wrong I was.

Kaylin finally started to eat and sleep better at six months, offering me at least four consecutive hours of sleep a night and a few peaceful moments during the day. Although delayed, our loving mother-daughter bond was fulfilling in ways I couldn't have imagined. Hopeful feelings surfaced!

Just when I began to "let down" and relax, out of nowhere, *it* happened.

I distinctly recall walking into our apartment kitchen to prepare a snack for Joshua, and a repulsive image hit the screen of my mind. I stopped, shuddered, and shook my head as if to shake the thought far from me ... but within moments, a repeat version flashed before me.

Terror entered my heart.

If someone wanted to destroy me, he would be immediately and entirely successful by harming my children in any way. I recoiled in horror when I heard news reports of missing and abused children. My imagination could scarcely contain the fearful possibility. So when in my kitchen, vile images dared to include the precious faces of my own children, I felt as if all the breath was sucked out of my lungs with each visual blow. Most incomprehensible of all, mine was the face of the perpetrator. There are no words to describe how disturbing this was.

I had no idea what to do to combat this continual onslaught of terror, so I began "rebuking" it. My mom "rebuked" any and everything that was remotely evil, whether words, deeds, or thoughts. I found myself rebuking continuously with little reprieve. I ran to the phone to call Mom for prayer, but the peace only lasted until the next terrifying image shattered my shelter.

I remained overly busy to try to forget the horrible thoughts that relentlessly pursued me. I was utterly exhausted and relieved for each night's end. However, no matter how hard I tried, I could not slow my frantic, unquiet mind. Depression and despair were familiar enemies that I had learned to live with. However, this altogether different beast was an unknown terror that held my racing heart tightly in its clutches. I was distraught to find myself still wide-awake for the 5:00 a.m.

feeding and pictured the difficulties that lay ahead just to make it through the day. Crying took too much effort, so I moaned softly as Kaylin nursed away.

That day, and the day after that, and the day after that, and the day after that, and the day after that continued on in the same hideous fashion. I ran from terrorizing thoughts all day and wrestled each night with no sleep in sight. I was sure I would die. Worse of all, I struggled alone because I couldn't possibly share these thoughts; they were just too horrific to verbalize. I felt that speaking the fear out loud would somehow validate it, so I remained enslaved to its demand for silence.

I could release only some of the anguish upon divine ears.

"God! Why is this happening? What is wrong with me? That's *not* me! Who is this person? Please deliver me from this evil; please deliver me from this evil ..." I begged.

Onward the cycle continued with crazy thoughts and compulsive responses. Whether I was quoting Scriptures or reading aloud, I felt as if I had to do something to stop the terror. My attempts at combating the fearful thoughts only perpetuated the problem, but I wouldn't discover this until many years later.

My sister Gigi suspected more than insomnia and probed deeper one day on the phone. I hesitated to say.

"Shell, hunny, tell me what's troubling you," she gently prodded.

"I ... I keep getting terrible thoughts ... over and over they chase after me ..."

"What kind of thoughts, hunny?" Gigi asked.

I couldn't formulate any words of explanation.

"Tell me, hunny. The fear will dissipate with exposure to light."

What she said offered hope, but it was contrary to the fearful instinct to conceal.

"I can't," I muttered.

"You can tell me, Shell."

Before I lost courage, I spilled what I could in fragments. "Awful, hideous thoughts of my children. Abusing and harming my own children. Atrocious sexual images ..." my words trailed off as I sobbed.

Gigi's quiet voice prayed, and then she assured me that everything was going to be all right.

I wanted to be strong. I wanted to dispel the ludicrous thoughts with laughter, yet I was held hostage to these fears as my mind replayed them against my control. I wasn't sure what frightened me most: the thoughts, the sleeplessness, or the fretting over what could be beneath it all. I knew something was terribly wrong and wrestled within myself for understanding. Yet, all my reasoning lead to further panic, self-doubt, and a lingering dread that I was losing my mind. I saturated myself with anything and everything "good" like Christian television and praise and worship music to try to overcome the evil in my head.

After a solid month of continual suffering, I stopped nursing and sought help for the insomnia through sleeping aids. I hoped to bring some relief from the cycle of terror with rest. To my dismay, the sleeping pills, herbs, and every other technique proved unsuccessful. But I was using only over-the-counter medications. I should have gone to a doctor and received some adequate prescription relief from the constant panic, but I was too afraid. Afraid to tell anybody of the madness in my mind, I found myself pacing our tiny apartment instead, quoting Scripture aloud. The louder my thoughts became, the louder I quoted. I was convinced that this is what hell is like.

I was too terrified to be openly angry with God for my plight. I felt that He was my only chance to make it through this thing alive. But in the deepest part of my heart I felt abandoned by Him, despite my refusal to admit it.

There were times when I would remind Him, "You promised me. You said if I trusted You, you would lead me to something good! What is this? What IS this?!? Why am I stuck in this hell? Please do not abandon me here. Please!"

My daily routine of caring for two small children, rebuking demons, and quoting Scripture was utterly exhausting. I felt as if I ran a mental, emotional, and spiritual marathon every single day, gutting it out to the finish, only to do a repeat performance the following day without any recovery in between. My biggest enemy was the sleeplessness; I feared my body would eventually shut down.

In the deep of the night with trembling lips and shaking hands, I pleaded with God to save me. I tried to quiet myself to hear a divine response of comfort or encouragement, but everything that I heard and saw in the recesses of my mind mocked and cursed me instead. I was petrified that I was somehow given over to evil. I repented for hours every night for my weaknesses, the fears, the thoughts, and every tiny conceivable grievance that I may have ever committed. This became another way to deal with the overwhelming thoughts.

My ability to act and mask kept everyone around me virtually unaware of the depths to which I was losing it. I recall blindly walking the aisles of the grocery store, looking at each face that passed by with longing, wishing I were normal like they were. No matter what I tried, I could not escape.

Paul's baseball season was nearing its end when he fractured a bone in his hand. What could have been a devastating injury only proved to be minor with having sufficient time to heal over the winter months. In fact, it seemed like a blessing in disguise, as worker's compensation offset expenses, enabling us to keep our apartment rather than live with Paul's parents.

Paul's having to resort to part-time work meant having full-time fun. And Paul was all about that with his kids. I resented his easy-going nature most of the time because of my survival mode of living. However, looking back, I am grateful that he continued to be the "jovial" part of our family, continually bringing laughter and humor into the lives of our children. I am also grateful that our future was hidden from us, because had we known the pain that lay ahead, we would have resisted the path and tried to find an alternate route. I had no idea our world was about to become even more bizarre.

—~m~—

My niece Heidi offered to baby-sit the kids one evening so that Paul and I could have a much-needed night out. My life was still a nightmare, so losing myself inside the big screen was a hopeful prospect. *Forrest Gump* had my full attention, except for the unusual interruptions as Paul repeatedly got up from his seat. The fourth time, I followed him out to the lobby. From the look on his face, I could see that he was not doing well.

"What's the matter? Are you sick?" I asked.

"I don't know…. but I gotta get this cast off…" he said as he desperately pulled and stretched the casing around his fractured hand.

He complained of shortness of breath, as if his throat was closing, and insisted that he needed to have the cast off NOW! His fingers looked raw from tearing at his cast, so I suggested we go to the ER and let them cut it off. I realized that he was having a full-blown panic attack.

He just shook his head in protest and motioned for us to get into the car. It was nearly 10:00 at night, and everyone was sleeping except Heidi when we arrived at Gigi's house. Paul took a B-line for the kitchen drawer, and I held my breath as he savagely sawed off the plaster with a steak knife! Heidi and I watched in shock, but upon seeing the considerable relief on his face when the cast gave way, we assumed it was for the best.

Paul never said anything about that night, but it was obvious from that moment on that something was wrong. He was withdrawn, silent, and serious. I felt as if an alien inhabited the body of my husband, because there was no trace of the Paul I had known. It was frightening enough to be "me," but to watch Paul suffer with an unknown fear was very worrisome. As vulnerable as I was, I always had the assurance that if I fell apart completely, Paul would hold our family together. Now that Paul was incapacitated, I had no idea what we would do.

Paul started a relationship with God at ORU his freshman year, but I was always the one in the family who "knew" spiritual things from my upbringing. In light of my recent terror "attacks" and now Paul, I decisively concluded that we were in a serious "spiritual war." I began digging deeper into the Scriptures to uncover ways to combat our enemy. Wrapping my condition in a "spiritual package" brought temporary relief from a continuous dread that I was going insane. However, this encouraged me to continue to strive harder to increase *my* faith and thereby justify my resistance to medical attention for my condition. I was trapped inside an illusionary world consisting of half-truths defined by fear.

Paul was not a reader, but he began to voraciously pound down as much of the Bible and other books of faith as possible. For the first time in his life, he encountered something he could not control. Driven to his knees, he sought after God with his whole heart.

Then you will seek Me, require Me and find Me when you search for Me with all your heart. I will be found by you, says the Lord, and I will release you from captivity ... (Jeremiah 29:13, 14)

One unsuspecting day a miracle came calling when my mom's longtime friend Linda rang to ask if she could drop by. The moment she stepped into our dreary apartment, life cascaded in behind her! This beautiful redhead became "all business" as she got out her flask of anointing oil and began to pray. As she prayed, we could feel the power of God in the room, which was unlike anything we had ever experienced before.

Within moments she said, "Amen," gathered her things, and was out the door. I stood in amazement and wonder as Paul's countenance literally changed before me. His eyes became clear and bright as his casual smile lit his face once again. He excitedly told me how he felt "something" leave him as she prayed, and he knew he was healed. From that moment on, he walked in total freedom from fear.

Paul and I found unity within the arms of our faith for the first time in our marriage. Out of the darkness, hope started to dawn within me that something good might actually arise from this disaster. I didn't however expect to hear words that could eventually alter the course of our lives.

Paul is a neat and tidy sort of guy. You never see food between his teeth or (heaven forbid!) anything on his face or clothes. One of his little idiosyncrasies is his need to towel-dry every square inch of his body before he steps out of the shower. He is appalled when I pull a clean tee shirt over my dripping wet back. That sort of thing makes his teeth hurt. So the day I saw his soaking wet body streaking through our tiny apartment, I knew something was terribly wrong. Or in this case, terribly right.

"What are you doing?" I questioned.

"I need a Bible," he said, scanning the room.

"Why?" I wondered aloud, staring incredulously at his dripping wet, bare body.

"I need a Bible. Where's your Bible?" he continued, instinctively covering himself as if I had never seen him before.

I laughed as I motioned toward the Bible. I watched in wonder as he stood in a puddle on the linoleum floor and read. He gazed up with a serious expression, placed the Bible back down, and briskly walked back into the shower without saying a word.

I wanted to howl in laughter, but my curiosity got the best of me.

"Heyyyyyy! Wanna tell me what *that* was all about?!?" I yelled into the bathroom.

"I'll tell you when I get out," he said through the hot steam.

Later he emerged and casually announced, "God just spoke to me, audibly, in the shower."

My jaw dropped to the floor because I knew that wasn't something that just "happened" every day. He continued to tell me that he had distinctly heard God's voice say, "*DO Matthew 10:8. JUST DO IT.*"

Grabbing the open Bible, he read aloud, "*Heal the sick, raise the dead, cure the lepers, and cast out demons. Freely you have received, freely give.*"

I sat, silent and incredulous, for several moments.

"You actually heard an *audible* voice?" I questioned.

"Clear as yours right now," he answered.

I was stunned. I don't know what surprised me more—that Paul actually heard God or that God would actually speak to Paul. I had a lot of mixed feelings about the whole thing. Clearly, some sort of spiritual awakening was happening in my husband. While it was what I had always prayed for, now that it was happening, feelings of jealousy and envy shuffled for attention.

Why did Paul get an instant miracle when I continued to suffer mental anguish on a daily basis? Why would God speak to Paul in such a vivid way after he has virtually ignored Him for years, while I have tried, albeit pathetically, but *tried* to seek after Him my whole life? Yet, I have *barely* heard the "still small voice" of God, let alone an audible response from the Maker of the Universe! It all seemed incredibly unfair.

Self-pity wanted to ruin the blissful moment, but I somehow pushed it aside momentarily.

Paul began experiencing one supernatural thing after the next. First he started having dreams and visions, and then when he stepped out in obedience to "do" Matthew 10:8, the palm of his right hand burned hotly. Time after time, people were receiving answers to prayer and healings from God through *my* husband Paul!

Looking for my own healing, I began clinging closer and closer to Paul as my connection to God. I continually placed his right hand on my head at night—a limp, mortal hand slipped onto my face instead of the burning hand of God. I held his sleeping body tightly against mine to try to stop the shaking.

I needed to know that I would make it through because despair like none other I had ever experienced began engulfing me in repeated waves. I wanted to believe God was waiting in the wings and that He would once again rescue me from destruction as He did that hot night in Columbus, Georgia. But where was He as I shook in terror, drowning in my fears? As I lay there, I tearfully wondered if He remembered *me*?

I had several books and devotionals all piled up beside me on the bed and I reached for my Amplified Bible and opened up to Isaiah 49, where my eyes immediately fell upon these verses:

But Zion [Jerusalem, her people seen in captivity] said The Lord has forsaken me, and my Lord has forgotten me. [And the Lord answered] Can a woman forget her nursing child, that she should not have compassion on the son of her womb? Yes, they may forget you, but I will not forget you. Behold, I have indelibly imprinted (tattooed) a picture of you on the palm of each of my hands. O Zion, your walls are continually before me (Isaiah 49:14-16, AMP).

I outstretched my arms upward toward heaven and prayed aloud, "God, I don't feel deserving of such Love, but I want to receive it. Please help me to know You, all who You are. Make me into something beautiful. I am such a mess, only You can do it."

Even before the last few words were muttered, a warm sensation slowly moved up and down my body twice. The warmth now covered and hovered about my head for a long time, and all the while a peaceful calm contained me like the shores contain the seas. Finally the sensation left, but when I lowered my hands onto my head, heat was still resonating from my scalp into my fingertips. I licked the salty tears that fell into my curved lips, and for the first time in several months I drifted off into a sweet sleep as I whispered, "Thank You."

CHAPTER 6

"Friend"

I rule the heavens, I made the earth
yet I stopped in wonder to dance at your birth
I hung the stars, I placed the moon
yet I look forward to long talks with you
I AM your Healer, comfort I send
Redeemer, Messiah, yet ...
I call you Friend.

ALL THE FIGHT had been sucked out of me after nearly four solid months of mental battling. I barely existed. Frankly, I didn't care anymore about anything but sleep. Obsessing about how many minutes of sleep I'd get each night became my full-time occupation, only interrupted by an obscene terror attack often enough to keep me sufficiently enslaved to both forms of torture. The hope of waking up from this nightmare wasn't manifesting and I regretted "the life sentence" description in reference to my marriage, because I would trade this current hell for an eternity of my former life in a split second.

Being able to point to Paul as the enemy all these years was easy and familiar; finding and eliminating the unknown cause of my mental deterioration was an altogether discouraging prospect. Isolating evil as the source continued my search for wholeness down spiritual corridors. What was confusing and later daunting was my inability to distinguish and apply spiritual truths without abusing them compulsively. I continued to refuse the option of medical care because of fear and faith. I was afraid to be honest about the severity of my symptoms, but my justification was easy to mask inside my narrow view of faith; I believed my faith would make me whole.

After our income and short-term lease ran out, our family of four found ourselves on the doorsteps of Paul and Michele Colaner's large Victorian home. Paul and Michele were best friends with my sister Maria and her husband Steve. Steve and Paul were stationed at Randolph Air Force Base in San Antonio, Texas, and during our courtship days Paul and I drove down from Tulsa to spend fall break with the four of them at Padre Island.

Saying that Maria and Michele are best friends is like saying there are a couple stars in our galaxy. I kid you not! With all the wonders of San Antonio—the Alamo, the River Walk, the endless rows of Texas Bluebonnets—nothing captivated me as much as the unique friendship Maria and Michele had. There

Maria and Michele

was nothing casual or trite about their relationship; they dove deep, straight to the heart of every issue, trusting each other implicitly. I was drawn and yet repelled at the same time by such intimacy. Of course, it's what my heart secretly ached for—to know and be known by another, but the prospect of rejection was much too great to be worth the risk.

Having witnessed them first-hand, how they interacted with each other so openly, honestly, and regularly (ten phone calls a day when they lived down the street from one another), it was no surprise when I learned that Maria had informed Michele of our current housing dilemma. We had to choose either to sign another six-month lease (even though we had less than two months before spring training and another relocation) *or* make a huge move across the country back to Iowa to stay with Paul's folks. Neither option sounded good, so when Michele gleefully told Maria, "They could move in with us for these couple months!" we weighed the offer seriously. We met with Paul and Michele and felt strangely at ease, as if we had known them all our lives, even though we had only met them on two prior occasions. With a little trepidation, we decided to accept their offer to stay with them in the cozy home they called "Wit's End." It seemed ironically appropriate in light of my state of mind.

Now Paul and I would get to know Paul and Michele up close and personal for ourselves. Paul and Michelle and Paul and Michele … our names alone caused hilarity and confusion. But it wasn't long before the humor grew tiresome, and nicknames became necessities. I became known as "Shelly" and my husband was simply "Meade." Their childfree sanctuary was immediately disturbed with Kaylin's ear-piercing screams despite my every frantic attempt to pacify her. I should have relaxed because they were two of the most casual, unfussy, and gracious people we had ever known.

Did I mention scary too? Michele was tall, loud, expressive, and unafraid to invade your personal space. Paul, well, he just plain scared me. He had a WWF countenance with his bare skinhead and multi-colored tattoos adding increased drama to fit the part. Moreover, his dry sarcastic humor was difficult to read, so I never knew if he was joking. My awkward insecurities were magnified in the presence of these larger-than-life personalities.

Michele had a disarming way about her, making her nearly impossible to resist. She was the most congenial, honest, openly loving person I had ever met. The first time she hugged me, I knew I was in for it. She wouldn't stand for my loose, one-armed, "pat- pat" hugs; she pulled me tightly to her chest and dug her face right down into my neck for a long embrace. I was mortified.

"I am just so happy you guys are here, Shelly! It's like having a little bit of Ria here with me!"

"Thanks for having us. It is so nice of you guys to open up your home for these couple months. We are so grateful," I replied.

It wasn't a *complete* lie, because a teeny, tiny, infinitesimal part of me was glad I was there. The other 99.9 percent wanted to run away and hide. It was one thing for me to be a basket case in the privacy of my own apartment; it was an altogether different thing to go through hell with an audience.

I tried to act as if everything was okay, but my masking ability was not flying above Michele's radar. I remembered Maria telling me how Michele had the uncanny ability to read people, and the personality to *do* something about it.

I walked around like a cat with cautious movements and carefully crafted expressions to conceal the raw, frayed nerves that lay hidden within, but I sensed she *knew.* Apparently Michele was not only aware of our ongoing troubled marital situation, but she also knew I was an insomniac. I was annoyed with Maria for sharing information about me. I was far more comfortable with anonymity and solitude; they were all I knew.

Michele's hearty laugh echoed off the ten-foot ceilings and resonated throughout their home. She had a way of finding amusement in every situation, laughing at commercials, her dogs, her husband's dry humor, my kids, and literally busting a gut over my husband. She thought he was one of the funniest people she had ever met in her life, and this irritated me to no end.

I had been married for nearly five years and I had laughed all of two times. Two! To me, my husband's humor was only an attempt to ignore the devastating issues in our lives. He joked to avoid conflict, and if there was one thing that needed more attention, conflict was it! How dare he try and make our horrible life any fun whatsoever. For the first time in my married life, I learned to look at Paul with different eyes, and Maria and Michele had everything to do with it.

Michele's vulnerability and welcoming grace almost made me feel safe enough to open up without fearing judgment. *Almost.*

I was so afraid of having a perverted thought that I refused to look anybody in the eye—including family, friends, and people on TV or pictures of Jesus in my own Bible! I knew all my thoughts and fears were irrational; yet I felt powerless to halt them. The more I tried to stop or defer, the more automated they became.

I was consumed with shame, as if I were guilty of these evils. My shallow raccoon eyes darted back and forth around a room, carefully avoiding any direct contact. I was screaming inside for help, yet silently suffering alone.

Paul was soon leaving the three of us behind as he prepared to depart for spring training once more. I was so painstakingly riveted in fear of each second that I couldn't bear to think about our future. Michele, however, was getting closer and closer to cracking my hard shell. I'll never forget that moment in her kitchen.

"I have to tell ya. You're safe with me, Shelly," she said in between sipping coffee. I refused to look up from my flurry of busyness as I continued to sweep the floor in slow, rhythmic movements.

"I mean it. It doesn't matter what you do or say. I'll still love you …"

I swept faster.

"You don't have to hide, Shelly. You are safe with me …"

I wanted to make an excuse to get the heck out of the kitchen, but there was no way to escape as she continued, "Shelly, put the broom down and look at me."

I knew I was no match for Michele, so my hesitation quickly gave way to obedience. Looking into her eyes of compassion was more than I could bear, and the dam within collapsed. The tears I hid came flooding out as she moved in to swoop me into her giant embrace.

"It's going to be all right. I am telling you, it is," she finally whispered after holding me quietly for a long time as I wept.

In those few moments, the oil of love seeped into the recesses of my soul and began loosening the chains. Formulating thoughts and words to describe the anguish was still difficult, but a month at Michele's without Paul left a lot of time for coffee talk. We watched Jane Austen movies, discussed books, poetry, gardening, and decorating ideas; and found we had much more in common than our names.

For the first time in years, I laughed aloud heartily as she described her relationship with her Paul in vivid detailed ways that only she can. Beyond entertainment, I was comforted to realize that others couples struggled with issues similar to ours. Sitting there in her front room, immensely enjoying her company, my heart swelled in the nurturing enfolding of *friendship*.

Ria called and announced that our sleepover party would be complete. She planned to join us for several weeks while Steve trained in Louisiana. I had already begun to adore Michele. And with my dear sister on her way, I felt as if God was smiling down on me at last.

"So I do all the work to get you to crack a smile and open up the teeniest, itsy- bitsy bit, and your sister will come to town, and you'll tell her all the *good* stuff ... what's really behind those dark circles! I just know it!" Michele said when we seated ourselves into our favorite chairs respectively.

As I fidgeted with a string on my shirt, I replied innocently, "I don't know what you are talking about."

"Yeah, sure you don't," Michele dropped sarcastically, then continued. "Listen, whatever it is, it couldn't be worse than the mess sitting right here." She said referring to herself.

"I don't know about that. *This* is a scary place," I said playfully, pointing to my head with raised eyebrows.

"Whose isn't? I'm half out of my mind every single day of my life," Michele insisted.

I kept looking down, but shook my head slowly from side to side in protest.

"WHA-A-AT is it?!?" she belted in loud, dramatic Michele-fashion.

I sat there, wondering what words would give her some indication of what I was experiencing without revealing the really awful stuff. Before I could reply she said, "Okay, just tell me what you're thinking right now."

Looking up, I shocked myself by blurting out the truth, "I have been afraid to look at you all morning because every time I do, I think 'pubic hair.'"

She tried not to laugh, but it was irresistible.

"WHAT?!?" she bellowed.

"Yeah, I am totally not kidding either. It has nothing to do with you or your beautiful black curly hair. It just happens to be the tormenting thought of the moment that ricochets off the corners of my mind ..." My eyes filled and my lips trembled as my words trailed off.

"Oh, Shelly," she said with a concerned voice and continued, " Hunny, everybody gets crazy thoughts. I get sick thoughts sometimes out of the stinkin' blue and I think 'Where in the world did that come from?' It's not uncommon. Really, hunny, it's not."

Michele began explaining her own overcoming as a way of comforting, but I ended up wandering off to a far away place. I was absolutely convinced that no one could possibly understand *this* madness. There was no way I could share what was really going on. I tried to pull myself back into the conversation by nodding in agreement at the appropriate times. I hoped the pasted smile would sufficiently cover for my lack of participation. With Maria here soon, I knew the conversations would be lively and constant, and I looked forward to the opportunity to sit silently on the sidelines.

In the meantime, I was busy completing my first ever "God assignment." While I was pregnant with Kaylin, God began dealing with my heart concerning the angst and bitterness I had toward Paul's dad. Over the years I saw a reflection of his father in many of Paul's mannerisms and behaviors. However unfair it may have been, when a marital argument ensued because of Paul's emotionless indifference, I provoked him by angrily accusing him of being "just like his dad."

Over time my heart grew cold and hard toward both. I was prepared to dig my heels in and retaliate with equal cruelty, feeling my position was justified. However, a higher authority checked my attitude.

As I waited impatiently through my final months of pregnancy, my heart was pricked with the truth:

"If you only love those who love you, what reward will you have? Have I not asked you to treat others as you yourself desire to be treated?"

I agreed, but ignored His point.
Later the subject was revisited with a divine request.

"I want you to crochet a blanket for Paul's dad."

I immediately shrugged off the instruction as my own silly conscience and proceeded about my life. Days later He repeated the very same thing.

"I want you to pray for Paul's dad while crocheting him a blanket."

"But I don't even know how to crochet!" I protested.

Nearly a year later at Michele's, I was finishing the final rows of fringe on this labor of love. Tears rolled down my cheeks as I passionately prayed for him. The piercing thorn in my flesh had now become flesh of my flesh as my heart affectionately claimed him as *my dad.*

Prayer is a mysterious wonder; the productivity and power are undeniable, yet the mechanism so simple and childlike that it confounds reason. The hardness of my heart softened with each and every stitch. This was my first real lesson in Love.

I carefully folded the finished blanket freshly washed in my tears, topped with a handwritten letter expressing my desire for a fresh start in our relationship. I openly admitted my failures and sought his forgiveness earnestly. I mailed the blanket and prayed it would be received in the spirit with which it was given.

—————

"She's here!!" Michele's voice belted out.

I hadn't realized just how much Ria had worked herself inside my heart until she walked through the door. The three of us proceeded to act like a trio of sorority sisters, staying up all hours of the night, yakking as if we were participating in some sort of "intensive therapy." At first I hesitated to partake of their openness; eventually however, I dared to dip my toe in to test the waters.

"I don't get it. Why do you think Paul's so funny?" I questioned Michele.

She started laughing aloud as she mimicked something he had said in Jim Carey fashion and continued, "He is absolutely hilarious, Shelly! I can't even believe you don't think so! At all, I mean ever?" she wondered.

"Nope. His silliness annoys the heck out of me," I confessed.

"It's because of the pain. She can't see past it, to see any of his good traits," Maria interjected.

"That's not true," I protested.

"Oh, yes, it is! When is the last time you looked at Paul and thought something sweet?" Maria asked.

"I don't know. But most people don't go around gushing over their mates, not in real life anyway."

"Ria does. She stinkin' kisses the ground Steve walks on."

Michele starts laughing and continued, "No, Shelly, it's the truth! I swear I've never seen a woman adore her husband more. Never, not even in the movies, and I am here to tell you, it's the real thing. When we lived with them for two months, the sound effects alone were way more than I needed to hear," Michele revealed with feigned disgust as Maria giggled.

I rolled my eyes in protest, "You guys are the exception and not the rule because ..."

"Maybe, but it wasn't always this way, and stop rolling your eyes to the back of your head!" Maria scolded.

"It can't simply be one-sided though, Ria ..." I tried to finish as she paused to suck in enough oxygen to interrupt me once more.

"Yes ... it ... can! It was completely one-sided at first. I thought I was literally going to puke when I was asked to kiss Steve on the lips. I wanted to punch his lights out when he came home drunk! I was told to stop nagging and preaching and simply love. And in my obedience to God, He promised to do the rest. It wasn't overnight, and at first Steve thought I was being insincere, but over time he saw that my response to him was going to be loving whether he deserved it or not."

"I am happy for you, but like I said, you are the exception and not the rule. I don't see it happening with us," I managed to interject.

"Only because you are choosing not to," Ria insisted.

"That's not true! I have tried to love, but it absolutely takes two willing people to make a relationship work! How can you tell me it only takes one to save a marriage?" I demanded, exasperated.

"Because it's the truth. Love is not a feeling and you cannot possibly expect your husband to make you happy! That is not his job. It makes me sick when people divorce, saying they fell out of love. Our feelings change day-by-day, even moment-by-moment. Love is a decision, Michelle. Period. You either choose to love Paul or you don't," Maria said loudly and emphatically.

"EASYYYYY, Ria! Geeeeeez! I am about to break out in hives just sitting here, listening to you!" Michele yelled out.

"But it's the truth!" Ria grinned, tossed her waist-length hair over her shoulder, and batted her large hazel eyes at Michele as if she were flirting with the ref in order to avoid a foul.

"It may be, but it is revelation you got from God and worked out through your own experience. Shelly's still in the nasty part, so EASSSSY! And I mean it, or I'll come over there!" Michele winked.

I asked sincerely, "It's just, what do you do when you've tried every possible way and get nothing? And I do mean nothing. I mean he chooses *not* to love. Am I supposed to be okay with that? Am I supposed to keep pretending by going through the motions when there are no feelings to back up my words? I feel like that is the highest form of hypocrisy. I am not being true to anybody."

"She has a point, Ria," Michele mentioned.

"AY! Whose side are you on anyway?!?" Ria scolded and continued, "Listen, hunny, I never said it would be easy or cut and dry. I cried myself to sleep more times than I want to remember. But slowly things changed as I consistently chose to love Steve regardless of his response to me. When you choose to love, God meets you where you are and does what only *He* can do, changing your heart and giving you genuine feelings. That's what you want isn't it? Paul's heart. Right? You don't want a fake response or a performance; you want him to love you from his heart."

I nodded silently, trying hard to resist the urge to roll my eyes back in cynicism. It was what I wanted, but I just couldn't accept that what she was saying was true. Love as she described was like taking a chainsaw to what was left of me. Michele's voice raised an octave with increased intensity, interrupting my thoughts.

"THAT'S going EASY?!! Geez, Ria! Shelly needs to vent. We've had each other to survive our husbands," Michele reminded.

"Shelly, you have me and Ria now. Not for just this time, but from now on. You can count on us. Call us anytime, even in the middle of the night. Call collect if you need to ... from anywhere and we'll be there. We promise to cry with you, laugh with you, and most importantly, we'll talk you down off the ledge as often as needed."

Michele's offer was sincerely touching and Ria nodded her head emphatically in agreement. I knew this was something special, more than a casual offer from a friend to "be there." I knew I was being invited into a friendship circle woven so tightly that you can't tell where the love and understanding begins or ends; it just is. I didn't know how to acknowledge their offer and the moment of silence was obviously my cue to answer. I had no idea what to say or where to start.

"Unlike the two of you, I don't always know what to say at just the right time," I said, regarding their over-expressiveness as if I were the "normal one."

"What you mean is that you don't know what you should say," Maria said, eyeing me pointedly.

Both sets of eyes were riveted on me when I snapped.

"I don't know how I feel!" I shouted, which was not typical in front of anybody but Paul. I ran my fingers through my hair and continued in a softer tone. "I have been living in survival mode for so many years now, I don't know how to feel anything but heartache, and most of the time I can't even admit, let alone deal, with my longing soul, so I just "do." I do what is needed and expected to get through the day. And these past couple months ..."

I paused and sighed before continuing, "I have been living in such a surreal place. I feel as if my life is some sort of science fiction thriller. On the outside I walk through my daily life as a mother and wife, but inside I have the mind of a hard-core felon. There are no words to describe the atrocities I behold on a daily basis. All right here," I managed to confess as I pointed to my head, grabbing large tufts of hair from each side.

I looked up and encountered compassion. Both faces reflected concern and sympathy. Their widened eyes filled with tears. After a couple moments of quiet, Ria belted out, "You do know you *need* to talk about it. You need to start talking about what it is that is terrifying you, so we can reassure you and remind you of the truth!"

"I can't," I muttered. I sighed long and hard and held my face in my hands and then looked up toward the ceiling.

"I don't know what's wrong with me. I feel like I'm going completely crazy," I said slowly and deliberately.

"I am not talking about the kind of crazy that people refer to casually. I am talking about the kind of crazy that makes you unfit for society. I am talking about the kind of crazy that necessitates locked-up isolation and heavy doses of narcotics to exist. I am talking about the kind of crazy that could separate me from everybody I love," I said, choking on tears.

I wiped my face and continued, "What I am experiencing is beyond words. And if I tried to describe the foul, insidious thoughts, I'd have to bring you into my hell and no one should ever have to go there."

They were both visibly moved and for once they didn't know quite how to respond.

I took a deep breath and continued, "You guys talk about sharing feelings, but I can't afford the luxury of feeling. If I unleash the floodgates, I won't be able to contain the devastation."

"Shelly, just take one small step toward freedom, then the next, then the next ..." Michele urged.

There was no such thing as small or manageable in my world. Everything from the sound of noises to a tiny criticism was repeated and magnified until it became overwhelming in my mind. I was trapped inside of myself, which was an absurd and hideous conclusion only fit for philosophical banter, not reality.

I took the first step: "Michele, you said something interesting: 'Acting like the pain isn't there doesn't help.' Well, I have been acting my whole life. I don't know how to be real. I mean, I've always tried to do the right thing whether I felt like it or not ... especially when I didn't feel like it. If I dare let my emotions have a voice, I'd crumble. I'd surely leave Paul, abuse and desecrate myself in attempts to numb the pain. I don't know how to let my soul have a voice while maintaining any sort of stability within. Do you guys know what I am saying?" I felt as if I were making a mess of my words.

"Keep talking. We're listening," Michele insisted.

"I'm probably not making much sense. I am just so tired, so incredibly weary. I truly forget what real sleep is like." I paused and ran my hands through my hair, massaging my head.

Michele said, "I can't even imagine what it's like, Shelly. I can't. And the way you love your children ... and doing it the way you do ... pouring yourself completely into them. It's utterly amazing, hunny. I mean it. A-mazing! I have watched you get up time after time and serve your family with raccoon-dark-circles under your eyes, knowing full well that you are the least of these."

Ria back-handed Michele lightly on the arm and said "She can't receive that compliment. She's thinking right now about the ten things she wished she had done differently with her kids. She's not even hearing you." Michele nodded knowingly.

Why was she always right? She was reading my mind, and it was ticking me off! Of course, I wasn't the mother, wife, or person I wished to be. I was a mess, a complete mess. I felt silence was my best defense against her accusation.

"You just won't cut yourself a break will ya, Shelly?" Michele asked kindly.

Ria answered for me, "No, she won't, and I'll tell ya why. She can't stand herself. Just give her another compliment and see what happens."

"Oh, don't think I haven't noticed," Michele scolded and pursued further, "But Shelly, honestly, can't you see your beauty inside and out, even just a little bit?"

I simply hung my head and shook it sadly and slowly side-to-side.

Michele was aghast. "Come on, that is just so wrong! I can think of a hundred different beautiful aspects of your character and personality right now on the spot. And I have always told Ria that there was always a 'Rachael quality' about you—the kind of stunning beauty that would make a man want to work fourteen years of slave labor for. I just can't accept that answer; you have to name me one good thing. At least one."

I managed to whisper, "Well, I have persevered and haven't quit yet. I guess that's good."

Ria chided, "More than most, but what I want to know is what you think about yourself, because I suspect it's all bad."

"You really want to know how pathetic I think I am?" I asked rhetorically. Looking at them squarely, I continued, "I look into the mirror and can no longer even find the disgust I once felt. There is nothing behind my eyes. Nothing. I used to wear shame like a garment, but now it's inseparable from my skin. So when you talk of how beautiful I am, I suspect you are both blinded to the truth," I admitted.

Michele blurted out, "Come on, Shelly! Honestly, if I were as hard on myself as you, I would throw myself out a window ... "

Michele couldn't finish before Ria interjected, "You pour out to everybody else, constantly loving and giving ... but it has to start with you, hunny. Love your neighbor as yourself. You've got to learn to love the person God created you to be. You've got to start seeing yourself the way He sees you: beautiful, valuable, precious, worthy."

My tattered heart sold me out, sending the bitter tears.

"Now look what you did, Ria!" Shel shrieked as she jumped up to smush me inside her arms. "Listen, you just tell me what's really bothering you. Whisper in my ear and I won't even tell Ria!" she teased, trying to lighten the moment.

"Yeah, right!" I laughed, and suddenly snot and tears shot unglamorously from my face.

"Lovely," Ria said as she threw me the nearby cloth diaper to wipe myself up.

I never got into more details of the mental anguish during that visit, but day after day, Ria and Michele were gaining ground. The laughter and the tears of these several weeks marked my soul in a way I could never have imagined. I was blossoming in the safety of their unconditional love and acceptance.

Three weeks into our sorority party, Shel announced that she had a special gift for me.

"For me?!?"

"Just for you, hunny. The Lord told me to make this for you," she said as she handed me a small, wrapped package.

I slowly unfolded the delicate rose paper to discover a handmade journal that was covered in muslin with beautiful and symbolic hand-crocheted daisies made of silk ribbon on the front.

"Daisies!" I smiled.

"Yeah, I thought it might replace the arrangement in the living room." She said with a wink.

It was obvious that Michele had kept the huge bouquet of daisies in the center of the front room to remind me of Paul's love. Knowing daisies were my favorite, he had searched all over town to give me a gigantic bouquet of yellow and white sunshine just before he left for spring training. Now the limping arrangement (probably drooping more from the decrease in oxygen from our continuous banter than from being three weeks old) was about to be replaced with a lasting reminder.

"Oh, Shel ... it's so beautiful," I said as I fingered the ribbon daisies and continued to flip it over and rub the natural muslin against my skin.

"This is a special journal. You are to write only the sweet things your husband says and does in here. Start savoring the good thoughts you have toward him. Even if it seems small or trivial, write it down and make a point of acknowledging the good. There is a lot of good there, hunny. I know you don't believe it, but the truth is that man of yours is ... and has always been since the moment he laid eyes on you ... madly in

love with you. You make his world go round, hunny, in every way. You really do," Michele said, looking directly into my eyes.

Ria sat quietly, grinning ear to ear with tender satisfaction.

"Thank you, Shel," I said, clutching the "thinking-of-him" journal to my chest.

"Shelly, flower delivery for you!" Michele yelled up one morning.

I came downstairs and smiled curiously as she held up a large, wrapped box.

"Aw, Paul remembered my birthday," I thought as I reached for the package. However, I noticed differently when I read that the flowers were sent from a *different* Meade. My frozen expression revealed my shock, as I stood motionless for several moments before opening the lid.

"Open it!" Michele and Ria both chided simultaneously.

Carefully lifting the lid of the box and peering inside, I discovered several dozen beautiful long stem red roses. I was speechless as tears slowly trickled down my face.

"Is there a note? What's it say?" they anxiously wondered.

There could not have been a greater response to my crocheted blanket.

"The roses say it all," I muttered. "Love never fails."
Dad.

—✐—

I only had a few more nights before Ria, Josh, Kayli, and I would depart for Florida to meet Paul at extended spring training. I desperately wanted to leave something with Michele as a *thank you* for all she had imparted. I grabbed a notebook and penned my heart. It seemed so insignificant and small compared to the love she had poured into my life in these few months that I almost didn't give it to her. Finally I left the hand-scribbled poem on her bed to be discovered and read at her leisure.

I silently thanked God for all He had done as we waved goodbye to Shel and her "Wit's End." I knew my soul was still far from mended, but through the love and tenderness expressed through friendship, I now knew I was not standing alone. Hope began to take root in my heart for better tomorrows.

I KNOW A HOME, I KNOW A PLACE
WHERE TROUBLED HEARTS DO MEND
IT OVERFLOWS WITH LOVE AND GRACE;
THEY CALL IT OUR "WIT'S END"

A FURROWED BROW, A TEAR-STAINED CHEEK
WEEDED AWAY AS THEY DO TEND
THE TRAMPLED GARDEN OF THOSE WHO SEEK
THE PEACE AND JOY OF THEIR "WIT'S END"

LAUGHTER ECHOES ALL THROUGHOUT;
OUR FATHER'S JOY HE LENDS
TO THOSE WHO ACHE AND ROAM ABOUT,
COME—FIND REST AT HIS "WIT'S END"

UNASSUMING AND SHY I CAME
HOPEFUL TO FIND A FRIEND
ALL AND MORE, I'M NOT THE SAME
LOVE'S MADE A HOME, AT MY "WIT'S END"

CHAPTER 7

"Surrender"

humbled heart, broken self
i lay my will upon Your shelf
wanting, longing to be filled
with Your spirit with Your will
take away the things that bind
as Your Word renews my mind
in Your hands i want to stay
willing, soft, moldable clay

AS WE PULLED AWAY from Michele's "Wit's End," Maria and I exchanged knowing glances. There was a glimmer of hope trying to emerge from beneath the painfully hard soil of my heart. My soul was still quite a mess, but I was slowly being equipped to receive God's love. These sweet meditations were quickly disrupted when trouble gurgled from the backseat.

Josh complained of a stomachache and Kaylin did what she did best, belting out siren screams to drown out life as we knew it. Maria and I stared at one another in disbelief.

"How in the world are we going to survive twenty hours of this?" I thought.

Kaylin threw each toy violently to the floorboard and effectively competed with each increase in stereo volume, matching and then raising her decibel level to let us know who was in control. Somehow Joshy managed to drift off to sleep, although I don't know how.

With our sanity hanging in the balance, Maria and I searched the car wildly for some way to distract or appease my little banshee in the back seat. I reached into the bag of snacks at my feet and located Kayli's favorite: pretzels. While she was in mid-shriek, I thrust a pretzel into each of her angry fists. I knew my salt-loving daughter well enough to know that little in life was more worthy of full attention than pretzels. I was right. They worked like magic. Shock. Delight. And then blessed silence.

Maria and I exchanged high fives just as Josh awoke with a yelp of his own. Before he could finish saying, "Mama, I don't feel ..." a mammoth eruption spewed across the back seat of the car. I screeched off to the side of the road as Josh proceeded to splatter the rest of his lunch all over the highway. Ria and I cleaned up the chunks using every last one of Kaylin's diaper wipes.

Despite our best efforts, we could not eradicate the foul smell; it was definitely going to be windows down for the remainder of the trip. Nineteen hours, three more vomiting episodes, two enormous over-the-shoulder poos (without benefit of diaper wipes, I might mention; use your imagination), and four and a half bags of pretzel rods later, we finally pulled into Winter Haven, Florida.

The delightful aroma couldn't deter Paul from swooping his two little munchkins up into his arms when we arrived. From his hotel, we drove to the condominiums under consideration as our next home. The ball field was in perfect view from the pool lounge chairs, and I smiled, "What else do I need to know?"

We moved our suitcases in and enjoyed a couple of lighthearted days of Florida sun before Maria prepared to depart to meet her long-lost Steve. From the way she pined for him, you would have thought they had been separated for years rather than a few short weeks. I envied the relationship she had with him. It's rare for a seasoned, married couple to be so openly in love the way they are. They kiss on the mouth every time they are in the same room, and say, "Love you, babe" 1,000 times a day until the rest of us want to throw up. Once a breath away from divorce, they are now a living testimony to the power of love and forgiveness.

Maria was the closet person to my heart, and within minutes of her departure, I immediately felt the pangs of loneliness. I missed her friendship, mothering, counseling, and encouragement that I had grown to appreciate and on which I had relied heavily in Paul's absence. I pondered the Everest-sized mountain that I needed to climb before I could have any real view of hope. How would I climb, let alone summit, without Ria? Despite my intense desire to bolt and run, I reluctantly turned toward Winter Haven alone.

I felt helpless and hopeless, running in circles from the fears that bitterly controlled me. My attempts to cope with the cycle of terror, a dead marriage, and the clinging despair were as futile as swimming up Niagara Falls. Dread filled each moment waiting for my endurance to inevitably fail me.

Night, when distraction melted away and quietude crept in, was the worst. Time was mercilessly slow. I was aware of every passing second. Yet somehow each dawn found me pacing the condominium parking lot, muttering aloud once more.

―――

Joshua greeted me one morning with an alarming discovery.

"Mo-o-o-m-m-m! I have red spots on me and they itch really bad!" he exclaimed while scratching. Chicken pox.

By the time I nursed Josh past his fever and incessant itching, Kayli picked up where Josh left off. Vomiting, she began her turn at the two-week cycle of the chicken pox.

While the rest of the world enjoyed sunshine, baseball, hot dogs, apple pies, and Chevrolets, my life was reduced to the loneliness and monotony of quarantine inside our tiny condo for an entire month. The isolation was more bitter than the medicine I gave my children.

Paul was assigned to extended spring training because the Indians wanted to explore his ninety-plus-mile-an-hour fastball. In spite of the drastic change, Paul adjusted well to playing only one out of every three or four games. If fact, he enjoyed the nonsense and camaraderie of the bullpen.

I continued to search fervently for something to write in my special "thinking-of-him" daisy journal that Michele had made for me, but occasions of praise were few and far between. Finding a reason to be grateful was like searching for a contact lens in a swimming pool.

The obscene attacks of terror slowly subsided, but insomnia increased to a level of frustration and paranoia that I had not yet experienced. My nighttime hours were spent in crying, pacing, journaling, and praying with ever-increasing frenzy. My newest compulsion was to pray through lengthy prayer lists, which consisted of every man, woman, child, cat, dog, and insect I had ever come into contact with. This took hours each night. The rules were that I could do nothing else until the lists were thoroughly prayed through, and if I skipped a name or went out of order, I had to start all over again.

Intensely weary from my daily drama, I became more and more emotionless. When Paul told me he'd been assigned to California and that we would have to immediately jump in our little car and drive two thousand miles across country, I felt as if I were going to implode. I looked at him as if he were the devil, shook my head slowly, and coldly announced, "I'm not going."

Still reeling from the trip to Florida with the children only a month and a half earlier, I knew there was absolutely no way my frayed nerves could handle the stress. I bolted out of the condo and ran as fast as my legs would carry me.

"I'm not going! I can't do it! I can't pack one more suitcase, drive one more mile, pull one more U-Haul, watch one more game, pray one more prayer, or endure one more night! I CAN'T DO IT!"

Seven miles of running and non-stop protest later, I finally returned and collapsed at the condo door to discover Paul packing our Dodge Spirit to the gills. I slammed doors and threw clothes into suitcases, refusing to speak with him. I knew he was just following orders, but I couldn't help directing my anger and frustration toward him. Baseball was god, and I was sick and tired of kneeling before its relentless demands. I wanted to tell Paul, his general manager, coaches, and managers to all "kiss my _ _ _ !"

I railed at God, "I know. I know. That's not nice. But guess what? I don't care! Why don't we talk about nice? My life is nice, huh? It has been one freakin' ridiculous nightmare after another … and You promised me differently! What do You have to say about that? What? I know I'm supposed to do the 'right' thing, but guess what? I'm not. Screw Baseball! I'm outta here! I'll go back to Michele's Wit's End!"

My raving quieted as Kayli pounded on the door.

"Mama! Mama! Mama!"

Tears dropped onto her bottle of milk as I cradled her and gently rocked her back and forth on the edge of the bed. Looking into Kaylin's beautiful hazel-green eyes, I heard His still, small voice again:

"Michelle, come unto Me and I will give you to rest. You must trust Me when I ask you to lose your life that you may find it. As you fling your burdens upon Me, I promise I will sustain you. Go to California in faith and see what I will do."

I sat there quietly, crying in the knowledge of His request. He was asking me to lay my feelings, my rights, and my personal agendas aside to follow Him.

"Whom have I but You?" I tearfully responded.

I carried Kaylin to her car seat and asked Paul what else needed done. He playfully slapped my butt to thank me as I began cleaning the condo in spite of myself. I had no idea what lay ahead, but decided to take it one breath at a time. I was at the end of myself and had nothing left to give. I didn't realize that the miracle ahead would not be based on anything I could give. A willing heart and simple childlike trust were all that were required.

As soon as we rolled out of Winter Haven, I felt as if all of the overwhelming, relentless cares I had borne were literally left behind. The depression, panic, confusion, anxiety, insomnia, and terror seemed like things of a distant past as I drifted serenely into a deep sleep for the first time in many months. I awoke several hours later to a peaceful car of happy children, and knew I was experiencing a miracle. Through the windows I beheld His beauty in the blue and starry skies as the moon guided our journey toward the West Coast.

I will praise you, LORD, for you have rescued me. You refused to let my enemies triumph over me. O LORD my God,

I cried out to you for help, and you restored my health. You brought me up from the grave, O LORD. You kept me from falling into the pit of death. Sing to the LORD, all you godly ones! Praise his holy name. His anger lasts for a moment, but his favor lasts a lifetime! Weeping may go on all night, but joy comes with the morning (Psalm 30:1-5, NLT).

It was a new day as the California sun rose over the Desert Mountains to greet us warmly. Our apartment would cost us every last penny and then some, but the scenery of the nearby hills and safety of a secured community were worth the extra sacrifice. I made up for lost dreams, sleeping eight to ten hours every single night! I had to pinch myself each morning as the sun cascaded in through the windows, and I realized that I had slept in peace and awakened in peace, and had a hopeful expectation of good. I surmised this unknown feeling as joy, and how sweet it was! I couldn't explain the drastic change that had taken place inside me since we left Winter Haven, but I was so grateful and appreciative to be released from hell that my love for God deepened. There was one heavenly word to describe my newfound peace: contentment.

Life was good.

Little concerns stayed little, and big concerns were amazingly shrunk down to manageable portions. I looked in the mirror and was stunned to find something beautiful trying to emerge from behind my eyes. For the first time in my life, it was okay to be me. Something beyond my comprehension was happening inside me. God was leading me into good, fixing parts of me that had been previously untouchable.

I was astounded at the way God fulfilled the word He spoke to me in Florida. Later I found the scriptural references and meditated on them, pondering His faithfulness:

Give your burdens to the LORD, and he will take care of you. He will not permit the godly to slip and fall (Psalm 55:22, NTL).

Come to me, all of you who are weary and carry heavy burdens, and I will give you rest. Take my yoke upon you. Let me teach you, because I am humble and gentle, and you will find rest for your souls. For my yoke fits perfectly, and the burden I give you is light (Matthew 11:28-30, NLT).

If any of you wants to be my follower, you must put aside your selfish ambition, shoulder your cross, and follow me. If you try to keep your life for yourself, you will lose it. But if you give up your life for me, you will find true life (Matthew 16:24-25, NLT).

Releasing control and laying my life down in *surrender* provided a beautiful, defining moment in my life, and the beginning of a real relationship with God.

My hopeful eyes in California with my grasshopper hunter.

Paul continued to spend much more time in prayer and reflection than he had during former ball seasons. One evening he was walking out under the stars, talking to God, when he got a vision of my sister Maria holding a baby boy named Jacob. After many years of heartbreakingly unsuccessful treatments for infertility, Maria began believing solely in God for a miracle child. She prayed Scripture over her womb daily and wrote in her journal the hope and heartache of believing without seeing as month after month, she encountered a period instead of her promise.

Maria was now living just two states north of us in Washington when Paul phoned to tell her that she would soon be holding Jacob in her arms. She received the message as an affirmation and the encouragement took root in her heart. She would not be dissuaded from her firm belief that God would be faithful.

〰〰

After a set of conference calls among family members, it was apparent that my baby brother Chris needed to get out of Tulsa ASAP. Paul and I both felt an urgency to have him come stay with us out in California, where hopefully his storm would pass.

When I met Chris at the airport in Los Angeles, I was unprepared for the deathly frail frame of my formerly athletic baby brother. He was barely recognizable. I couldn't see his eyes beneath the limp hair that covered his face and hid his own damaged soul. Chris filled the drive back to Bakersfield with wild, unbelievable stories of his life. He was only twenty years old, but he had already lived a lifetime brutal enough to leave him world-worn and weary. Time and distance from the world that sucked him in gave Chris the advantage of perspective. Rest from the rat race, home cooked meals, and unconditional love nurtured him toward wholeness. Transitioning from single life into family life went smoother than I anticipated. He fit right in. Well, almost.

"Michelle! What are you doing? Either I'm hallucinating or you just shook a box of Cheerios directly onto the floor!" Chris said, rubbing his eyes in disbelief.

"Oh, I guess I should have warned you. I used to pour Kayli's Cheerios into a nice little bowl only to watch her furiously throw it to the floor and insist upon eating them there. She screamed and kicked a fit as I painstakingly picked all six hundred of the tiny demons up off the carpet, only for a repeat performance minutes later. I finally got smart," I proudly announced.

This is what Ria sarcastically referred to as my "natural immunization plan." I would expose my children to a diversity of dirt and germs in trace amounts. Their little immune systems would slowly strengthen, and they would be good to go. Chris, however, was not buying it and remained mortified.

"I am sorry, Shelly, but that's just not right!" he said as he got on all fours to pick the small O's up off the floor.

"Single guy with no kids," I thought as I walked away.

⁓⁓⁓

One afternoon I received the greatest phone call of my life. My sister called to announce that she was six weeks pregnant! I was thrilled and shocked at the same time. No one but God knew that she had already conceived when He had given Paul the vision. Once again He proved Himself faithful, making a true believer of me yet. Might as well start knitting blue.

⁓⁓⁓

Chris had dabbled in modeling while in Tulsa, and I convinced him to go to Los Angeles to try to find work. I accompanied him. Bantering it up, we traveled the length of

chic Rodeo Drive. In the middle of our hoopla, I urgently had to
go to the bathroom. After searching for a few blocks, I gave up
looking for a public restroom and simply popped a swat right
there between two parked SUVs. Chris was a bit disturbed.
"Shelly, what are you thinking?"

Impulse (without good judgment) was one of the hallmarks
of my mood swings. I often did things when I felt good that
were very uncharacteristic of my conservative prudence. This
was one of those moments.

Another example was when Chris and I were traveling
with the children to Seattle to visit Maria and Steve. I started
to get carsick part way through the trip as we wound our way
up and around some mountainous terrain. Instead of pulling
over until I felt better, I opted to have Chris take the wheel,
switching places mid-lanes speeding down the treacherous
roadway, in spite of the fact he did not have a driver's license or
much experience. I was oblivious to the danger; I giggled over
the thrill, and then rolled over and went to sleep. Thankfully,
we made it there safely, in spite of me.

It was always a comfort to see my sister. I was looking
forward to all the fun and camaraderie I had come to expect.
However, I soon discovered that since the nausea and fatigue
kicked in, the only thing she enjoyed was lying on the couch,
rubbing her growing belly. We still laughed a lot as she micro-
managed her life from the horizontal position.

The rest of Paul's season was painful to watch. Nearly
every time he went out on the mound, he got absolutely
hammered. It didn't matter what he threw or how hard he
threw it, they somehow managed to rock him all the way back
to the bullpen. At first it was a little disconcerting, but then
amazingly we both put the game in perspective and decided
we were going to enjoy the journey rather than agonize about

some future destination. It was beautiful to be able to give up two home runs in one inning and still have joy.

Baseball was no longer god, and I had finally made peace with Paul's passion. This was a significant mile-marker on my journey of trust. Letting go was more liberating than I ever could have imagined. All those years I had struggled to maintain control, thinking that control would bring contentment. However, when I finally waved my white flag up to heaven and said, "Your will be done, not mine," a peace that passed understanding flooded me from the inside out and I started to truly live.

CHAPTER 8

"Everything"

I AM Truth, I AM Love,
I AM what you have need of
give Me all, not just part
I will live inside your heart
every worry, every care
all your burdens I will bear
just your ashes you can bring
I'll breathe life in Everything
I AM Everything.

CALIFORNIA DREAMING was wistful delight. I savor and remember our time there as safe haven from the storms of my life. A quiet mind afforded me the simple, cherished, sacred pleasures of life that most people take for granted— laughing with my kids, listening to music, reading, being still, and watching sunsets. Having existed as an agitated observer for so long, it was such a thrill to live.

The season came to an uneventful conclusion, and we made our way back to Ohio for the off-season to stay with Paul and Michele once more. It had been seven months since I had driven away from Michele's "Wit's End," but it felt more like seven years. I pushed memories of my troubled past into the recesses of my mind as I buzzed busily with all sorts of activities and projects, including co-writing a book with Paul: *How to Become a Dangerous Hitter.*

I had extraordinary drive and felt invincible. Having stared death in the eye, I ravenously tasted the marrow of life and it was good. The eyes of my children, the arms of my husband, and the beauty of creation awakened my senses once more. Baseball? No problem. My marriage? Ah, I guess it'll do. Our future? Promising. What a drastic difference in perspective from seven short months ago.

We went back to Iowa to be a part of Paul's younger brother Tony's wedding celebration. It was a beautiful ceremony—the first time I had attended without suicidal thoughts. Progress!

We enjoyed Paul's family and talked about all the possible scenarios for our future. Paul was three classes shy of his bachelor's degree, and we had often discussed his going back to school. We could stay in Iowa and live with his parents until he graduated, found a job, and settled into a predictable middle-class life. Or, we could move back to Canton and try to make our own way.

My Paul wasn't pulled toward any particular option, so he obliged my pleading eyes to head back to Ohio at least for now. Family was the single allure of moving to an otherwise forgettable place. My parents had moved back to Canton, and a few of my siblings still resided there. Michele and Paul were like family to us now and offered their home for as long as we needed.

We then took a monumental step with crazy abandon and made an offer on an eighty-five-year-old, thirty-two hundred square foot Georgian brick beauty. It was nothing short of a miracle to get a loan based on the miniscule seasonal income from baseball, not to mention Paul's precarious job situation with the Indians. One October day we moved the few pieces of furniture we owned into a house that we purchased on a wing and a prayer. Granted it was in dire decorative disrepair and located in what I affectionately referred to as the "ghetto," but at last our gypsy family was pausing long enough in one location to have a permanent mailing address.

Paul fielded, pitched, and hit the last baseballs of his career during that spring training. His time with the Indians came to an end. He could have pursued different teams and other options, but ultimately chose to put his glove quietly to rest. I couldn't understand how he could casually walk away from a game that had meant everything to him, never to look back. Not even a single glance. I was stunned that Paul could be fully devoted, yet completely detached at the same time. Strangely enough, this brought a temporary comfort, for he treated both of his life's loves with equal indifference.

In my new home I became a wacky version of Martha Stewart with a sledgehammer. At first my demolition was limited to ripping down the hideous, dark, '70s style paneling, but then I began tearing down walls and ceilings with the expertise and credentials of an occasional HGTV viewer. Needless to say, I was in way over my head, but I loved every minute of it. I had about twenty projects going simultaneously and felt completely unstoppable. The only pause in the furor came when I discovered I was pregnant with baby number three.

Paul was absolutely thrilled to expand our family. I was a little apprehensive, but took the news in stride. From the moment Elianna graced my arms, the fears began subsiding, and I knew she embodied the meaning of her name. Elianna is the female version of Elijah and translates "God answered me."

As wonderful a baby as Elianna was, this proved to be a tricky time in my life. Between the post-partum blues and an unfulfilling marriage, I felt like I was balancing my emotions on a high wire, teetering precariously from side to side. I was trying to believe the best, but there was very little I could find to write in my special "thinking of him" journal Michele had made for me. Reality was often hard, cold, and difficult to reconcile against all the romantic hopes I still held in my heart for a real relationship with Paul.

It was during this time that someone special came into my life. Her name is Zazoo Pits. She's actually a fictional character (an alter-ego) I developed as a way of dealing with my so-called life. I created Zazoo out of memories of my animated Italian aunt raving about "Zazoo Pits" in reference to everything that

Zazoo Pits™

The Chaos of Life

was untidy in her life. I never had any inkling that my aunt was referring to an actual person, a prominent comedienne of the early to mid-1900s named Zasu Pitts. I simply made the obvious connection between "mess" and "me" ... and "Zazoo Pits" was born. I dreamed of syndicating a column to bring humor and encouragement into the unappreciated and unglamorous world of motherhood. I invite you to share the laughter and tears of my life through the eyes of "Zazoo Pits."

Mercy Me

It began just like any other day. With my puffy, tired eyes still closed, my feet methodically followed the sounds of whining and arguing that began early that morning in the family room. I squinted just enough to survey the damage. Toys were strewn about and covered every square inch of flat surface. The raised voices of Kaylin, Josh, Barney, and Baby Bop simultaneously swirled together. It began to sound like the background fuzz of a bad station. I decided to save my breath. Instead, I waved around the biggest wooden spoon I could find. Then came the blaming and excuses ...

"He not be loving to me. He hut my feedings. He-he-heee not give me dat!" said the two-and-a-half-year-old tyrant, pointing to a teddy bear. Joshua gave a more accurate description as he tattled on. He described her various demands and then her ensuing attacks after those demands weren't met with adequate speed. (She didn't get the bear she wanted, so she socked him.)

Before I could turn to the lil' darling, she quickly reverted to her famous hypochondriac/healing spiel used exclusively to avoid punishments and gain sympathy.

"Mama, Mama, Mama! M-m-m-my finga hurts, Mama. M-m-m-my belly hurts, Mama. M-m-m-my dis hurts, Mommy..." she said, pointing to a scribble tattoo she had specially "designed" with permanent marker.

If I had let her continue, she would have covered the entire human anatomy.

"Yeah, and your butt is about to hurt too," I said preparing to dole out the punishment.

"B-b-b-but, Mommy, you pray for my ouchies, Mama?"

Only a trained professional could overlook her rather convincing attempts at distraction and move effectively forward. Now wide-awake, I put on a video for the lil' tear-stained sweetie and left to dress Josh for school. It seemed as if only seconds had passed and in walked Kayli. Her guilty face caused the hairs on my arms to stand up, alerting me of trouble ahead.

"M-m-mama, da BCR is boken."

I walked fast and furiously to the family room, repeatedly asking, " What did you do to the VCR, honey? You didn't put anything inside of it again, did you?"

Her silence made my stomach ache, confirming my fears. My voice started to rise to that extremely high pitch that can only be detected by small dogs and other irate mothers. To my horror, I discovered there were marbles inside. Not just one or two, but as many as could be jammed into the machine. I angrily told her to take her butt upstairs and wait in her room. With every extracted marble, I felt fire sweltering within.

Having only a day ago removed bread crusts from this very same opening, I mumbled aloud as I fidgeted with the contraption.

"It's not right that I know this much about the inner workings of a VCR, yet I don't have time to shave my legs!"

After the seventeenth marble was carefully extracted, I stormed upstairs and found my mother standing in the kitchen. I saw large puffs of ratted hair sticking out from behind her apron, accompanied by suspicious sniffling sounds. When I realized that Kayli disobeyed yet again, I began to get wacky with rage.

"Kaylin Briana Meade! Didn't I tell you to get your rear end up to your room?!?" I demanded, madly waving around the wooden spoon in one hand as I leaned forward to grab her arm with the other.

Quietly my mother reached for mine and whispered, "Mercy."

"But Mom, she knew better! It's not like it was the first offense! I mean, how many VCR resuscitations are necessary before she learns her lesson?!?"

My mother wrapped the sobbing hairball tightly in her arms and began to comfort her.

Again mom whispered, "Mercy, Michelle. She's sorry. Have mercy."

I went back down to the family room to finish the delicate surgery. There were exactly twenty-three colorful marbles in all. Then, to my utter amazement, I put a tape in and it worked!

I went up to Kayli's room. From beneath her blankie, where she was buried, she said, " I sorry, Mama. I be dood. I not bake the BCR no more, Mama."

I thought about what my mom had said about mercy and then thought of my own many, many failures and God's mercy. I reached down and scooped her up into my lap.

Hugging her tightly, I said, "I forgive you. And guess what? The VCR works!"

Kaylin quickly squealed out, "See, Mama? I payed God to heal the BCR, and He did, Mama!"

I laughed aloud and thought to myself, "He just might have!"

The Lord is merciful and gracious, slow to anger, and abounding in mercy (Psalm 103:8).

Paper or Plastic?

In retrospect, it was absolute lunacy to attempt to grocery shop with three small children in a limited amount of time, but I was desperate. We had devoured the last of the Fruit Loops and were down to the scary stuff in the back of the refrigerator that resembled some sort of fungus more than food. The way I saw it, I had no choice but to go for it.

"Okay, listen to me very carefully. No yelling, no arguing, no pushing, no hitting, no scratching, no biting, no spitting, no touching ... "

I gasped for air and continued, "No grabbing, no taking, no asking, no begging, no stealing ..."

"But Mama," said my two-year old, interrupting my list of commandments.

"No time for questions. Let's go! Move it! Move it! Move it!"

Glancing at my watch, I realized only twenty minutes remained until the baby would have to be nursed again. I was herding them so fast, little feet tripped and Kayli flew down onto the slushy pavement. Never mind the wet mess. I handed her a few sticks of stale gum I found deep in the recesses of my coat pockets, and all was well.

Once inside the grocery store, I was in rare form—making three-pointers into the basket, weaving carefully in and out of the narrow aisles, and progressing at a record pace—when suddenly my world began crumbling around me. My five-year-old tattled that the two-year-old swallowed her first piece of gum and that the second piece was stuck in her waist-long hair.

Kayli then proceeded to cry about the tangled gummy mess and complained that she had to go potty. If that weren't enough, baby Elianna was awakened by the chaos and joined the chorus of crying. I surveyed the damage and came to the conclusion that I was in too deep to turn back now.

I opened a bag of chips out of the cart while simultaneously shoving the pacifier into Ellie's mouth. I found myself nearly sprinting down the aisles, narrowly avoiding collisions at every turn. With about six minutes to spare, I entered the last leg. It was here at fresh produce that my mission should have been aborted. I should have run out of the store while I still had the chance because in a matter of minutes, things went from bad to worse. In a battle over ownership, the bag ripped in half, and sour cream and cheddar-flavored chips erupted into the air. Then as if a giant-sized alarm clock rang out, Elianna launched the binky out of her mouth and began wailing loudly for the real thing.

By the time I reached the checkout line, Ellie was sobbing uncontrollably, Kayli had peed her pants, and I realized I was out of checks. I finally found my bankcard, but only after dumping the entire contents of my purse onto the conveyer belt.

Lost in a daze, watching my worst shopping nightmare become a reality, I barely heard the clerk say, "Ma'am, I said, do you want paper or plastic?"

Dumbfounded, I turned toward the bagger in a stupor. I have heard and answered that question hundreds of times before, but now suddenly it seemed absurd. I just stared at her. When she repeated the question the third time, I was ready to ask her if she really thinks I give a flying rip whether I get paper or plastic?!?

While nursing the baby in the car, after all that had happened, I realized that I was most irritated by the clerks' insensitivity. Paper or plastic? Whatever! How could she possibly think I'd care about such an insignificant choice when my world was falling apart?

I began pondering the concept of the bigger choices in life, the Serenity Prayer came to mind: "Help me, Lord, to accept the things I cannot change, change the things I can, and the wisdom to know the difference." This prayer has taunted as much as guided me over the years.

The overwhelming desire to "fix" people and situations, to sculpt them all into my version of acceptability, has always been more important to me than dealing with myself.

My plank or their speck? The choice is mine, yours, and ours. What a kinder, more compassionate world we'd have if we knew how to make the right choices.

So, what'll it be? Paper or Plastic?

Zazoo Pits always had a way of making her experience a classroom of learning, gleaning wisdom, and finding humor in the chaos. I, however, was not so triumphant in real life. Shortly after Elianna was born, I found myself fighting off a looming depression as if I were wrestling for my life. I busied myself with the needs of others, renewed my mind and attitude nearly moment-by-moment, and willfully refused to let my emotions control me. In spite of my best efforts, however, at the end of many days, I sobbed into the carpet.

Having a huge house was a mixed blessing of more square footage to clean, as well as an abundance of extra rooms, often filled like hotel rooms with guests. Many family members and several groups of friends ended up living in our house with us at various times during our eight and a half years there. My brother Chris moved into our basement apartment and was part of our household, often eating dinner with us and hanging out. Being intimately involved in our daily lives, he also found himself in the middle of situations, which I am sure he would have rather avoided. One particular incident earned me the nickname, the "Onion-Tosser."

I was progressively getting better at managing my outbursts of rage and usually left the house to lift weights or run when I felt an eruption was imminent. I hadn't exploded in a long time. But that control was about to slip again.

Overwrought with newborn care and Kayli's continual misbehavior, I began to fester at the stove one evening. I was making dinner while disciplining children when I heard laughter in the next room. We had turned the formal dining room into a recreation room, and Chris and Paul were innocently playing ping-pong when I slammed the door wide open to disrupt their fun.

I was deaf to their protests as I reached for the softball-size Vidalia onions that were heaped in a basket on the floor and began hurling expletives along with the onions as hard as I could at Paul's head. At first Chris laughed, thinking I was joking, but when he saw that I was serious, he began trying to block my throws with his paddle to protect Paul. After the entire basket was emptied and my wrath satisfied, I quietly left the room. It wasn't until later that evening, as I scrubbed splattered onions off the walls and floors, that I began to weep. I despised myself. Why couldn't I act like a normal person? Why didn't I calmly go in and simply ask for help with dinner? I wept and longed to be different than the constant mess that I was.

God continued to pursue my heart despite my fledging and failed attempts to be the kind of person I felt He would be proud to call His own. Although I could not accept His Love with open arms yet, He had successfully removed several rows of iron that surrounded my soul with His persistent gentle response. He always left me feeling as if there was hope for me yet. He continually told me that all His Heart yearned for ... was mine.

 " *Agape* "

help me Lord to be true
to Your command to love like You
to forgive, selfless and free
surrendering all thoughts of me
to bear the arrows of offense
reflecting grace as recompense
to keep perspective from above
for i am nothing without Love.

1 Corinthians 13

ALTHOUGH I APPRECIATED THE RESPITE from the hurricane gales of total insanity, there was one constant wind that relentlessly buffeted me. My marriage. It was a continuous source of anguish and depending on my pendulum moods, life swung back and forth from bearable to unbearable. When it was unbearable, I was not a version of myself I would want openly displayed for others to see. Crying spells and endless hours of quiet desperation surrounded me.

Paul's sister Lisa remembered my love affair with a Robert Doisneau print from Paris in the 1950s that she had hanging in her home and gave it to us as a housewarming gift. I admit it; I am a hopeless romantic, and despite the obvious signs my husband was unlikely to ever come around and play his part—my prince on the white horse—I couldn't resist hanging the passionate black and white print on our bedroom wall. I hoped it would breed hope in me to believe, and ignite desire in Paul. Unfortunately, no matter what I tried, Paul was absolutely uninterested, and the print only succeeded in mocking me.

After months of refusals, one night I looked down at my negligee and then over at my sleeping husband. I jolted him awake with pillows and foul language aimed to hurt. My tantrum eventually wound down, and after I changed my clothes, I sat at the foot of the bed and wept.

"Michelle, please don't look at me like that. Come on, hunny, it's going to be okay," he offered.

"No, it's not going to be okay. I have been telling myself that absurd little lie for over six years now. I'm done, Paul. I'm done. I cannot live this ridiculous charade one more day. I have done everything in my power to show my love to you and it's like running repeatedly into a brick wall. What in the hell is it? What is wrong with me? Do you have any idea how brutal and hurtful your refusals and lack of response are? Do you realize that I am only human and that I have limitations? I've reached my limit, Paul. I'm done," I soberly announced.

I retreated to the top floor and gazed out the windows at the huge moon that played hide and seek between the hundred-year-old tree branches that hung only a foot from my reach. I wanted so badly to endure through the storms like these trees had. I knew that their roots were deep and firmly secured to prevent collapse. I pressed my face up against the icy panes of glass as the pain flowed down my cheeks. I thought my roots were growing deeper in God these past few years, anchoring my troubled soul, yet how often I found myself at this same precipice of despair.

Though far from where I needed to be, I knew I was not the same person I used to be. Yet, my occasional "bursts of bad behavior" made me feel like I was incapable of real progress. Thoroughly sorry, I determined it would never happen again, no matter how badly I hurt or how angry I was.

In the quiet, I looked up at the twinkling sky and remembered the letter of heartache I had written eight months earlier while overlooking the very same precipice:

Dear Lord,

You know how absolutely awful everything has been. Feelings of rejection, hurt, pain, and hopelessness are so sobering to me. Paul doesn't want me.

I know I can't force him to love me, and I guess that's what I've been trying to do all these years. I have forgiven so many times that if I were to measure, it would resemble a starry sky. Each twinkling star would whisper, "Mercy. One more try."

To lessen the ache, so that I might not despise myself so much, I sometimes pretend he's like that with everyone. But the truth is he's generally kind and patient with everybody except me. I'm the black mark on his soul.

And now the struggle intensifies deep in my heart again because of the child I carry within me. I know why… it's so painful to see Paul lavish his love upon our children while scorning me.

As he did with our other children, he ignores the baby while I'm carrying her in my womb, but the minute she is separated from me, someone should post flood warnings … because his love rages with tender affection and care toward the child. It's me. It must be me, the leper of love.

So what do I do? Add another star up there with all these tears? Continue for the long awaited rains? You created me this way. I need love. I need it. Just like all of Your creations must be watered by Your loving care or else they die, so too will I. Then remember me, Lord. My roots are so dry that my soul is no longer getting moisture. Don't let my heart wither up, and grow hard and cold. Don't let our marriage die. Help me to respond to Paul with divine love. Help me to bloom in the desert.

Your girl, Michelle

Now here I was again only eight months later, looking at the same black starry sky. The recipe box beckoned me as I stood up to return to bed. Glancing at the clock, I sighed and closed my eyes. It was nearly 3:30 in the morning and how soon 6:30 would roll around to begin yet another day. I reluctantly grabbed my sister's handmade gift from my desk and lovingly touched the creative accents she had added. Opening the lid, I read her handwriting on the recipe card.

RECIPE: from the kitchen of yo' sista Ri.
'To walk in Love'
SERVES: God. Starting with your husband.
B.E.S.T. (Blessing, Edifying, Sharing, Touching)

IF you love someone, you will be loyal to him
NO MATTER WHAT THE COST. You will always
believe in him, always expect the best of him,
and always stand your ground in defending him!
Love never fails. (1 Corinthians 13)

This Scripture, 1 Corinthians 13, offered no excuses or defenses. Maria's capitalizations, emphasizing all that I wanted to forget, were most irritating at moments like these. Indeed, how great the cost would be.

"Love is a decision, Michelle, not a feeling. Choose love."

I quietly slipped into bed and curled up next to Paul's warm, sleeping body. I thanked God for averting another potential disaster—impending divorce threat #202—and drifted off to sleep with a silly smirk on my face as I imagined Zazoo's version of tonight's events. She would overcome, even if I did not.

I continued to search for God. I couldn't satisfy my intense hunger to know and be known by Him. I particularly loved reading the letters of Paul. He once had such hatred for Christians that he sanctioned their deaths. Now in Philippians 3:8-10, he espoused passionate arguments for Christ, declaring his sole purpose in life is to *know* Him.

I was driven to know what caused such a radical transformation because if God could change the heart of Saul of Tarsus and turn him into Paul the Apostle, then I knew there was a chance He could do something with me. Yes, even me, Zazoo Pits.

I began to pray Scripture over myself daily, personalizing it by inserting my name and speaking in first person. How shocking and unacceptable were the real-life responses to these prayers. God wanted me to glorify Him through the mundane and repugnant issues of life? At first it was difficult to imagine I was accomplishing great things for God by reading *Cat in the Hat*, playing Barbies, kissing ouchies, and changing dirty diapers. It all seemed so trite and unspiritual. However, the lessons learned in kingdom values during this time were invaluable.

Pouring myself into my children, holding the door open for someone, or allowing a shopper to cut in line in front of me in the grocery store when they had six items and I had a cart full became very deliberate and holy acts. My whole perspective began to change. I wanted to leave a legacy of love wherever I went, whatever I did. As my eyes became affixed on the needs and hurts of others, my own needs and hurts diminished in demand and scale, and were put appropriately on the altar for God to redeem.

I was slowly learning to do the *One Thing*: love God with all my heart by loving others. *What an amazing discovery it was to realize that God's greatest pleasure is to be received.* Simply receive His love, mercy, and grace, and then pour it out!

It was pure joy to practically hold the keys to the kingdom! I was so close to the answers my heart had always longed for that I could almost smell the freedom. So many deceptions had fallen away over the years as my perception of God was being corrected. He had been remaking me all along this treacherous journey of trust, and I would never turn back now. It's just ... well, there's "one thing" to this *One Thing*: complete willingness to be humble, transparent, and real—a burnt offering of *100 percent* of my heart. There's no pretending in the throne room; it is just His heart and mine.

I could do the *One Thing* with the 'one thing' (all my heart) except for one tiny, minor *one thing*. Okay. It happened to be a glaring, significant, cancerous relationship called "my marriage." I had legalistically slid under the door by "loving" Paul with all the self-sacrifice of a true martyr for years by serving and submitting, laying my life on the proverbial wedding altar as expected. My itsy bitsy problem was that it was all a performance of righteousness, lacking the most crucial ingredient of all: my heart.

Early on in our marriage, I attempted to give my heart, but crushing disillusions and disappointments sent me seeking safety inside my shell. The only two people I let in were Michele and Maria, and I barely had the option to deny them with their forceful determination to make a home in my heart. But Paul? Oh, the merry-go-round on which we have tortured each other!

The refusals were the most painful. Instead of my boundless sex drive being a blessing, it became a curse. He didn't want me. No matter what I tried, he remained completely detached and disinterested. Unless you've experienced this kind of continual rejection, it's impossible to understand the despondency, self-doubt, vulnerability, and depths of heartache that follow.

Finally after Elianna's birth, I succumbed to a looming lie that I was somehow a "leper of love"—unlovable, untouchable, and unreachable. I surrendered in defeat in a symbolic ritual on a dark, cold winter day in 1997.

Anger and rage unmasked themselves in a silent ceremony as I tearfully removed the large romantic Doisneau print from my bedroom wall and then carefully went through dresser drawers and closets, removing every item that was remotely alluring. I packed them away in a large lawn and garden bag and threw the bag deep into the black of an attic cubbyhole.

The whole "I don't need you" charade was really a well-orchestrated defensive maneuver to avoid further bruises of disappointment. Denial is such a foolish escape because it is only an illusion of peace, and proves to be an intensely dark, narrow hallway of regret.

From Paul's point of view, the waters were smooth sailing. He didn't miss the romantic print, the sexy negligees, or my advances. Things were great for him as I quietly continued to serve him. But one day, the fault lines shifted and all the years of placating and pretending came to a dramatic end when the truth reared its ugly head in full view.

"What is going on? What did I do now?" Paul questioned when he walked in the door from work and found me throwing his clothes into suitcases.

"What *didn't* you do is more like it," I seethed.

"Michelle, where is this coming from? Things have been going fine ..."

"I am not even going to bother explaining myself because you are so freaking clueless. Just grab the rest of your things and get out before I lose it and say a bunch of things I'll regret later. Just go. Please. I can't bear to even repeat the same garbage one more time. It is too painful to live in the same house with you anymore, so you have to leave," I said in an even tone, looking at my feet.

"I don't know what you're talking about, and I'm not going anywhere until you tell me what's wrong, Michelle."

"Paul, consider this a warning. I am devastated, angry, and ... not in working order right now. Please go. Please," I begged, hoping he'd oblige.

"I'm not going anywhere until I know what brought this on. We can talk about it," Paul said.

"Buh-bye," I said, holding the bedroom door open for him.

Pushing me toward the bed, we landed with force. Paul tried to get me to look into his eyes. It was all I could do not to spit in his face. I struggled to break free as his grip tightened around my wrists until they throbbed in pain. I kicked and wrenched free, and ran upstairs to my office. I would bolt the door before he could catch me. As he chased me upstairs, I threatened to call the police.

Just as his hand reached for me, I slammed the heavy door on what I think were his fingers. I quickly latched the lock and paced the tiny room in a fury. I tried to calm myself down, but when Paul started pounding on the door, threatening to knock it down if I didn't open it, every last ounce of decency and self-control evaporated in destructive rage. I began kickboxing the solid oak door with repeated jabs of my fist and feet.

"You stupid _ _ _ _ _ _ _! I hate you, Paul Meade! I hate you! I hate you! I hate you!" I screamed each phrase as I kicked the door with such force that my body bounced off the wood. I continued to kick and punch the oak door, badly bruising my flesh, but I wanted something else to hurt worse than my heart.

"I hate you! I hate the day I met you, the day I married you and every _ _ _ _ _ _ _ day since! You piece of _ _ _ _ ! There is no excuse for you! None! How could you tell me you love me and treat me worse than _ _ _ _ ? Do you have any _ _ _ _ _ _ _ idea how many _ _ _ _ _ _ _ hours of my life I have spent crying and mourning over a love I can't have?!? I hate you, you selfish, _ _ _ _ _ _ _ waste of a person! Why don't you buy a gun and put me out of my _ _ _ _ _ _ _ misery? Do you understand me? I hate your _ _ _ _ _ _ _ guts! Do you hear me, Paul Frank _ _ _ _ _ _ _ Meade?!?" I screamed as I repeatedly thrashed the door with all my might.

There was no reply, but I knew he was behind the door. I whirled around the room and grabbed everything that was not attached and threw it against walls and windows, doing as much damage as possible. Then I returned my rage to the door, throwing up some final blows so violent that I thought I broke a bone from the sharp stabbing pain. Sweaty and breathing hard, I leaned up against the door and slid down onto the carpet in exhaustion, yet still writhing with rage.

"I'm sorry, Michelle," Paul apologized with a cracked voice and continued, "I'm sorry for hurting you. I never meant to hurt you."

I silently shook my head in pain and disbelief, not even sure I was going to bother to respond. But as I sat there pondering his apology, I knew I had to tell him: "*I'm sorry for hurting you, I never meant to ...???* That is such pathetic bull_ _ _ _, Paul. I have seen you successful in absolutely everything you put your hands to. Sports, careers, fatherhood, you name it. Your desire always exceeded your lack, always. You have an amazing will and drive for everything in your life, everything except ... me. I hate you for that. I hate you for destroying me. I hate you for taking the tiny parts of myself that I esteemed valuable and obliterating them into worthlessness. You are the most ignorant stupid _ _ _ _ I have ever met."

I snickered as I imagined his gigantic, well-deserved loss when his very breath walked out the door holding the hands of their mother, and out of his life forever.

"If you were halfway smart, you would have made some tiny effort, even if insincere, to preserve the family you hold so dear. You are going lose your kids, Paul. I will see to it. I will take them to the ends of the earth to keep them from you. You will see how _ _ _ _ _ _ _ miserable it is to be unloved and alone," I said with such bitter, seething intensity that I felt as if I were going to vomit every time my mouth opened. Had wickedness finally overcome me?

Silence held us both captive for a few moments. More quietly, I continued, "Paul, how can you possibly plead ignorance for the four thousandth time? Isn't that rather incriminating? You have eyes, but you do not see. You have ears, but you do not hear ..." I let my words trail off. What a futile effort this was. Was he still behind the door? Was he listening? Did it matter?

He had nothing to say. Absolutely nothing.

I continued coldly in his silence: "You know as damn well as I do that love is intentional. It's a choice, Paul. And my dear, you've made your choice exceedingly clear. Day-by-day for seven hellish years, you have refused me. By God, Paully, you've achieved your goal, you have single handedly managed to destroy me. Congratulations."

"And as for your apology, you can keep it, fold it neatly, and tuck it up your _ _ _. Don't bother to pull it out again because your apologies have been reduced to meaningless lies that mock my forbearance. Now, please take your bags and get the hell out or ... whatever ... just please for the love of God, go."

I closed my eyes to rub above my eyelids to lessen the pain that shot from my feet to my fists and finally to my temples. I hurt everywhere, but nothing compared to the intense pain that seized my heart.

I began to weep as I thought of the starry sky letter. I couldn't possibly imagine adding this monstrous star up there for gazing! Not this time. This was like a galactic explosion that altered time and space. I could not get up, wipe myself off, and go on as before.

And then my mind spun through the heartache of the letter to the closing, "*Let me bloom in the desert. Your girl, Michelle*"

How could I dare call myself "His girl" and act like this? This was my worst tirade to date. The honesty of the ugliness ripped my soul to shreds. More sincerity of heart was expressed toward Paul in those foul four-letter words than all my noble service, submission, and words of forgiveness and love spoken out of duty.

Waves of remorse and hopelessness washed over me. I was a wretched, miserable, hopeless mess, and our marriage received the same pathetic verdict. Trying my utmost to live a life worthy of God seemed futile in light of my repeated failures.

I sat motionless, paralyzed by indecision. Do I unlock the door or just stay here until I disintegrate into the fibers of the carpet? Hit Paul square across the face? Make him leave? Maybe pack my own bags? Demand counseling? Demand change? Cry uncontrollably and despair? Not even Zazoo Pits could escape this one victorious.

Giggling children walking up the stairs interrupted my thoughts. Our precious loves were innocently unaware that a mere thread—a simple, frayed, fragile thread—held their happy world in place. I rolled my head back as far as it would go and stared up at the ceiling. Could I shatter their world to make mine livable? Those same words had once altered my self-destructive plans and saved one precious boy and joy, but now there would be three casualties. There was no such thing as a painless escape.

Elianna, Kaylin, and Joshua's happy world.

 **"I Know"**

all the hurt and all the fears
I know them all, each trail of tears
I took each one and made them Mine
I cried with you each single time
I AM aware, I Know the cost
the sacrifice of all that's lost
so when your down and cry in pain
"Remember ME," call out My Name
no better place that you can go
than in My arms, because I Know.

AFTER A HORRIBLE FIGHT with Paul, I usually sulked quietly for a few days and then went straight back into "Martha-mode," serving with such conviction, I fooled myself into believing it was love. But this time was different; I simply couldn't do it.

I couldn't even work up the nerve to pray. Every time I felt the urge to be with Him, shame kept my feet firmly shackled in place.

I was a certifiable mess. All my ambitions of knowing God, doing the *One Thing*, and serving Him with all my heart were shipwrecked upon the shores of a failed marriage. Paul was the glaring target of my blame, and this fueled my anger.

I knew the bottom lines were love and forgiveness. God commands we love and forgive others if we want to be forgiven, and oh, how I needed to be forgiven. However, if I chose to forgive Paul fully and freely, then why would I leave him?

The black and white logistics were one thing; my reeling emotions and broken heart formed an altogether different picture. At best, I could hope for something tolerable. Real love, real communication, a real heart-to-heart love relationship? Absolutely impossible. The mental reeling back and forth was more than I could take. I chose to live a staged life of denial once more ... until Maria called one day.

"Hey, Mom said you and Paul had a major blow-out."

"Yeah. It was pretty ugly. I still have the bruises to prove it," I confessed.

"Ewww. What happened? The same old stuff?" she questioned.

"Sort of. But it was intense. A frightening side of me surfaced. It builds and builds and builds silently underground, until I explode and my world breaks apart. I just can't pretend and go on this time. I don't think I can do it, Ri. I know I can't," I said slowly, bracing myself for a backlash.

"What are you going to do?"

"I don't know. I want to walk away and never look back. I want to forget his name, his eyes …" My words caught in my throat as a sob tried to surface.

"Hunny, you're hurting, I know, but you've got to realize that's impossible. Your children, Michelle … they have his name; they have his eyes. You can't change that," Maria pointed out.

"I know. I just can't deal with reality right now because it is simply too painful …"

"You don't have a choice, Michelle. What's your alternative? Go back to masking the pain, hiding your heart, deceiving yourself until the next explosion?" Maria chided.

"That's what I love. The one choice I did make as an adult has effectively silenced all my choices since. There are no words to describe how much this sucks," I cried.

"I understand. I do," Maria began.

"No. No, you don't. And I am such a fool for believing things could be different, that I could be different. For hoping …"

"No, Michelle, you haven't been a fool, but you'll be a huge one if you give up now. God is incapable of lying, Michelle. Do you think He's built you up, given you hope, opened your eyes to His love and promises only to fling you down to crash and burn?" Maria asked.

"Of course not. Do you think it's what I want? You think I inventoried all my options and concluded that yep, quitting is definitely my best choice? Maria, I feel as if I'm cornered with no way out. I just can't keep pretending; it's killing me," I admitted.

"Well, hunny, now is the time to stop pretending. You want to run. And I don't blame you, but I am telling you, now is the time to stand and face your pain and deal with your relationship with Paul honestly. It won't go away or disappear. Face it," Maria said.

"I just don't even know where to begin. We're talking seven years worth of crap sitting under this rug."

"So you keep walking over it and by it, covering up your nose to act like the smell isn't there? Yes, it'll hurt, but the pain of remaining the same is far greater, isn't it? And you have a secret weapon inside you. God will empower and enable you. You are not alone. Now... talk with Paul even if it takes you 1,000 tries to express your heart. Do it! I'll talk to ya later, hunny," Ria closed

"I gotta go too. Thanks. Love you. Bye."

Elianna needed to be awakened from her nap so we could pick Kaylin up from kindergarten, but instead, I sat motionless on the floor as tears rolled steadily down my cheeks. I fingered the buttons on the phone and wondered if I would actually succeed in dialing Paul's work number. Fifteen minutes later, still quietly weeping, I knew it was now or never.

"Hi. You've reached Paul Meade. I'm not at my desk right now, but if you leave your name and number, I'll return your call as soon as possible. Thank you."

The beep came and went as I held the receiver in my hands wondering what, if any, message I could leave. Before I realized it, the annoying constant beeping announced my phone would soon be off the hook.

I said out loud, "Okay, Michelle, get up. Get up, get Ellie and pick up Kaylin. Now. Go."

I knew talking to myself was not a good sign. I truly felt paralyzed in every way. The heaviness inside made every step feel as if it were an exaggerated movement. As the day began to pass, I determined that tonight I would share my heart with Paul. There would be no screaming and crying and pounding on doors. There would be gentleness and truth. I psyched myself up for an evening of heart-to-heart conversation, so once the kids were tucked into bed, I prepared for his late arrival. I cooked one of his favorite meals, had a fresh gallon of orange juice prepared (he is the thirstiest man alive), and even managed to shower and blow out my hair, which was nothing short of miraculous.

"Hey."

"Hey."

"How was your day?"

"Long. Something smells good," he said as he leapt up the stairs to kiss the kids and change out of his work clothes.

I had a hot plate sitting at the table and was getting his drink when he came bounding into the dining room, reaching for his plate. My heart sank as I heard the familiar click of the remote. I wanted to admit defeat before I even began.

"Hey, I was hoping we could talk a little bit tonight."

With a mouth full of food, he looked my way and nodded.

"I wanted to apologize for the other day. I am so sorry."

"It's all right," he muttered between chews.

"No. No, it's not all right. Nothing about that was right. Nothing. Not my rage, bitter ugly words, the violence ... none of it. Please forgive me."

Turning to me with a gentle look in his eye and a nod, he accepted my apology. I sat on the edge of the sofa, poised to lay my heartache bare when his full attention shifted toward the television. Once again disappointment wanted to discourage me from going any further, but I forced myself to "stay in the game."

Once his plate of food was empty and a commercial appeared, I reached for the remote.

"I'm muting it just for a minute. I really have a lot more I want to say."

He shifted back into the sofa and continued to look at the silent moving screen.

"I'm not doing okay. The other day was an explosion of the turmoil I have been hiding inside. Paul, we have no relationship. None. And it grieves me beyond words. I've acted like it doesn't matter and even tried to convince myself that it doesn't, but it does immensely. I have given up on so many aspects of our relationship, forfeiting them in lieu of a peaceable living arrangement. But I have only been fooling myself. There is nothing peaceable about the state of my soul right now. I have been trying to avoid conflict and arguments, but at the same time ..."

He reached for the remote to return the sound, and I felt heat rush to my head.

"Paul, this is pretty important. Can't the show wait?" I questioned.

"I'm listening. Go on," he said.

I was unconvinced as his eyes were firmly affixed on the screen ahead.

I stood and slowly walked up to the television armoire and slammed both doors.

"Aw, Michelle, come on. Don't be like this!" he said, frustrated.

"Don't be like what ... a human being? I am asking for just an ounce of respect," I said as I began to walk away.

"Okay. Michelle, don't leave. I'm sorry. Finish what you wanted to say."

"It wasn't important anyway," I muttered as I walked out of the room. At the stairs I paused long enough to hear Maria's voice echo in my head.

Seconds later Paul repeated, "Please, Michelle. I'm sorry. Come back. I'll listen."

"Did you hear anything I said?" I asked as I returned to the couch.

"Well, you said you weren't doing well ..." he admitted sheepishly.

"Yeah. I'm not. I want to give up on us. Expecting real change or masking the pain and continuing to go through the motions are both unthinkable."

"Why is everything such a drama with you, Michelle?" he asked.

"Our relationship has become an endless drama because it has been neglected and ignored for so long. Do you have any idea how much it would mean to me for you to give me some attention. I'm not greedy. I'll take even the slightest bit of affection ... a touch, a hug, anything whatsoever. Maybe a real conversation once in a while?"

"Most men just aren't like that."

"That's not an acceptable defense. Love gives. Always. Love is kind. Love ... Wait a minute! I could be assuming here. Maybe we aren't talking about the same thing. Because I am talking about a marriage commitment where we vowed to love each other until death do us part. If men aren't like that, then why enter into a covenant relationship with someone, promising to put their needs above your own, promising to be there in sickness and health ... not just physically be there, but an active supportive presence?" I demanded.

"You seriously kill me. You always have the right things to say! How is that even possible?" he said, chuckling.

"I don't get what's funny."

"You. Michelle. You should have been an actress or a lawyer. Maybe both."

"Whatever, Paul. Are you committed to a real relationship or just a legal piece of paper? I want something real. I can't bear the thought of existing as roommates who barely like each other. I want something real. I know it won't be easy, but I am willing to do whatever it takes to make it happen. I am desperate for something more," I said.

I wondered if he had magical X-ray vision and could see through wood because he stared motionless at the armoire doors.

"Don't you have anything to say?" I questioned.

"Michelle, what do you want me to say?"

"My God, Paul. Just answer however you think or feel," I said in exasperation.

After a couple minutes of silence, he turned to me and said, "I'll try."

"That's all I ask," I said with hope in my voice. I smoothed my hair and positioned myself comfortably on the couch, poised for some real heart-to-heart conversation.

"I'm glad we talked," he said, kissing my cheek.

Before I knew what happened the armoire doors were wide open and the volume on the television had been restored.

"Wait a minute. What are you doing? You just said you'd try to respond, to address some of these issues."

"No. That was my response. I said, I'll try. And I mean it. I'll try to be a better husband. I'll try. What else do you want me to say?"

I was dumbfounded. I opened my heart let him know how vulnerable and desperate I was. There was so much to discuss and so many problems to solve, and the discussion was over!

"You know I'm not like you, Michelle. I can't sit here and talk all night. I heard you. You're miserable and I said I'll try harder," His sentence was punctuated with finality. He felt like he'd made an effort and was probably pleased with himself for giving up half of his favorite show. I sat there dejected and in despair.

"Okay, glad we talked," I said, dripping with sarcasm, and left the room.

Safely in the confines of my office, I fell to the floor and wept. The conversation confirmed my every fear: it was absolutely hopeless. Our so-called relationship was a useless joke. I had no other choice but to sever this marriage and go on. After my sobs died down, I heard His still, small voice.

"Humanly speaking, it is impossible. But with Me, everything is possible."

"Shamefully, I'm not there right now. I'm just not."

I sat in the darkness, looking out at the branches playing hide and seek with the moon and was undone when I realized that He was still here. Even after the most destructive rage of my life, here He was by my side with His pursuing Love.

"You know, I'm always surprised that You still talk to me, even after ... after ... all the horrible stuff. I'm so sorry."

His unspeakable kindness never failed to melt my heart into a puddle of repentance.

"Make me new. Only You can."

Then He gently repeated, *"All things are possible to them that believe."*

My mind said, "No way. Just give up. Look at the evidence," but my heart simply couldn't refuse Him. After all my blatant failures, He still continued to woo me with His love. His faithfulness to me tore my heart enough to at least try to express His love toward Paul.

"Okay, I'll give whatever shreds of belief I can. I can't believe for tomorrow, but I can believe for this moment."

I felt His affirming embrace as I tucked myself in. Victory. I had chosen to stay another day and face the dawn. One moment of grace at a time, I made my way back into covenant commitment.

The days and weeks passed pretty uneventfully as I faithfully went through the motions of duty until the evening that my world suddenly collapsed. After tucking the children into bed, saying their prayers, picking up toys and clothes off the stairs, and re-tucking the roaming toddler back into bed, I was making my way downstairs when out of nowhere *it* hit me: A hideous thought of terror.

Despite my history of these episodes, I was struck off-guard by this gnashing blow as if it were the very first assault. When it came to this, denial had been a necessary coping mechanism. I had all but forgotten the awful past. It was the only way I could go forward. And now without warning, I was blindsided again.

I immediately felt sick, as if I would dry heave on the stairs.

"No. No. No. Uh-uh. Not happening."

I began to get up, but immediately another vision knocked me back down. Fear nearly consumed me. I shook my head in disbelief.

"No! This cannot be happening. Not again. I can't do this again. God, please," I pled silently.

As I did my housework, I recited every Scripture I had committed to memory. But when I paused in silence, re-runs of horror played through my mind. Paul worked late for another hour and most of my chores were already completed, yet I didn't want to stop and rest. I feared that inactivity would allow my mind to have its way with me. I picked up the phone and casually asked my mom for some prayer. I hung up the phone amazed by my hesitancy and secrecy. I wanted to cry on my mom's shoulder and confide in her, but the powerful urge to conceal was driving and forceful. My old foes, fear and shame were knocking on my doors once again. How could this be happening? What did I do to allow this? By now, symptoms were raging full force. Heart palpitations, trembling, cold sweats, and difficulty breathing all told me that I was going back to "crazy land."

Finally, Paul came through the doors and a flood of relief washed over me. I ran and flung my arms around him before he even made it through the entryway.

"Hey, hey, hey ... easy," he joked as I held on to him tightly. He pulled away and could tell by the look in my eyes that I was not doing well.

"What's going on?"

"I'm not feeling right."

I just couldn't tell him how freaked out I really was. I wanted to. I wanted someone to understand, to tell me I was going to be okay, but I was paralyzed by fear. I released him with a small, practiced smile, and he went upstairs to kiss the children and change out of his work clothes.

"Don't tell anyone. They'll lock you up. They'll take your kids away," I reasoned silently. I convinced myself that silence was my only option.

The worst thought of all tortured me: "You will become what you think. For as a man thinketh, so he is."

I warmed up Paul's plate of food and hoped to drown out the noise in my head with some TV and fall asleep at his side. My hopes were soon dashed as disturbing, vile, perverted thoughts attached themselves to whatever face was flashing across the TV screen. I lasted about three minutes before I mumbled that I was going upstairs to read.

"God, I can't do this again. I'd much rather die than attempt to endure this hell. Please take me," I begged quietly as I walked up the stairs to my office.

I thought about God's strength being perfected in my weakness and was left wondering if this could be a weakness. This seemed much worse than a weakness, but I could not allow myself to consider the possibility of a debilitating psychotic illness. It was just too overwhelming and frightening; I reverted to spiritual reasoning instead, concluding demonic influences were waging war against me. The cycle began, the waters crashed over me, and I was trying desperately not to drown.

The demands of motherhood forced me to go forward during the day, but the night was insufferable with the disturbing quiet of the house combined with the maddening hell in my head. By now, my family was aware that I was struggling. I told everyone that insomnia and anxiety were the culprits, and it was truthful enough without being explicit or incriminating. Each moment of the day, I dangled a deceptive carrot before me: "Just get through today. Tonight you'll sleep, and tomorrow you'll awake to normalcy."

However, when my weary body, chaotic mind, and trembling flesh lay tossing and turning for the fourth consecutive week, inconsolable grief overcame me and I began preparing to die. I pictured Paul finding another wife, the children having a new mom, and life going on for everyone but me. All of these thoughts were strangely comforting, and I knew it was just a matter of time. I could no longer weep or offer up prayers. I felt as if I were slowly, silently slipping away.

As I lay watching the gigantic oak branches sway back and forth in the midnight shadows one cold, starry night, something mysterious happened. It had nothing to do with me; my will dissolved into nothingness. My attitude was anything but positive. My determination had slowly disintegrated into despair. My character ... well, it looked very little like the character of God despite my best effort.

But here is where the love story blossoms. My God refused to let me go. Unlike me, God wasn't gazing at my failures, He was gazing at my heart, and it moved Him. He was determined to fulfill all my purpose. He met me right there in the frozen garden in the middle of the blackest night.

It was as if a supernatural surge of strength and hope filled my entire body. Cleansing tears accompanied repeated waves of hope. I felt as if I were being pushed upward toward the light of the water's surface after having sunk to the depths of darkness.

A will to live emerged, and for three months I fought valiantly.

As courageous and determined as I tried to be, there were still moments when I cried out with bitter anguish and begged Him to make the torment cease.

Well into my third month of continual suffering, I became aware that the line from mental anguish into insanity had been crossed. Hallucinations were not uncommon, as was confusion to the point of disorientation. I remember calling to Jesus, fully expecting Him to appear through my walls. The darker side saw demons on every turn. I blamed the chronic insomnia on my increasing mental collapse to still the mounting fears.

My only comfort, my sole source of peace, was devouring God's Word. While everyone else slept, my new nighttime ritual was to dive into intense Bible studies that required my full concentration. I had already filled several large legal pads full of notes and my insatiable appetite drove me to eat up ferociously.

This spiritual buffet was my saving grace, enabling me to go on. The downside, however, was my slow withdrawal from normal life. I intensely feared walking outside my surreal world of super-spiritualism, or letting anyone else in.

Paul went from frustrated and angry to despondent over my lack of interest and involvement in life outside the pages of my Bible. I was watching everybody else enjoy and participate, yet I was on the outside looking in, and that disturbing feeling triggered my compulsion to be alone with my Bibles and books.

When I allowed no other, He would hold my face and say, *"I know."*

CHAPTER 11

"Remember ME"

I brought you out, parted your sea
My power smote your enemy
your God, I AM, I'll always be
turn your face, Remember ME
through the wilderness I led
Heaven's Manna you were fed
recall My Word, all that I've said
turn your face, "Remember ME."

THE WEEKS PASSED and to my surprise, I grew in faith in spite of my fears, which were oh, so many. I used all my energy to perform for my family while hiding the devastation that ate at my soul. The acting job was Oscar-worthy: all the appropriate smiles, nods, and small talk to stay below everybody's radar. Nobody knew, nobody but God. I was well groomed, well spoken, and well liked. None could have fathomed in their wildest dreams the inner leprosy and mental deterioration that I have laid bare in these chapters. I was determined that no one would ever know my secret shame.

I literally pined for time alone, so evening couldn't come fast enough. It was only then that I was able to let down, take off all the masks, and weep openly before the only One I dared. I had come to know the Heart of God a little better these past few years, and my faith consumed my life. But it was so close to my face, right up next to my eyeballs, that my vision was skewed. I couldn't see that I was missing the most vital aspect of what God truly desired. He didn't want complicated theologies, or dutiful service, or radical faith. God simply wanted my heart.

Many times over the years, God made His intentions known in small and profound ways, yet I still didn't get it. Perhaps if even a small amount of His Love had penetrated, I would actually have been able to take my broad statements of faith and apply them to me. Oh, I *said* I believed; I acted like I believed. And I truly wanted to believe that all those marvelous aspects and promises of God were truly for me, but my heart refused. I never doubted God's ability to deliver; I doubted His willingness to do it *for me*. I didn't realize this disconnection existed.

In "the church," we have a way of putting our best "confession" forward ... even when our hearts belie us. God patiently waits for us to stop our strivings, and to humbly come and allow *His Spirit* to forge a genuine faith that is alive and active in our hearts. This faith leaves our minds—where doubts, fears, and confusion have the capacity to corrupt—and fills the entirety of our hearts, where it works protected in *"The Secret Place."* This kind of faith can't be snuffed out by circumstances, nor can it be "hyped up" through emotionalism. It simply knows God, and through intimacy with Him, trusts implicitly. I just couldn't grasp this relational theology God was initiating with me because of the massive scar tissue still surrounding my heart.

The physical effects of my distress were long reaching. The most debilitating by far was the continued insomnia, but next in line was my inability to eat. I forced myself to chew each tiny piece deliberately, resolved my stomach would not bring it back up, even though my body continually resisted. My mom taught me the importance of feeding a depleted body whole foods to fight off whatever ailed you. I obediently drank nutrient-laden concoctions while holding my nose. I hoped my brain would respond positively and receive whatever was obviously lacking. My weight was continuing to plummet, and my bare reflection in the mirror was unsettling. I was skeletal and pallid, but I felt I couldn't seek treatment or openly share my plight to receive prayers and public support. No, this cursed ailment ate at both my body and soul in private. My only prayer was for a flat out miracle. I needed God to come rescue me as He did David.

Do not stay so far from me, for trouble is near, and no one else can help me (Psalm 22:11, NLT).

Quoting Scripture aloud remained my primary defense during the day as I scampered about in continuous motion of duty. When I was not quoting, I was singing, for there was a release in my soul when I sang. It was extremely therapeutic and seemed to have a soothing effect on my brain and its frantic and disturbing thought patterns. I didn't understand my experience, but when I recognized relief in any form, I clung to it.

For the first time in my life, I began writing songs. The melodies often came before the lyrics. It was an automatic response, and often when the words emerged they came out so rapidly and naturally, I forgot them as quickly as they came. These songs were often written as scribbles on used napkins and paper plates, bill envelopes, and gas and grocery receipts. I grabbed whatever was available at the time, and it became my memory.

My beautiful Elianna full of life.

Later in the evening hours I started to transcribe the scribbles onto the computer for saved reference. I didn't know why I did it, but I just felt compelled to do so. I felt as if they were sustenance from the skies poured into my barrenness. It was a distinct sign that I would survive.

Some days were worse than others. I remember going through lengthy periods of time where I felt I could not look at my children or be alone with them. The very thought of it would send me into a panic. My eyes darted back and forth, but refused to settle on them for fear that an associated "thought terror" would attach itself to their image. The most disturbing were the sexual images. I dreaded changing a diaper or giving baths like one would dread being skinned alive and set on fire.

Elianna was a toddler now and had a cherubic face if you ever saw one. My mother's heart longed to munch on those delectable chubby cheeks and look deeply into her languid blue eyes and fall in love. And here I was, the woman who bore her and cared for her, prohibited from loving her. I had no choice but to feel nothing at all. Numbness was more tolerable than inconsolable grief.

One Sunday morning I laid in bed listening to the bustle of activity of our house. Paul and the children were giggling as they prepared for church and all I could do was pull the covers over my head and plug my ears. Children laughing, birds chirping, the sunlight streaming in through the large windows were all bitter reminders that life was good, and I was forbidden from partaking of its luscious fruit.

"Michelle, why are you still in bed? Aren't you coming to church?" Paul asked.

I could hear the swishing sound of his leather belt rubbing against his trouser as he pulled it through the loops.

"Nope, I don't feel good." I mumbled beneath the comforter.

"I think you should come. It would be good for you," he added.

"Sorry, I just … I can't. Please take the kids without me, okay?" I muttered, trying to fight off tears. I had to restrain myself. If I let on to the tick-tock time bomb within, Paul would be alarmed and barrage me with questions I didn't want to answer.

Thankfully, he conceded, and as soon as they were safely gone, I threw back the covers and unleashed the compiling anguish of these many months, and it was a terrifying display. Everything that could be ripped from its place was hurled against walls and shattered upon floors in crashing explosions that were drowned out by my desperate screams. Had we lived in a safe, suburban neighborhood, I am sure that neighbors would have called the police.

Leaning up against the wall I hit the side of my head with forceful blows while screaming, "Stop it! Stop it! Stop it! Stop it! Stop it!" Exhaustion lowered the volume on each "Stop it!" until the last one was a mere whispering plea.

Completely spent, I limped into the bathroom and splashed cool water on my sweaty face. I purposely refused the mirror the opportunity to scorn me. I didn't want to see the vacant stare of the bloodshot eyes and ratted hair of this tormented soul. I had no idea who I was anymore. I knew what God and other people said about me, but then there was the constant evil gnashing in my mind that said everything but.

My thoughts were rapidly slipping toward suicide. Suddenly I wished Paul would decide to turn around and come home, or maybe my mom would drop in, or if only the phone would ring. But no, there were only the voices in my head all competing for attention. The realization that I was alone was a frightening one, because never before in my life had I felt so desperate to end the madness as in that exact moment.

For a brief second I thought of calling a help-line, but thought better of it when I considered where it might lead. If I dared to be honest with a medical professional, I feared being put away in a mental institution.

In my world of extremes, everything was very black and white, all or nothing. I chose to fling my all upon God and to place medical help into the recycle bin as a deleted option. Even when my desperation exceeded my feelings of "faithlessness," the stigma of mental illness remained like a heavy veil across my eyes. I simply couldn't lift the veil and risk exposure. Once again, fear and shame immobilized rational thought.

Hamstrung by indecision over my next move, I heard His voice emerging above the noise.

Quietly and gently, He said, *"Just touch the hem of My garment, Michelle. Get dressed and come."*

Truly unbelievable.

In one split second, His voice silenced all the others and gave me a reason to live. I brushed my teeth, threw on whatever clothes were nearest, and flew out the door. Worship had gone over time and there was a quiet hush all throughout the sanctuary. I slipped in beside Paul in one of the back pews. I had just settled in when a stunningly beautiful middle-aged woman stood up and walked quietly over to the microphone. Her beauty distracted me—her striking black skin complemented her light brown hair and unusually light eyes. It wasn't until these words spilled out that she regained my full attention.

"I have been ignoring this all morning, but I can no longer ignore the Spirit of God. He is telling me that there is someone … a young woman … who is suffering in her soul so intensely that the anguish is unspeakable."

My heart instantly began to pound within my chest as I wondered, "Is she talking about me?"

Fully engaged, I listened carefully as she continued, "She feels she won't get through it, but I am here to tell you the

Lord is in the midst of you, and if you dare come forward *to touch the hem of His garment ...* "

Her words were still coming through the microphone, rattling the atmosphere, but I heard nothing as I quietly moved out into the aisle and slowly made my way toward the very front of the church. I didn't care anymore that every set of eyes were riveted on me as I walked. I didn't care anymore about the whispers and speculations. I cared about nothing except making my way to *Him.*

My head was bowed very low as I approached. On all fours I crawled the last step or two, landing my face upon her feet. She rocked me back and forth in her arms in rhythm to her soothing humming, which accompanied the soft piano music that still played from the stage. The large auditorium was absolutely silenced. I almost forgot where I was, as if it were just the two of us. I wept quietly in her arms for what seemed like a very long time. Like a protective mother not quite ready to release her wounded child back into harsh reality, she held me tightly to her chest, refusing to be rushed by the demands of time. When she sensed I was ready, then, and only then, did she gently unfold me as she stood up, reclaimed the mic, and began to pray.

I don't remember the specifics of her prayer or much else, but I remember calmly walking the long aisle back to my seat, thinking in my heart, "He knows. He heard my cries, and He answered me."

As much as I longed for an instant healing and to have walked out of those church doors completely free, it didn't happen that way. My healing proved to manifest through a process. However, more than anything else that day, I needed the assurance that I knew *His* voice. With all the madness, it could be argued that I never heard God at all, that it was just another "voice in my head." He proved otherwise. The disturbing thoughts, and tormenting voices were in my mind. His gentle voice of Truth resonated from deep within my *heart.* This critical distinction became more and more crucial as my journey advanced. Without a doubt, I needed this divine validation to boost my courage and strengthen me to get through the next couple weeks.

Once more, running became a constructive release. I would go until my mind finally released me. Maybe this was endorphin related, but inevitably I reached a point in my run where I no longer felt as if my mental assailants were chasing me. I was free from their control and for a few sacred moments, I could be at ease.

My main sanctuary still remained my office after dark, when all were asleep, the house was quiet, and I was alone with God. Most evenings were productive and comforting. However, some days had been so destructive and exhausting that by the time I made it to evening, I literally fell into a heap upon the floor. One such night I cried:

"Do YOU hear me? I am calling out to You. Do YOU hear me?!? My flesh cries out, my soul cries out, my spirit cries out! If You do not hasten to save me, I'm done. A dead body cannot declare Your wondrous work. Can a dead mother tend her children?

"I believed You when you said You came to give me life. I believed You when You said that if I dared to trust You, then You would lead me into paths of good. I believed You when You said that if I was willing to lose my life, I would find it. I believed YOU.

"I don't mean to sound ungrateful for the rescue the other week ... what You did in church ... touching the hem of Your garment, but I can't wait. Do you understand that I cannot wait? I need You to show Yourself true to me. I need hope now. I need help now. I need You now. Right now, I need You."

I know that prayer moved all of heaven. Not because of the language or the tears, but because for the first time in a very long time, I poured out the unedited fullness of my heart. In desperation, my pain provoked honesty, and I truly laid my heart bare, not caring if I sounded presumptuous, not worried that I was challenging God on His Word; I simply cried my heart.

After the tears dried, an unprecedented stillness kept me pressed to the carpet for over an hour. I continued to lay in the quiet, waiting, expecting, yet there was absolutely nothing. I slowly emerged from my prostrate position and sat in my computer chair, wondering if I should dare attempt to go to bed and seek rest. Tossing in misery was like surrendering to defeat. I absolutely had to redeem the time with something productive to minimize the pain.

I grabbed my face with both hands and sighed deeply trying to determine my next move. Then, I heard His tender voice:

"Michelle, Remember ME. Bind your testimony around your neck that you might always remember My love and faithfulness."

He then led me to Deuteronomy 8, which is the command to remember the Lord. As I read and re-read this entire passage, several things stood out to me: Our humbling and painful experiences aren't without purpose. As stated in verse sixteen, ultimately the experience is meant to "do you good in the end." And in the process, we learn to trust in His faithfulness. The testing reveals the true nature of our hearts that we might come to personally *"know"* God. I tucked it all away inside my heart and pressed on.

I started to sleep a couple hours a night, and the thought terrors began subsiding. I still struggled with the onslaught of irrational fears, panic attacks and the like, but those were

Oscar nominee with her precious family.

tolerable in comparison to the horror shows. I was still writing songs, and I even contemplated bringing Zazoo Pits back from the dead for some creative writing release. These were all signs of improvement and tangible hope that I would be okay once more.

Slowly I began breaking free from isolation by attending some "Mom-and-Tot" groups. It was a challenge to leave the safety of my house because a panic attack away from home was twice as difficult to manage. Also, packing up for a day out with a toddler meant car seats and diaper bags. And then there was my own paraphernalia. Hidden in my oversized backpack were ridiculously large volumes of books, Bibles, and notebooks. They were my connection to what was "real." They were getting increasingly difficult to carry and even more difficult to conceal. But I needed them.

During worship one Sunday morning, the pastor stood up and said, "The Lord has been imparting gifts for the edification of the Church, yet you are refusing to be used. Freely you have received; freely you must give."

My heart immediately began beating faster.

"Not me? Not the songs? No. Those are for me, right?" I argued inwardly, feeling more and more uncomfortable with each passing moment.

I squirmed all service and finally at the end, I slowly and sheepishly approached the stage toward our worship pastor, who was still sitting at the piano.

"Hi, Michelle."

"Hi Kevin, I ... uh ... well, after hearing the pastor talk about gifts this morning, I thought I'd mention ... uh ... I get songs."

"You get songs?"

"Ah, yeah. First the melodies and then the lyrics, and they are mostly praise and worship, comfort and encouragement types."

"I want them."

"You want them?" I repeated incredulously.

"Yes, I want them all," he said with a reassuring smile.

"Well, okay then," I said and quietly walked away.

"Well, that wasn't as painful as I expected," I thought to myself.

It didn't occur to me until later that because I didn't read or write music, I would have to actually sing into a tape recorder. The thought was mortifying. I hated disappointing anyone, but disappointing God? No, I would swim with sharks, jump into volcanoes, and eat slimy bugs if it would please God. I figured embarrassment was a small price to pay. I printed out all the songs and to my surprise, there were nearly ten completed. Then when my children were asleep, I used their karaoke machine to record them. Within a couple of weeks, I handed our worship pastor the package of songs, and he thanked me.

A few months later I got a call for him. "Michelle, I just want you to know that with your permission, we plan to use at least three of your songs on our next CD. And we'd really like to use 'Run to You' as the title track."

"Ah, okay. That's great," I said in shock.

"I am using some creative license with the arrangement. I hope that's okay. You can pop in on Thursday if you'd like to hear it before it's sung on Sunday morning," he said.

"Ah, okay. I'll come Thursday if I can," I said and hung up.

I tried to slip in quietly into the dark back pews of the sanctuary, but Pastor Kevin saw me and called me up to the stage.

"Everybody, this is Michelle Meade. Michelle, this is our worship team. Michelle wrote several of the songs we have been working on, and I wanted her input here tonight."

"Hi," I said and quickly found a seat.

Some very beautiful piano music began, and Kevin said, "This is 'Run to You.' Let me know what you think."

The arrangement was different, but as soon as they began singing, I got lost in the song as I always did.

"So ... what'd ya think?" Kevin asked.

"Beautiful," I replied.

The remainder of the evening continued to be surreal. One right after another, I heard songs I had sung alone in the privacy of my home from my heart to His. Soon an entire congregation would join in worship with them. And once recorded on the CD, untold people would minister and be ministered to.

The drive back home was very quiet. As wonderful as it was to see others worship with these songs, it was still very strange for me because they had been so intensely personal.

"That's the point, My love. I pour Myself into your pain so you can pour into theirs."

I nodded silently as I brushed away the lone tear that escaped.

I understood for the first time the "purpose in the pain."

That Sunday, Kevin introduced "Run to You" to the congregation, and when I opened my eyes near the end of the song and looked around, scanning the rows as far as I could, there were no dry eyes. Arms outstretched, every person was completely lost in worship and taken to another place with Him.

I knew at that precise moment I was beholding the *"rainbow in the rain."*

A Heart's Cry

MANY A TEAR MANY A SIGH
TIMES OF WONDERING QUESTIONING WHY
IS THERE PURPOSE IN THE PAIN?
WILL THE SUN COME OUT AGAIN?
ALL I SEE IS STEADY RAIN
HEAR THIS FAINT HEART UP ABOVE
HEAR ME CALLING OUT TO—LOVE.

Love's Response

YES MY LOVE YOU'LL FLY AGAIN
HIGHER AND FARTHER THAN YOU'VE EVER BEEN
ABOVE THE MIDST OF THE PAST
YOU'LL SOAR WITH ME FREE AT LAST
DON'T GIVE UP, DON'T GIVE IN
KEEP THE GROUND YOUR STANDING IN
I'M RIGHT HERE NEXT TO YOU
HOLDING YOU UP, SEEING YOU THROUGH
WITH EVERY BREATH TRUST IN ME
WITH EVERY STEP PRESS CLOSER TO ME
LOOK FOR THE RAINBOW IN THE RAIN
AND HEAR LOVE CALLING OUT YOUR NAME.

CHAPTER 12

"*Joy*"

Joy... living in love

He is my portion
no sorrow can dim
the light of the Love
found only in Him

"REMEMBER ME ... Bind your testimony around your neck that you might always remember my love and faithfulness."

"Remember ME ..." stirred over and over in my spirit. I knew He was telling me something personally profound, and although I got bits and pieces from Deuteronomy, chapter 8, I knew there was much more.

In the meantime, I checked all the local stores for a "special something" to wear around my neck. I left disappointed. I felt it needed to encapsulate all He had done and taught me personally on this Journey of Trust, and a regular piece of ordinary jewelry would never do.

The days were still particularly trying. It seemed not one more Scripture could be quoted, not one more song sung, and not one more minute borne. At the end of one of these exhausting days, I collapsed in my computer chair and starred blankly at the screen, feeling numb and desolate. Even though I rather suspected that God had forgotten me, in the very depths of me, I could not succumb. I needed to hear from Him more than I needed air to breathe. Quietly, I waited.

Instead of words or instructions, beautiful images came to mind. I instinctively reached for a pen to try to sketch what I was envisioning. I was surprised to count over forty pictures. They were different in form, but all had a similar feel. They ranged from abstract figures kneeling or praising, to a tear bottle, a lamb, a mended heart, and so on. It was apparent that they were symbolic, so I listened for more understanding.

I reached for my pen again and found myself writing a specific name beside each symbol along with accompanying Scriptures. To the casual observer (or anyone else, for that matter), it was all chicken scratch. But as I gazed on this scribbled piece of yellow legal paper, I knew I was beholding treasure. My first thought was how on earth would I wear all these around my neck?

I didn't have many answers to explain the meaning or significance of this experience, but for the moment, I had hope in my heart, and that was all that mattered. As usual, it was the wee hours of pre-dawn when I climbed into bed with my two-foot high stack of Bibles and books beside me. But this time I grabbed the legal pad from atop the pile and kept it next to my chest. I could face tomorrow. I had to. I had to know what those symbols were for and how they would lead me to wholeness.

My answers to these uncertainties came in a treasure hunt of sorts as He began detailing and explaining His intentions with His Word. I was absolutely compelled to follow this path lit before me. Though the mental storm still raged, this was a break in the clouds, a beacon of sunshine spotlighting the pouring rain with a bow of colors.

> "...LOOK FOR THE RAINBOW IN THE RAIN
> AND HEAR LOVE CALLING OUT YOUR NAME."

Instead of managing levels of grief, I found myself excited over the development of something so much bigger than my pain. Only someone who has been consumed in a bottomless pit of sorrow would understand the profundity of such a statement. In the world of chronic suffering, there is nothing larger than *your pain*. For something to overshadow such a dominating debilitation, it has to be acknowledged as a miracle.

"Remember ME" was my miracle.

Every sleepless hour was now energized with productivity. The first several weeks I studied each symbol and its accompanying Scriptures and found hidden meanings to be absorbed. And then, in the many months to follow, the third and final aspect of what was to become "Remember ME" Jewelry was revealed: the poetry.

This part of my journey lasted nearly a year, and I am just as moved today, recalling how intensely personal and passionate God was in pursuit of my heart. He gave me poems to expound the concepts He revealed, bringing each symbol magnificently to life. Each symbol highlighted beautiful facets of God's love and faithfulness. Often these poetic revelations came deep in the night as lifelines, preserving me with the comfort and encouragement needed for that precise moment. These were not merely doctrinal truths scribbled onto scrap pieces of tear-stained paper, but living Hope inscribed on my soul by the finger of God.

The very first poem was "I Know," the tear bottle representing the compassion of God.

A WEARY MIND, TEARS YOU SOW
DOWN YOUR CHEEK THE PAIN IT FLOWS
TATTERED, ON YOUR KNEES YOU GO
HE'LL HOLD YOUR FACE AND SAY, "I KNOW"

I always had great difficulty in believing that the God of the universe would consider my meager problems, let alone care enough to capture my pain with His finger and place them in His bottle.

I wanted to believe it, but my heart refused. My weaknesses and lack all indicated failure. Why would He bother with a mess like me? Staring at this penned tear bottle, pondering the probability (or rather the *improbability*), His Father's Heart poured over me:

"*I love you. When you see your children in distress, do you not run to their aid? Do you not hold them close, and calm their fears? Yet you think I could respond any differently? The problem is that you don't know My Heart. Situations and circumstances appear cruel and meaningless at times, and you doubt who I AM. Who I AM never changes. Though the seas should dry up or the skies fall from the heavens, I AM. You shall trust in the unshakable constancy of I AM. All throughout my Word, I foretold of my intentions to redeem you from the anguish of sin. My Son is the very manifestation of My love for you."*

Finally my heart was pricked with the Truth. I had spent all these years pursuing knowledge about God, trying to unlock the secrets to wholeness, when all I really needed was to *know* Him—to simply know His Heart. The search was on.

John 14 says that we see and know the Father when we see and know the Son. It was as if I was reading an altogether different book, but it was the same Bible with the same worn pages. The difference was that I was looking with new eyes. According to John, if I wanted to understand God, then I needed to look at Jesus and His ministry here on earth. I re-read the gospels not to attain knowledge, but with ears to hear for the first time what His heart was saying.

Let's start with the stable delivery for the King of kings. Though his blood was so royal that it could not be found in earthly veins, Emanuel, *"God with us,"* was not born in a palace. Instead, God humbled Himself to be born a baby of insignificant birth, by an unknown teenage girl, in a tiny town of Bethlehem. He was born not in a simple inn room with a bed, but in a stable surrounded by barn animals.

How I love Him.

Consider the upbringing of the Son of Man. He experienced hunger and pain, and grew and learned like any ordinary Jewish boy of that day. God had His diaper changed? God fell down and skinned His knee? God walked into the very Temples erected for His worship and taught there? God learned a trade and constructed with the very Hands that created the wood? God chose to grow and learn and live an ordinary life for over thirty years without expressing His deity?

How I love Him.

And my favorite discoveries of God's Heart lie in the beautiful way He interacted with people. There were no waiting lists or political hoops to jump through or consultation fees. No fanfare, no schedules, no refusals.

How I love Him.

What about the "sinners," people you wouldn't find seeking after God in a church pew? In fact, their behavior indicated they couldn't care less about this God. Yet, He sought after them, finding and touching them right in their emptiness. In His Presence, all became painfully aware of their need by His personification of all that their hearts cried for. God dined with crooks, defended an adulteress, remembered the forgotten, and touched the untouchable. None was too far-gone in sin to be found by Him.

How I love Him.

And finally let's consider what God looked for when He handpicked His followers. Did their resumes reflect schools of higher learning, superior skills, and flawless character traits? "Superior skills" won't include the ability to eloquently communicate as the famed of their day, but if you needed to catch and scale some fish, them were your boys!

God's handpicked followers emerged from all walks of life, but none of the caliber we would imagine. I mean, where were the philosophers, orators, poets, sages, warriors, and priests? By comparison, the line of twelve looked more like a scraggly bunch of "nobodies" than a group of men who were destined to change the whole course of history and affect the destinies of untold millions for God's Kingdom.

How I love Him.

Doesn't your heart just lurch when you ponder these truths? Mine did the kind of fluttering that can only indicate one thing: the awakening of true Love. All this information pointed to one significant earth-shattering point: *God is a relational God.*

His very identity expresses relationship among Himself, His Son, and His Spirit—three in loving communion as One. Not a Dictator, demanding honor and service, but a humble King who selflessly gave, served, and loved His people hand-to-hand, eye-to-eye, and heart-to-heart. The Old Testament said, "Do as I say," but the New Testament revealed a God who taught by example, tasted our pain firsthand, and said, "Do as I do."

How I love Him.

The perfectly detailed, exquisite, costly Temple built for God to dwell in the books of the Old Testament foretells a magnificent love story. Holy and worthy of all imaginable beauty, God chooses to dwell in the corruptible, messy hearts of you and me. Hope surged through my veins with forceful abandon when I dared consider the timeless Christmas story a living reality. God could dwell in *me?*

This whole concept of "relationship" was slowly demolishing traditional religion and its stranglehold on my heart. What an ironic revelation to discover that "religion" was essentially all about me and constituted man-made institutions and theologies! These theologies focused on *my* ability, *my* faithfulness, *my* duty, and *my* devotion to God. This brought all new meaning to the term "self-righteous."

Oh, how glorious it was for the tables to be turned to their rightful positions! In an intimate love relationship with God, *my heart* is the only requirement. The entire focus was God, His Faithfulness, and His ability to work in my heart through His Spirit and to change me from the inside out. It was *His work* to make me righteous, loving, and productive for His Kingdom. All I had to do was bring a willing heart.

Stunning, shocking, and earth shattering were these revelations!

Now as I held the picture of the "I Know" tear bottle once more, these basic foundational truths seemed to support this absurd notion that God might actually understand *my* pain.

In the meantime, I moved forward in faith to establish "Remember ME" Jewelry, Inc. as a business identity, registering for corporate status in the State of Ohio in November of 1998. I recognized God's fingerprints all over it, and I wanted mine only seen as they entwined with His through obedience. The first step was to get the images drawn precisely so that the jewelry molds could be made.

I did my best to tell Maria all that was unfolding before me—how these symbols and accompanying poetic writings were a culmination of the meshing of His divinity with my humanity, as our two hearts collided. God came near to me not in a church, but in the wreckage of my tattered soul.

I repeated His instruction: "Bind my testimony around my neck that I might always remember His love and faithfulness."

Maria was very receptive and encouraging as usual. She agreed to pray to discover how she could be used.

Early in spring of 1999, I got my first real confirmation that "Remember ME," was going to happen. My stomach did a flip-flop when I picked up the mail and saw a large package from Germany. I knew it held my sister's renderings of the Symbols. Carefully I opened the box and pulled out each 8" X 11" inch drawing in black ink. I starred in wonder.

My "chicken-scratch" was ridiculously useless in truly conveying what I envisioned. I just knew that God would show her exactly as He had shown me. Yet, still there was a profound sense of awe when I received the fullness of what I believed for. To my utter delight, each and every "Symbol-Art" piece was perfectly formed. From the modern, cutout shapes to the fluid lines that had just enough detail, but were abstract enough to inspire personal ownership, it was all above and beyond what I could have asked or thought. I was speechless.

Up until this point, no one knew about "Remember ME" Jewelry except Maria and Michele, from the little bits and pieces Maria would e-mail to her. "Remember ME" was an outward manifestation of an inner transformation, and therefore very personal and sacred. I didn't want anything to contaminate what had been up until now so pure and sweet. However, in my efforts to protect, I was leaving my husband completely out of the loop. "Remember ME" contained too much of my heart. I hadn't yet been willing to trust Paul with it. But my excitement exceeded my reservations, and later that same day I showed him Maria's drawings.

"What are these?" he asked, holding them up to the light and scrutinizing them very carefully.

"Symbols. They all have names and meanings and will be made into sterling silver jewelry. Many months ago in the middle of a personal struggle, I cried out to God and He answered me in an unusual way. He said, "Remember ME," and instructed me to bind my testimony around my neck that I might always *remember* His love and faithfulness. Well, a few weeks later, I got all these images, names, and Scriptures to go with them. And finally, I got poems, which accompanied each piece, making up the total package of "Remember ME" Jewelry," I said as I handed him a poem.

Paul read the poem and looked at the symbol again, and then clearly impressed, said, "Wow, this is really amazing, Michelle. How long has this been going on?"

"Well, I felt strongly enough about it that last November, I registered "Remember ME" Jewelry, Inc. as an S Corporation in the state of Ohio."

"So this is what you have been busy working on every night up in your office?" he asked.

"Well, yeah mostly."

"I am really impressed. What do you plan to do next?" he asked.

"Well, I have a lot of information written in my prayer journals, detailing the business, the marketing strategy, and the vision statement that will lead the company forward. Now I just need to wait for the money to come in," I said feeling a little uncomfortable.

Up until now Paul had been unusually supportive and seemed genuinely excited about what was going on; I was nervous that the tone of the conversation was about to change.

"What does that mean? You expect a check to come in the mail?" he asked.

"Maybe."

"Michelle, I can see that this is a spiritual endeavor, but it's going to take money. I think it is a unique, creative, solid idea that could easily get funding. Don't rule that out," he said.

"Well, I know I probably sound ridiculously naïve, but I believe this business belongs to God. I have poured my heart into it, but I have repeatedly told Him that if He wants it to happen, He's going to have to make it happen. In other words, I'll do what I can, but everything outside of my ability and resources ... well, it's up to Him to provide," I boldly said.

"Michelle, that's great, hunny, but God uses people and banks too, right?"

"Look, God can use any method He wants to provide the money. I just know in my heart that He will and He's going to bring the resources to me. I'm not going to have to go search them out," I said.

Paul said in resignation, "Okay." Clearly, he thought I was guilty of "super spiritualizing" again.

Walking away with the sketches held closely to my chest, I determined it would be best if I kept "Remember ME" to myself and out of Paul's reach. Because of the unhealthy nature of our relationship, I felt I couldn't trust him with my heart, at least not yet.

Relating The Father's Heart of Love to this generation, that they might turn and Remember God— radically Trusting in His Love, obeying His Word, and possessing the promise of their future in Christ.

This Vision Statement was the punctuation mark to everything given pertaining to "Remember ME." Now all I needed were the financial resources. Show me the money! And you'll hardly believe it, but He did. It wasn't but several weeks since that initial conversation with Paul that I received a most shocking answer to my prayer.

Tears rolled down the familiar path of my cheeks after I opened a letter addressed to me in an unfamiliar handwriting. I unfolded the sheet of paper that said, "Use for the Glory of God for 'Remember ME.'" Tucked inside was a check for $12,000. I read the name on the signature line and was moved even more deeply. The person who wrote this check was not a wealthy woman with unlimited resources, but a hurting woman still reeling from the brutality of divorce, dealing with the financial uncertainty of her own future. Out of her own need, she sowed this unbelievable seed of faith. I was stunned, but not to silence. I threw on shoes and ran as fast as I could the several blocks from our home to the car dealership where Paul worked.

Emerging from his office, he looked concerned at my tear-soaked face.

"What's the matter?"

I simply released the check into his hands. He looked at the check, and then looked up at me. We shared this glory moment until his attention was required elsewhere and I quietly walked back home in stunned silence.

CHAPTER 13

"Overcomer"

Lord, You know i'm pushing on to run this race

i fix my eyes on You in everything i face

even when my feelings say it isn't so

Your Truth that beats inside my heart

won't let me go

with every step of faith, You strengthen me

along every mile of trust, You're remaking me

tho a trail of tears mark the path that i've come

until in Your arms ... i'll continue to run

I UNDERSTOOD MY RACE of faith to be a marathon and not a sprint, and was learning how arduous and painful it was, overcoming obstacles and difficulties along the way. Yet, emotionally and mentally, I was constantly challenged beyond my capacity to control. This continued to be a razor thin tightrope walk between faith and fears, facts and truth, wholeness and illness for the next several years as I struggled along. Yet, I continued to believe the He would rescue me somehow, someway.

It is so precious to me as I recall how faithfully God continued to encourage me throughout this difficult journey. Making my way to the grocery store, the windshield wipers were struggling to disperse the pounding water from a thunderstorm. I pulled over to a side street to get my bearings as I looked up at the sky between the fast moving blades. The dark ominous clouds seemed to represent these turbulent years, struggling to survive. Before I could declare my questioning heart, He spoke.

"Michelle, the sky is always blue."

"It's stormy and black right now, literally and figuratively, in my life."

"The sky is always blue," my Lord repeated.

"I don't mean to argue, but if it's blue, I simply can't see it."

"The sky is always blue," the Lord said for the third time.

All throughout the day, I pondered those words and asked for understanding. I knew it must have been important to be repeated three times. He wanted me to lay hold of a powerful spiritual truth to fortify me, to enable me to use the same massive winds that were meant for my destruction, and to rise up with wings to soar above the present clouds.

To grasp this truth, I had to close my eyes and remember the time I had boarded a flight with apprehension because of thundering, blackened skies. The plane only bounced a few times in turbulence before it plowed effectively through the billowing clouds, climbing safely above the threatening weather. At this altitude, my view was altogether different. The storm was still raging below, but from a place of security, I calmly looked out at a peaceful sea of blue. God showed me that the only difference between what I saw from the ground versus what I viewed from those heights was my *perspective*.

Perspective is defined as the relationship or relative importance of facts or matters from any special point of view; the judgment of these facts, circumstances, etc., with regard to their proportional importance. It is a matter of judgment, then, to determine which is greater: the threat or My God, the changing circumstances or My God, my weaknesses or My God.

My God is the only denominator in any of life's equations that does not change. Ever.

The sky is always blue.

I remembered what He told me months before: *"Situations and circumstances appear cruel and meaningless at times and you doubt who I AM. Who I AM never changes. Though the seas should dry up or the skies fall from the heavens, I AM. You shall trust in the unshakable constancy of I AM."*

Both of these truths intertwined beautifully together, anchoring my troubled soul in the immutable character of God. God's Love and Faithfulness were permanently branded on my heart with this singular directive:

The Sky Is Always Blue.

Between the spiritual metaphors of the "starry sky" and the "blue sky" was my natural affinity for the vast above. I took every opportunity to lift up my eyes and behold His splendor. I watched the white puffy clouds sway and dance with the motion of the wind. And the evening sky … sigh, I cannot number the countless, sleepless nights I have spent gazing up at the twinkling lights and shining moon, and aching to know

Him more. Who is this God that created all of this? And He cares about *me*?

When I look at the night sky and see the work of your fingers? the moon and the stars you have set in place? what are mortals that you should think of us, mere humans that you should care for us? (Psalm 8:3-4, NLT)

Above all my desire to be delivered was my desire to know Him. However, my real heart's longing was constantly sidetracked by symptoms that kept me spinning and battling for survival. Rather than leave the battle in His capable hands, I continued to speak Scripture obsessively, and strove in my own power to see it manifest. It somehow became all about the size of *my* faith. Instead of taking His yoke of control and learning how He received from the Father, I did it my way. I continued to walk 'round and 'round the mountain, striving to *do* more, *read* more, *believe* more to *possess* more ... until my struggling reached a climax. I was nearing the end of myself.

I would like to have skipped this whole chapter of the book because of its ugliness. If I were writing the story of my life, this is how it would have gone: On the heels of receiving the check, Michelle also receives the fullness of God's love for her. She is miraculously healed from the mental illness. And she founds "Remember ME" ® Jewelry, Inc., and lives happily ever after. The End.

Not so. On the heels of receiving the check and all those glorious revelations about the Father's heart, Michelle is still fighting to survive.

There are no words to express the heart-wrenching disappointment and shame I felt for being a constant failure.

"Why can't you be normal? Eat, sleep, think like a normal person? What is wrong with you, Michelle? You are such a mess!"

My spiritual frenzy induced a seven-day complete fast. I figured I was like the epileptic boy in Matthew 17 who threw himself into the fire, and this must be what it was going to take. Never mind that I was already thin and weak; I was gonna stop eating and pray like I have never prayed before. I was determined to receive my deliverance if it was the last thing I did ... and it nearly was.

By the seventh day of this fast, I was an absolute mess and didn't know which end was up. My thoughts bounced lightly every millisecond like a ping-pong ball, leaving me in the dust of managing a continual, twenty-four-seven panic attack. Anyone who has experienced a panic attack knows that the seconds crawl like hours and you feel as if every moment, your heart is going to explode in your chest and there is no way around it: you are gonna die. This was my life. I was so used to hiding my condition, it didn't occur to me to tell Paul that I was spinning completely out of control.

Instead, I helplessly spun and spun and spun until I couldn't stand one more second of it. Not one more second.

I went to an upstairs bathroom and started screaming at the top of my lungs. If I had been screaming incoherently, it would have been damaging enough. But I screamed vile profanities for all of heaven, earth, and hell to hear. I raised my hands toward heaven, doing what Job refused to do after being afflicted much worse than I, and openly cursed God. I used the F-word repeatedly and mixed it with others equally disturbing. I slung these slurs at His very throne, against His very character and His very name. Reeling with rage, I tore the bathroom apart, breaking whatever could be broken, throwing the wreckage about the room violently.

In the ravages of this tirade, I caught a glimpse of myself in the mirror and paused long enough to peer into my soul. My eyes were piercing with a troubling glare I had not witnessed before. During other episodes, though damaging and violent, I had never seen myself. I only knew the devastation of the aftermath. Here I was—looking into the mirror at a monster. She looked like someone I might have known, but her nature was so debasing and beastly that I would have sworn I never knew her. Yet, when the rage subsided, I could not deny those were my own wounded eyes peering back at me from the mirror.

I wanted to hide. I wanted to go low. I wanted to run. But I was paralyzed. I found myself crawling into the nearby closet and hugging my tiny frame as tightly as I could. I began rocking back and forth, moaning incoherently. For a few moments, there was utter quiet, as my mind had not caught up with my body. An eerie stillness as I have never known charged the atmosphere as I rocked back and forth, back and forth, back and forth.

It seemed as if the tirade had peaked and that I was moving into some form of recovery mode, but unfortunately it was not yet over. The stillness turned to noise, then into a mixture of disturbing voices. I covered both ears in vain, unable to silence them. My own voice began rising once more. I grabbed large tufts of hair with both fists and pulled as hard as I could.

Piercing screams shattered the air: "NO MORE! NO MORE! NO MORE! No More! No More! No More! No More! No more. No more. No more. No more. No more. No more ..."

My words slowly quieted into nearly inaudible whispers.

"Michelle! Let me in!"

I heard loud knocking and my mother's familiar voice calling outside the door. Apparently Maria heard me wailing in the bathroom and ran across the street to get Mom to try to get me out. There was too much debris to push open the bathroom door, so my Mom called repeatedly with her most authoritative voice until I finally emerged from the two by two foot closet space, creating a path as I went, so the door could be opened.

I don't remember much except that I wanted to die.

They had called Paul home from work, and all three of them stood around my bed and prayed.

There was no aftermath like this aftermath. No regret like this regret. No despair like the one I faced now.

What a mess. I was sick and needed help, yet still I refused.

It's like the story of the man lost at sea, treading water and praying for rescue. He passes up the first Coast Guard cutter, waving them on, saying, "God is going to save me." Then he does the same to a fishing boat and finally a cruise ship, informing them that God was going to save him. Eventually, he drowned. When the man reached heaven, he asked God why He didn't rescue him. God replied, "I attempted to rescue you three different times. First I sent the Coast Guard, then a fishing boat, and finally a cruise ship."

That was me. Sick, helpless, yet still refusing to allow God to help me with any of the medical resources He's created. Yes, part of my refusal was wrapped in my warped sense of faith. But much of it was raw fear. I was terrified to find out what was really wrong with me. I feared the worse. I feared having to be institutionalized somewhere long term, away from family and friends. I feared a slow death in a heavily medicated state. I feared being branded with the stigma still associated with mental illness. I feared. I feared. I feared.

I was not in a place to be reasoned with. And even if I had been, those around me—particularly my husband Paul—had no real understanding of how sick I was. I didn't tell him. He could only observe what I allowed him to see, which was a performance. I was the greatest pretender ever. Yes, I was nervous, distracted, and not myself. But overall, I appeared okay. I got up, functioned, took care of the kids and house, and acted my way through life just well enough to avoid discovery.

So when I sat in bed that day, wanting to die, and Paul grabbed my hands and asked me if I was going to be all right,

I lied through my teeth. I knew something was drastically wrong with me—something way beyond my control. I knew I needed help. Yet, I hid. I hid everything: the real horror, the real devastation, the real fear behind all my quotations of faith.

There I stayed in my pain. It was familiar and comfortable and mine. I owned it. It belonged to me, defined me, and dominated me into submission. God had rescued me in the past, even in all my stubbornness. He somehow found me and coaxed me out with His gentleness, forgiveness, and love. But now, I wondered if I had crossed the line. This time was different to me. Most other times, I blamed Paul for my pain, damning and railing on him. But this time I blamed God in a very personal, flagrant assault.

Thinking about the vile and blasphemous way I cursed and mocked God was unbearable. I simply couldn't recall any portion of that episode without wanting to die, so once again I found myself in full throttle survival-performance mode. Fake my way through the day—do, say, and act whatever way is necessary to endure another twenty-four hours. As pathetic at that sounds, it was all I could do to exist.

The days passed painfully and slowly, but they passed. The sun still rose every morning and set every evening, and much to my shameful dismay, *the sky was always blue.*

He wouldn't leave me.

I cursed Him in a seething rage, yet He wouldn't leave me.

I reviled Him for abandoning me, yet He wouldn't leave me.

I blamed Him for all my suffering, yet He wouldn't leave me.

The sky was always blue; He was constant, unchanging, faithful and true.

Love refused to give up on me. Love refused to let me go from His firm grip of grace.

CHAPTER 14

"Whole"

run to W)e, I'll hold you close
curing your heart's ache
with W)y tender knowing touch
I'll sew up every break
memories - scars they fade
like the end of day
when W)y Love is planted there
the pain is washed away
I AW) your prince of Peace
The Lover of your soul
let W)e in, I'll mend your heart
W)y Love will make you whole

AS ALWAYS, GOD BROKE the blackened skies with some kind of sunny reprieve. He sustained me once again, using "Remember ME" to shift my focus from my failure to His faithfulness. I bore down hard, using 120 percent of my energy and determination to work on the necessary business elements. As I formatted each poetic writing and symbol to be printed on cardstock, the messages seared my heart with His compassion and love.

Praying about the process also kept me preoccupied enough to push aside my symptoms. The discrepancy between the details that needed attention and my lack of knowledge was so vast that I had no other choice but to rely solely on heavenly wisdom. Foolish at it sounds, I began a habit of having nightly "business meetings" with God. I got out my yellow legal pad and wrote down question after question and then waited for replies. I didn't get them immediately, but they always came when needed. I knew if this was ever going to happen, He was going to have to make it happen.

Though I was beautifully distracted from my troubles by dealing with the business of "Remember ME," God is never distracted from His purpose of transformation. He wanted to do some business of His own with His girl heart-to-heart, and gently He pursued. The healing process was continual. As I allowed more and more of His love to flow in, the bitter sweetness of life became much less bitter and ever increasingly sweeter. He opened my heart to matters of His in fresh revelation.

During this time, there was an ironic reversal of fortunes: Michele and Paul were now living at our "Wit's End." We had that small basement apartment open to "whomever" in need, and they accepted the opportunity to stay there to reduce debt. I, of course, was thrilled. I loved Michele dearly and relished every chance to be around her. I didn't know that God had much bigger plans to work things in them and through them for His glory.

Meanwhile, I realized that the jewelry line was to include rings. Once again, the mystery of His Love and revelations surrounded me. Beautiful images, names, and writings continued to fill cracks and crevices inside me that were unknown to anyone else but Him.

Guard my teachings as your most precious possession. Tie them on your fingers as a reminder. Write them deep within your heart (Proverbs 7:1-3, NLT).

Michele was the very first person besides me to be ministered to by "Remember ME" Jewelry and His Father's Heart of love. She first agreed to draw the rings, and then she embarked on a personal journey of her own. Scriptures from Exodus 31 inspired Michele that God would equip her to make our master models the way He equipped the artisans to build His Tabernacle.

A local jeweler, who had been rendering custom designs for more years than I have been alive, relayed to me the difficulty of such precision. He warned us there was no way a novice could do it. Yet Michele believed and stepped out in faith.

Unskilled and inexperienced in jewelry making of any sort, Michele sat in the back room of our basement, cutting away. She often paused to remove the protective goggles to wipe the tears that fell as revelations of God's love filled her. It was a slow, patient process to take each drawing and then precisely cut, file, and sand a magnesium version with a Dremel and a few sparse hand tools.

We were both moved by God's faithfulness the day we took Michele's work to the jeweler who said it couldn't be done. After closely examining the pieces under a magnifying glass, he concluded (much to his chagrin), "This is some of the finest work I've seen."

It was a great witnessing opportunity to relate how God used an ordinary person to do something extraordinary.

Michele possessed a humble, willing heart, and God magnified her abilities.

Slowly creeping out of survival mode, I began doing some active ministry. I was filled with joy to be able to share some of the truths I was learning along my journey. Michele was a captive audience for two reasons: one, she was walking through her own valley at the time, and two, she could not avoid me if she wanted to. We were living under the same roof. ☺

There is something powerful about speaking His Word aloud, not in the way I had been accustomed to abusing it compulsively. It was powerful to share what He deposited inside me by Spirit revelation and allow Him to take that very life and deposit it inside another. Great and wide were the leaps and bounds of healing and growth at this time.

Come Away My Beloved and *God Calling* were two devotionals I read until the pages literally fell off from use. Not only was I fed and encouraged in my daily walk, but I was also provoked to wholesome jealousy. If these women could hear from God in such a close and personal way, I wanted to too. The problem for me was that real intimacy required transparency … and well, the actress in me wasn't ready to retire.

I was able to skirt the real issue in our marital conflicts. When push came to shove and I wanted to "bag out," I would either threaten to leave him or go through the motions, and sometimes did both. Repeated rejection and disappointments had me thoroughly convinced that the root problem was Paul and his unworthiness of my heart. God revealed, however, that the root of our marital problem was my lack of trust in *Him*.

Oh, that was not something I wanted to hear! I wanted to trust God with all my heart, and this meant that in order to do so, I had to stop withholding my heart from my husband. I didn't need to decide whether or not Paul was worthy of my trust. I need to decide whether or not the Lord was. This was getting way too uncomfortable!

I flunked half of the time, but slowly wholeness was becoming a reality as I dared to allow God into the broken places. I didn't exactly come running into His arms of Love. My tattered heart looked more like a brothel than a Temple. How objectionable this was for me to allow His Holiness in there! My prideful refusal was challenged the day He asked if He could wash *my* feet.

It was as if He were looking into my eyes as He did Peter's that day. Never did His Love pierce so deeply.

Before the Passover celebration, Jesus knew that his hour had come to leave this world and return to his Father. He now showed the disciples the full extent of his love. So he got up from the table, took off his robe, wrapped a towel around his waist, and poured water into a basin. Then he began to wash the disciples' feet and to wipe them with the towel he had around him. When he came to Simon Peter, Peter said to him, "Lord, why are you going to wash my feet?" Jesus replied, "You don't understand now why I am doing it; someday you will." "No," Peter protested, "you will never wash my feet!" Jesus replied, "But if I don't wash you, you won't belong to me" (John 13:1, 4-8, NLT).

I didn't want God to visit me in my wretched condition—wracked in pain and filled with hatred for Paul and myself—let alone allow Him to dirty Himself in the process. But in a most personal and heart wrenchingly beautiful way, this is exactly what He was asking me to do. He was asking me to willingly let His divinity be marked by the filth and stains of my humanity as I released the ugliness of my pain.

My heart broke at His request. In a place of sweet abandon, He Himself would do the work of washing me clean, and replace the bitter with His sweet. Willingness to come to God in my brokenness was the first step to wholeness.

The second step to wholeness was a full heart response to God's love. Here's where I really had some issues. He revealed how I continued to wear the garments of self-worth based on my past and others' opinions and acceptance of me rather than clothe myself in God's say-so. I am precious not because Paul values me or says I am beautiful or accepted or worthy of love. No, I am precious because God values me and says I am beautiful, accepted, and worthy of love. I have a future not because my determination met up with my ability, but because God's ability and tireless determination to transform me (in all of my weaknesses) into a vessel of His Glory met up with my willingness to let Him.

Responding to the fullness of God's love *for me* also meant accepting God's Fatherhood over my life. Romans 8: 15:16-17 explains that I am a daughter of God not by chance, but by the will of God. Ephesians 1 emphatically states *God chose me* from the foundations of the world to belong to Him.

Again, I had crystal clear head-knowledge about all of this, but my freedom was subject to my heart's willingness to *receive this truth for me.* God loves me passionately. God wants me and has always wanted me (despite the fact that I looked more like Zazoo than a disciple).

This is incredibly weighty stuff, and I had to choose whether to really believe it in my heart and *receive this truth for me.*

*For as many as are led by the Spirit of God, these are sons of God. For you did not **receive** the spirit of bondage again to fear, but you **received** the Spirit of adoption by whom we cry out, "Abba, Father." The Spirit Himself bears witness with our spirit that we are children of God* (Romans 8:14-16, NKJ, emphasis mine).

Possessing my future has everything to do with accepting God's view of me, and His Fatherhood over my life, marked from the beginning of time.

"Chosen"

I find great delight
in knowing you are M)ine
chosen and appointed
to bear fruit upon M)y Vine
hidden in M)y Love
I hear your every cry
a part of M)e you'll always be
the Apple of M)y Eye

A significant healing process was underway, though it was not the tidy, sutured, quick fix I had wanted. God was doing an "inside job," tending wounds I hadn't even fully realized. He continued to massage His soothing love into my bleeding heart when I would dare come and allow Him to "wash my feet." As much as I wanted to, I couldn't by-pass this process and still become whole. If I were ever going to risk offering my heart to my husband, I needed to know that I was the desire of God's heart, complete and secure in Him first, so that my world would stand unshaken regardless of Paul's response or lack thereof. The impossible was slowly becoming.

Another part of God's wholeness plan for me was completely unexpected and caught me by total surprise: the Meade family expansion continues with baby number four! I struggled in my heart when I first heard this news, but God quickly came along side of me with courage:

"Do not merely accept my will with resignation, but purpose your heart for acceptance with joy."

I am thrilled to tell you that this pregnancy and delivery were markedly different in every way from my previous ones. Somehow, as I chose to accept this pregnancy with joy as a gift from my Father, my heart and attitude fell in line. More miracles followed—unprecedented emotional well-being, limited nausea, and even excitement! Excitement stood in such stark contrast to the dread and gloom of before.

But the most precious miracle of all was trusting God with a home birth. From early on in the pregnancy, I began sensing a nudge to have this baby at home. Paul, however, was totally opposed. He didn't like the uncertainty and risks he thought would be inherent in a home delivery. He much preferred birth with trained professionals in the "safe" environment of a hospital. The more I tried to convince him, the more resolute he became. The answer was no.

I never did take no for an answer very easily. This time, however, instead of demanding my way with threats and manipulation, I began to pray that if a home birth was God's plan, He would change Paul's heart. I can't explain this urgency to have a home birth except that I felt it was coming from God. I am in no way discouraging hospital births; I just felt that this was a very special occasion for a very specific purpose.

At nearly eight months along in my pregnancy and as large as a house, I was still hoping for a home birth ... even though there was no sign of it happening. Paul was repulsed by the whole idea, and I was getting nowhere in my search for a certified midwife in our area. Just as I was about to resign myself to the fact that it probably wasn't going to happen, God made a way.

Shopping at a local secondhand store to stock up on some basics for the baby scheduled to arrive within five weeks, I stumbled upon my answer when I unintentionally eavesdropped on a conversation between the cashier and her customer.

I interrupted excitedly, "Excuse me. I don't mean to intrude, but did you just say you were a nationally certified midwife?"

She confirmed with a smile that I had heard correctly. We talked briefly; I took her card and hoped for the best.

"Nope. How many different times and different ways do you expect me to say the same thing? I don't feel good about it, so you just need to drop the whole thing," Paul said in response to the business card still in my hands.

"Okay, I'll drop it if you just agree to meet with this midwife on your lunch hour. That's it. One hour of your life, and I promise I will drop it for good."

"Come on, hunny, you know I never take a lunch break. I can't get away."

"Ple-e-e-ease. All I'm asking is one hour and that's it."

"All right, Michelle. One hour," Paul acquiesced with a sigh.

I tried to keep my optimism in check, knowing it would still take a miracle. I giggled on the inside as we approached her house. Linda Bruckmier (not her real name) was one amazing lady—the kind that makes frontier women look like posies. She home-schooled all ten of her children, whom she literally delivered by hand herself.

I asked a few questions and she answered them as completely and professionally as I had hoped. What surprised me was how Paul's interest took a sudden turn, and he began to shoot tough questions directly at her. She fielded them as smoothly as he had fielded ground balls. I could tell that he was impressed. At least a full hour later than promised, Paul was still engaged in heavy conversation when Linda brought it to a close with her final statement.

"Well, that's about everything I can possibly tell you. Get back with me as soon as possible if you are considering this because obviously there is little time to spare."

Just as I was saying we'd let her know in two weeks after we returned from a much- needed family vacation, Paul looked at me and said, "We don't need to do that. I'm fine with it, so if you want to, just get things going now. That would be great."

I about fell off the couch.

How I love Him.

I had such peace. I mean there were no irrational or even rational fears about this. I was living in a place of such protection and peace that I felt completely hedged in, behind and before, with God's hand resting upon me. Day after day and week after week passed until the day finally came.

I called Linda and told her my contractions were progressing, and I felt that this was definitely "it." I walked the neighborhood to lessen the discomfort and quicken the labor process, waddling over to the dealership to tell Paul that it was time for him to come home and meet his new baby. We walked, talked, swung on our patio swing in the full blooming garden, and enjoyed the morning. By early afternoon I could tell by the intensity and progression that I should move upstairs. Linda was sleeping peacefully on the couch, which symbolized the comfortable and relaxed atmosphere. The calm nonchalance left me feeling as if we were going upstairs to watch a movie, not to deliver a baby. Much less, *my* baby!

By the time I climbed the two flights of stairs and reached my office, pressure began bearing down on me. I was nearing transition and contrary to every other experience, I was absolutely blissful! Instead of sounds of agony, there were laughter and prayer. Linda sat on the floor, casually reading a book. My mom sat in the corner deep in prayer, and Michele paced right along with me, capturing the moments on film. It was such a sacred time. I could almost see myself rounding third base, picturing only three pushes away from home plate.

"Ah … Linda, I think I need to push," I said in a deep voice still trying to breath through the rapid, intensely painful contractions.

"Okay, then push," she said barely looking up from her book.

"Ah … aren't you going to check me or something … or tell me what to do?" I prodded, a bit agitated.

"Hunny, trust me. Your body knows what to do. Listen to your body," she said calmly.

As the pressure bore down and the contractions refused to let up, I awkwardly made my way to the little vintage rose loveseat Paul and Michele had given me. My mom held one knee as Paul held the other and I pushed. Then I pushed. And I pushed some more.

I was all psyched up for just a few pushes, so when the minutes passed into an hour, and still I was failing to progress, I found myself utterly exhausted. Linda remained calm, but after another additional half hour of intense pushing, her countenance changed. She soberly announced, "I think the baby is transverse; that's why we're not progressing."

I didn't know exactly what that meant, and I didn't care. I wanted this baby out, and I wanted it out an hour ago! I thought that Linda had exhibited all the "calm nonchalance" I could stand. I was about to pull out all the hysterics of a woman writhing in pain when Linda suggested that I get into the tub and push lying on my side to see if the baby would turn on her own. I pulled Paul into the tiny bathroom to be with me alone. As I lay in the tub, tears fell in helplessness. I grabbed his face closely to mine and said, "Paul, please pray for a miracle."

Paul prayed a simple prayer from his heart, and after a few more pushes, I emerged from the tub and resumed my position on the loveseat.

Linda gleamed with excitement, "I can see a ton of hair! Keep going! Come on! You're doing great. Just a few more ... Hold it, hold it, hold it ... Okay now, with all your might! PU-U-USHHHH!!!"

There was no greater feeling in the world than when the baby slipped out into Linda's hands. She immediately placed the warm, wet bundle directly upon my chest. I could feel three distinct beats of love as our hearts and the pulsating umbilical cord surged with the presence of new life. I was so relieved that I could scarcely take in the moment. Beaming faces and exaltations of joy spontaneously erupted. Caught up

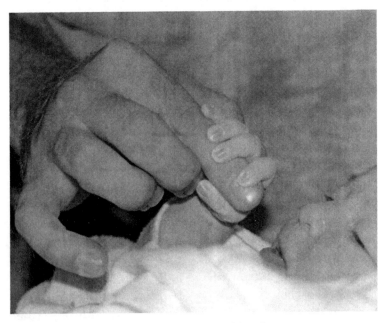

Isabella gripping her daddy's finger.

in the glory of the experience, it was several moments before we realized that we hadn't looked to see the sex of the baby.

"Linda, boy or girl?" Paul asked, not wanting to disturb the beautiful baby still lying peacefully on my chest.

"I don't want to steal your joy, look for yourself," she said quietly.

Paul cautiously turned and lifted his precious gift, and then held her out for me to see that we had a *Jessie*.

"Another girl! Hunny, what do you think?" I questioned, wondering if he was disappointed that he didn't get just one more boy.

His face said it all as he gazed down at her perfection and beheld her beauty. She clutched his finger and astonishingly, for a newborn only minutes old, she stared directly at her father's face. He carefully cut her cord and finally handed her over to Linda to be weighed and measured.

"She doesn't look like a *Jessie*, though, does she?" we questioned amongst ourselves as we pondered her appearance.

"She looks just like your mother. Faye, don't you think she looks like you?" Michele exclaimed.

"Oh, I don't know ..." Mom replied.

"Oh, I'm telling you she does!" Michele insisted.

We had planned on naming her *Jessica*, but after seeing her strong ethnic features and stunning head of jet-black hair, it was apparent that our original name for her would never do.

"Well, maybe we should name her *Rafaella* then, after you, Mom," I said.

The look on Paul's face immediately changed from contentment to concern as I put him on the spot.

"Oh, hunny, I don't know. Maybe that could be her middle name," he suggested as diplomatically as possible.

"Okay, then what do you think about *Isabella*?"

Rolling her new name off my tongue just felt right. Paul agreed, and it was almost settled. After a phone call to our nephew Mikey and his wife Toniann, who assured us that they had no objection to our using the same name as their four-year daughter, it was truly settled. There she was—perfect in every way, all nine pounds, eight ounces of her! She peacefully emerged from her world into ours, and it wasn't until she was being cleaned did we hear the first precious wee sounds of whimpering.

The sun gleamed through those same three attic windows through which I had watched the towering oaks play hide and seek with the moon night after night, resisting despair. Now the glistening, deep, azure-blue sky was smiling at me. It was an exquisite end to an exquisite day as I held the exquisite Isabella Rafaella Meade closely in my arms.

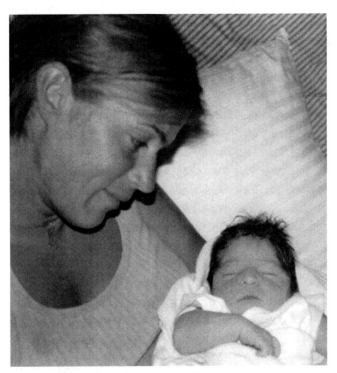

Holding the exquisite Isabella Rafaella Meade.

CHAPTER 15

" I Will Praise "

when i think of Your Faithfulness
i have to sing and shout
to declare, i'm aware,
of where You brought me out
when i think of Your Kindness,
i fall onto my knees
heart contrite, with all my might,
it's You i long to please
when i think of Your Goodness,
heart and hands i raise
i'll take this chance, with You i'll dance...
and give You all my Praise!

WEEPING MAY ENDURE FOR A NIGHT, but joy comes in the morning (Psalm 30:5).

I cannot pinpoint a specific time, but somewhere nestled within the months prior to my pregnancy with Isabella, my deliverance had dawned like morning rising. It was like the subtle changing of the autumn leaves; each tree dressed in vivid coats of red, orange, and burnished brown. And then one day they stand bare in their bark, unashamed. It happened so softly and so sweetly.

Daily I marveled at the tiny victories. I could leave my house without my backpack of books and be in public without the fear of an oncoming panic attack. I could think. Yes, I could think! My mind was processing one intentional thought after another, and I could hardly stand the ecstasy! My nights miraculously lengthened from one to three hours of sleep to an unthinkable eight or nine without having to keep ritual prayer lists or my gigantic stack of books in bed! The compulsive behavior was but a memory. This was the closest thing to "normal" I had experienced in over five years since California. My morning had come and I was determined to hold onto it indefinitely.

Unexpectedly, one day I got a call from Pastor Mary Kay, the pastor of women's ministry at church. She wanted to know if I would share my testimony, including "Remember ME" Jewelry, at her fall women's event in a couple months. This was amazing to me on so many levels.

I remembered running mile after mile, trying to escape the mental torment. I would hear the Word of the Lord prophesy hope into my soul.

"You will be speaking before multitudes, telling of my Love and Faithfulness…"

My speaking before crowds of people? I wanted to believe it, but at the time, it was utterly laughable; I was barely functioning. I was an absolute mess. The suggestion of public speaking implied a triumphant end to the madness, and that hope kept me going.

I had only begun to share "Remember ME" with a select few, as I felt led. One happened to be my Pastor Mary Kay. I walked into her office with a simple binder full of computer-scanned images and poetry. I related enough of my struggle for her to realize that what she was about to see and read was not a self-accomplishment. Her eyes widened with wonder, then filled with tears as she read and looked, and read and looked some more ... until she finally asked if she could keep the notebook and use the poems during her quiet times as prayers. I was honored. Her response was so beautiful and most dear to me. Her heart had been touched with His. Priceless.

Now, months later, I received her phone call—the fulfillment of so many promises beginning to unfold into lovely reality. It was almost too wonderful to take in all at once. I said yes so fast, I nearly fell over myself in excitement. It wasn't until I hung up the phone that I began to process the nuts and bolts of it. And suddenly they were not fitting together very well. I had a two-month-old newborn baby and a jewelry business that was more a figment of my hopeful heart than a real business, and I would actually have to articulate my journey before a room full of women. I was in way over my head!

I had no clue what I would share. I would definitely have to clean up my story to make it more palatable. I planned to focus on the glorious splendor of my newfound relationship with a living God and tell them how He pulled me out of a desperate pit ... so if He rescued me, He will rescue you. The end. Thanks for coming.

I certainly wasn't being asked to stand up before a room full of women and bare my ugly soul? I assured myself that God would never require that of me. My comfort and assurance lasted a mere three days until I stole a moment alone and began asking Him what He wanted me to share with those women. Never did three little words bring on such defensive backlash in my life.

"All of it."

I rolled the words around in my head and tried to loophole my way out of such a request. Despite every twist and turn, there were no exclusions to the word "all," and that made me exceedingly nervous. It wasn't until I looked back at "that place" that I realized, once again, it wasn't about me.

Like it was happening to someone else, I recalled a deathly thin, gaunt, frail woman rapidly pacing a familiar room in unconstrained confusion. She was so daunted by her circumstances that she was barely coherent, yet there she stopped in the middle of the chaos, and, raising her hand toward heaven, made a declaration that shook the spiritual realm. His heart so filled hers that despite her situation, she could not stop the overflow from spilling out.

"Lord, I want souls! I am asking for souls as my recompense. For every second of torment, I am asking for one soul. One by one by one, I am calling forth every wounded, battered, and lost soul to be found by You. I am asking for the captives to be set free, for the sick to be whole, for the blind to see. I am asking for one soul in exchange for every second of torment I have endured. Souls, my Father."

I blinked away fresh tears and the recollection. I knew I had to trust and obey, no matter the personal cost. These weeks of preparation were so full of validation from His throne that I felt the applause of heaven cheering me on. And believe me, I needed all the cheering I could get because attempt after frustrating attempt to outline my talk left me a mere three hours over the maximum ninety-minute time allotted to me to speak. This, of course, became my justification for cutting out the most disturbing parts in order to make room for the encouraging, good stuff. Yet at the end of the many days of wrangling, I found myself on hands and knee, scraping up the edited cuts that lay scattered and crumpled on the floor.

"*All of it*" meant *all of it*.

Finally, I grasped the literal nature of my training. Sharing my testimony was not a separate narrative of my "Journey of Trust," but it was in fact a pivotal and climactic part of this journey. I was still very much in progress, and this was all divinely part of it. I was on the ledge, ready to jump into His arms full throttle, and never before had I felt so free. I abandoned my notes, outlines, and everything else to His care.

It was a good thing I released the story content into His hands because this freed up my time to attend to the product … or in this case, the lack thereof. I encountered some difficulties getting molds made and jewelry poured, turning an already long and trying process into an even longer and trickier one. There were many times when I felt certain that the Lord was leading me in a particular direction, only to reach an unexpected end.

One such case was our first casting house. I was drawn to one particular casting company, and no matter how I tried to ignore their tiny mom and pop outfit, I kept being drawn to them. Finally, Paul and I made our first business trip by driving over 500 miles from our home in Canton, Ohio to a suburb near Hartford, Connecticut to meet Terry and Gavin of G&T Casting (not their real names or business name). We expected modest facilities, but nothing prepared us for the tiny cramped quarters of a damp, darkened basement. Could this be the humble beginning of a jewelry outfit that had a global destiny? I was a bit dumbfounded, but rather than doubt, which would have been my obvious natural response, I walked fearlessly forward. "Remember ME" was unlike any other aspect of my life, for here I had such inexplicable courage and faith that I remained undaunted when faced with impossibilities.

Our trip was full of adventure, and we learned a lot about the jewelry process and business. After handing over all the hand-sketched images and magnesium molds to two unlikely candidates in an act of utter faith, I smiled inwardly. This seemed so like my God.

Once the business had been accomplished, we took them out to dinner where we had the opportunity to share The Father's Heart behind "Remember ME." Looking into their eyes, I told them that God breathed life into a hopeless mess and created this beautiful line of jewelry to share His love and faithfulness with an entire generation. They had only known traditional religion, so this whole concept of relationship was new and intriguing. We shared for quite some time and left the conversation and the state of Connecticut, hopeful that God was definitely at work there.

A few months later, we held the first real pieces of jewelry in our hands, carefully wrought with Gavin's large, nubby ones. Tears fell again. This was really going to happen! The high was so high that the unhindered view declared His Glory with crisp expressions of His love and faithfulness.

I was caught completely off-guard when I got a frantic phone call from Terry. She said Gavin needed emergency heart surgery and that it wasn't going well. Her tearful plea for prayer was her last hope. And pray I did. I prayed over the phone with her and continued a vigil of prayer for hours. I emerged from the prayer, confident that God would bring Gavin through, that Gavin "would live and not die and declare the works of the Lord."

A day later, reeling from shock, Paul and I prepared to leave once again for Connecticut, this time for a funeral. It was so surreal. There seemed neither rhyme nor reason. All I could do was believe that the Lord somehow watered those seeds we planted that evening in the restaurant. Sitting in a quaint, white, hundred-year-old countryside chapel, I looked around at the fifty or so people and wondered if they *knew* Him. My heart began to ache for every person who stumbled through life purposelessly only to face an unexpected end.

Then I heard His tender voice say, *"Tell them."*

I argued inwardly because it seemed so inappropriate for a "stranger" to stand up at a funeral and testify. But after the select few speakers stood, I found myself standing, presenting evidence that God was real.

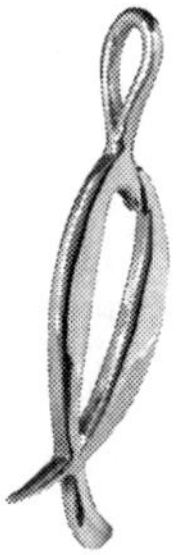

"*Testify*"

tell them, tell them, Testify
give them every reason why
you believe, make it known
how I made your heart my home
with all my love, I forgave you
by My Power, I remade you
how My Truth has set you free
won't you tell them about Me?

I was doing the unthinkable. As every eye turned toward my intrusion, I simply opened my mouth. Then, a miracle happened and out poured the grace, compassion, and love of my Father, drawing hurting hearts toward His Son. I shared briefly about my connection to Gavin and how his life, even after his death, will bring life through "Remember ME," Jewelry to countless others. I closed by reciting the "I Know" poem. After pressing the "I Know" tear bottle her husband had made into his wife's hands, we quietly left. Still to this day, I have two of Gavin's original samples; they are precious to me. God used him to use me ... and around and around His matchless ways and purposes flow.

Now months later, with a new casting company in Israel, we were hoping against hope to have some of our symbols and rings in by the November event. This women's event was God's sovereign choice for "Remember ME" Jewelry's public birth. Here before hundreds of women I would share my testimony for the first time, introducing "Remember ME." However, the weeks were ticking by, and it became a painful probability that we would not have any jewelry. How could we have a delivery with no "baby" to follow? I waited for His response. It was beautiful.

I awoke one morning, preparing to embark on a week's worth of activity in one short day, and found myself waiting before Him instead. I've learned: the busier I am, the more time I need apart. As I listened, I heard Him tell me that He had something else in mind ... or rather, someone else in mind. His heart was hurting for our senior pastor who was reeling in grief over simultaneous blows of a splitting marriage and a splitting church.

The Lord's instructions were very specific, so I got busy printing the "Overcomer" Symbol and Writing onto a quality cardstock, and then proceeded to tear the edges and tastefully frame the print. It turned out beautifully, and I waited for the appropriate time to give this gift with a handwritten letter, expressing God's swelling heart of pride and pain over His Son's journey of faith.

Once the assignment was complete, I held the framed print in my hands and smiled. One of the most meaningful writings of my life was now about to expand beyond the borders of my own heart and touch another's. Humility and gratitude seized me once again in the wonder of it all. But then something surprising happened in the following moment that trumped the preceding emotion. I began laughing aloud when it hit me!

I thought it was about the jewelry, and having the jewelry there to represent the transforming work God did in me, but it wasn't about the jewelry at all! It was about the meaning behind the pieces, the poetry, and Scripture that encompass it. The jewelry is simply a tool for the message to be worked in.

I suddenly realized the provision that was being handed to me, and excitedly went to Paul, Michele, and few others involved to share this concept of putting together framed prints for the November women's event. The torn edges were symbolic because of the tearing and repairing in my own life, but there was more. When someone suggested that we burn the edges instead, that was all she wrote. My home became one continuous smokehouse for the next several weeks as we frantically printed, tore, burned, and framed nearly three hundred prints.

As the *official* birthday for "Remember ME" Jewelry neared, one very special young woman from our women's group at church shyly approached me with a most dear and unusual request. She was a massage therapist, and she said that she felt like she was supposed to give me a massage on the eve of the event. Of course, unable to afford such luxury, I readily agreed to the extravagance. On a portable table in my top floor office, she had soft music playing, candles burning, and all my children safely out of earshot. It was pure relaxation. It was ironic that as she worked through all my weary muscles, she spent an inordinate amount of time on one side of my neck. She worked and worked and worked and finally said, "You have a gigantic knot that is resisting stubbornly!"

How revealing this was. My stubborn stiff-neck. Running and running from His tender embrace all these years, keeping my face swiftly turned from His eyes of love, my head was cranked in the opposite direction. Too ashamed to release the horror in His presence, I tried tirelessly to bear the pain and shame alone. Oh, I used His Word for comfort and relief, but I could do that and still keep my heart elusive. It was intimacy He desired and that was all too daunting for me.

After the massage, I spent the remainder of the night conversing with God. During this time, He revealed the purpose behind Isabella's home birth. All my life I had run from the pain. I searched for all alternate routes and exits prior to any entry that hinted of discomfort. Never is there a more predictable, guaranteed doorway to intense pain than childbirth. It's larger than life; there is no stopping the process; that baby nestled inside you must be born from an insanely small opening into a painful world.

Having Isabella at home was a direct confrontation with my past and a triumphant entrance into my future. I was embracing the oncoming pain for the first time in my life—without denial, blame, or abuse. Instead, I trusted with my heart that I was facing it with my God. I might have failed, but He would not fail me. I may have left, but He would not leave me. I might have been faithless, but He would remain faithful.

The sky is always blue.

He was trustworthy. Having Isabella with Him was a treasured display of our intimacy. I was finally beginning to trust Him, releasing the pain to make way for wholeness.

Now it was time to birth another baby. And just like Isabella's home birth, I would have to trust God with the oncoming pain. I realized November 3, 2001 would change my life forever. I could never return to the anonymity I relished; everyone was about to know me in all my secret shame. Yet despite the trepidation, I knew My Father had planned this day and that it would be a significant altar building moment on my Journey of Trust with Him. There was no going back for me. This baby was bursting within; it was time for her to gloriously emerge into the light of day

It was a beautiful, defining moment in my life as I stood in front of a bathroom mirror in a corridor room off the sanctuary stage. After years of loathing myself, finding every opportunity to hate the reflection that peered back at me, I now regarded myself in absolute wonder as His work of grace. She was gloriously, stunningly beautiful. And she was … me. Yes, Michelle Meade, the self-proclaimed *"leper of love,"* was basking in a private moment of divine recognition. I felt His approval, and it moved me. I hadn't even done anything yet, hadn't spoke one word, and hadn't prayed over one soul. Yet I felt His approval, and I was undone.

A knock on the door indicated that it was time. I smoothed the dark grey suit with my hands one last time, taking one extra moment to touch the shiny monogrammed buttons. No detail was spared for this event. God provided intimate little surprises no one but He knew I would appreciate so much. I knelt one last time.

Nerves were not an issue until I emerged from my "sanctuary" into the large sanctuary filled with endless rows of women. I silently prayed that God would help me resist the overwhelming urge I had to run scared through the double doors. As they worshipped, I did my best to concentrate, but my mind was not cooperating. Outline headings and subheadings were flashing back and forth, taunting me to fall into their safety. Michele Colaner tearfully introduced me, and suddenly I found myself walking up the stairs and onto the stage.

"You may think you are in a church, but today this place is called "Wit's End." "Wit's End" sounds like a scary place because lack of control is perceived as either unwanted vulnerability or failure. I am here to tell you that "Wit's End" is actually the launching point for intimacy with God. It is the place where authenticity replaces pretense, where abandoned trust replaces control, and where His perfect love replaces every fear. I didn't realize that I had to be completely at the end of myself in order to come and truly receive from God. Today, here, in this place called "Wit's End," my prayer is that you will come, maybe for the first time, into His Presence, just as you are and receive His love."

"I have my tidy outlines and notes, but God has different plans, and this is what I have to say about that ..." I said as I flung large index cards across the stage, indicating I was letting go and letting God have His way.

"Instead, ya'll are gonna take a little journey along with me. I'm gonna start this day just as I've started the past 365 days, declaring my desperate need for God. Just as I do in my living room, I'm gonna do it right here, right now."

The music began to play, and I felt the same way I did every time I heard Leanne Rimes' haunting melody. I flung my arms up and swung myself around as I sang loudly along, "I Need You" with all my heart.

All the nervousness evaporated as I swayed and danced across the stage, lost in surrender. I knew it was the point of no return for me. I had run from the pain my entire life, resisting control, resisting the unknown, and resisting true love. Now it was all culminating in this climactic moment when I would choose to abandon myself in delight entirely to God.

It's tempting for me to want to replay the entire scene exactly as it happened on the morning of November 3, 2001. However lovely and meaningful the details were that memorable day, I'm forced to summarize the nearly three and a half-hour saga into a few pages.

All you Type A personalities are cringing at the administrative nightmare of this event scenario. How do you 'damage control' such a thing? I mean, there was this woman baring her soul before hundreds of other women for hours on end.

These perfectly manicured ladies were stoic a fourth of the way into the drama. Halfway through, however, one could quickly tell which women didn't use waterproof mascara, as raccoon eyes across the sanctuary stared back at me in teary empathy. They might not have related to my situation, but they certainly related to my pain. In those hours, a common denominator tied our hearts together in a synergetic harmony. One-by-one-by-one, the countenance of every woman changed before my eyes. My transparency and vulnerability provocatively called to every longing soul for a response.

I broke up the journey into three parts: the Shaking, the Breaking, and the Making. The Shaking emphasized the early years when it was "all about me." I retold of my pain and self-hatred. This included all the lies and eating disorders that revolved around my obsession with my appearance.

The "Breaking" described the part of the journey where I was learning about the cost of love. I shared my heartache over a loveless marriage and how I performed and manipulated my way through over ten years of wedded folly. Most revealing was the ugliness of bitterness, how it can turn an innocent, hopeful heart into the stone cold heart of a murderer. I told how my desire to be loved was slowly being transformed by the healing power of God's love. As He endlessly poured in and I received from His heart, I was slowly equipped to pour out in pure, sincere, undiluted love for the first time.

The "Making" told of the molding, the fire of the kiln, and the chiseling until the deepest part of me was finally prepared to receive the deepest part of God. Verbalizing for the first time my mental struggles was difficult and raw, but also intensely liberating. The stranglehold of fear that kept me locked in silence for over ten years suddenly broke. The shackles fell as hard and fast as my words. I explained that it was here in this darkness that The Father's Heart of Love, revealed through every symbol and ring writing, began truly penetrating my brokenness. Here in the ash heap, "Remember ME" Jewelry crystallized into a crowning jewel in my soul.

And finally, the closing—the linchpin of it all. Please follow along as if you were here with me that day:

> "You may be wondering how my story applies to you? I'll tell you. God is mindful of your pain. He tasted your pain, and still shares in it. I thought there was absolutely no way God could understand my pain. It was centered on evil—heinous, vile, terrorizing thoughts, disturbing obsessive behavior, and a stain of shame deeply embedded into my soul. How could He know my pain? Jesus cast out demons from the afflicted and tormented, but He Himself couldn't possibly know the affliction and torment ... or could He? There is more, so much more, than the atrocious physical suffering of our Lord.
>
> "Whatever suffering was not experienced walking amongst us for thirty-three years as the Son of Man, He experienced in those six hours on Golgotha. He knows more intimately than we could ever imagine the horror of sin, for it was embodied in His flesh as He hung on that tree. He who knew no sin, became sin, that we might become the righteousness of God.
>
> "There is no anguish too deep, no act too vile, no thought too repulsive. He experienced them all. There are no exclusions. Every brutal tragedy conceived, intimately known. So you think, like I did, that it's impossible for anyone to know and understand your

pain? I tell you it's impossible for Him to *not know* and understand. *He knows your pain. He's tasted every part of it.*

"In Hebrews 4-5, I read and finally understood the reason that it had to be done the way it was done. After all, a spotless blood sacrifice was the only legal covenant requirement for atonement of sins. Couldn't He have been beheaded, so that His Blood could have been spilled quickly and painlessly? No, the prophets foretold of His gruesome, shameful death, and indeed it had to be. But why? The Spiritual Transaction was far more complete than you or I could have ever imagined. Yes, sin, death, and the power of the devil were defeated as Christ rose triumphantly from the grave, but it was the *process* of His life and death that enabled Him to be our High Priest before the Father. Hebrews 4-5 says that God understands our propensity to sin and every one of our weaknesses, having been tempted in the exact same way. Therefore, *He knows by experience* how frail we are. There is nothing we can't bring to Him in full confidence of being understood and sympathized with. Fathom the depths of suffering God endured in order to *relate* to *you and me.* I tell you, God knows your pain.

ALL THE HURT AND ALL THE FEARS
I KNOW THEM ALL, THIS TRAIL OF TEARS
I TOOK EACH ONE AND MADE THEM MINE
I CRIED WITH YOU EACH SINGLE TIME
I AM AWARE, I KNOW THE COST
THE SACRIFICE OF THAT'S LOST
SO WHEN YOU'RE DOWN AND CRY IN PAIN
"REMEMBER ME," CALL OUT MY NAME
NO BETTER PLACE THAT YOU CAN GO
THAN IN MY ARMS BECAUSE "I KNOW."

"Every aspect of His suffering was for you. If that kind of love and sacrifice does not translate into love, then you can't possibly understand. The 'world,' mentioned in the famous John 3:16 verse, is not a generic term, but an all-inclusive one, just as 'whosoever' is. It is saying that there is no one excluded, regardless of race or background or sin.

"The most disturbing aspect of all of His suffering, which He willingly embraced for our sake, was the separation from His Father. No words can express the horror. They have been One since before time, created all that there is, shared together in all God's splendor ... and then the unthinkable: Jesus was rejected. Heaven's Darling was shunned. God's only beloved Son, in whom He is well pleased, forsaken.

My God, my God, why have you forsaken me?

"God turned His Face from His Beloved in order to be able to turn His unveiled face toward us, to make us His sons and daughters."

Behold what manner of Love that the Father has bestowed upon us that we should be called children of God! (1 John 3:1)

"I Love You"

for your sake I took the scorn
the mocking of the crown of thorns
piercing through both flesh and soul
I hung and died that you'd be whole
what else could I possibly do
to express My Love for you?
you are the reason that I bled
My "I Love You," written in red

"Now you must choose for yourself. Today you must choose what you will do. Will you leave every excuse behind and run into His arms today and receive His love for you? Will you turn your face from religion and all that binds you and enter into an intimate love relationship with The Living God?"

The music started and I opened up the altars for a heartfelt response as I sang the song the Lord wrote for me many months earlier, titled appropriately, "Remember ME."

WHEN I LOOK AT THE STARS, WHEN I GAZE AT THE MOON
THEY PALE IN COMPARISON TO YOU
FEEL MY BREATH IN THE WIND, TASTE MY KISS IN THE RAIN
LET MY LOVE IN TO HEAL THE PAIN…

BRIDGE
I'M TRYING, WON'T YOU LET ME IN. YOU'RE CRYING,
ANGUISHED WITHIN
YOU'RE DYING TO BE FREE AGAIN.
IF ONLY YOU'D TURN TO ME….

CHORUS
YOU WERE DOWN AND CRIED IN PAIN
I RAN WHEN YOU CALLED OUT MY NAME
MY LOVE FOR YOU IS STILL THE SAME…
REMEMBER ME

I TOOK YOUR TEARS AND MADE THEM MINE
ASSURED YOU THAT YOU WOULD BE FINE
I ANSWERED EVERY SINGLE TIME…YOU CALLED TO ME

VERSE 2
I LONG FOR YOUR HEART, I TREASURE YOUR SOUL
I'LL FORGIVE YOUR PAST AND MAKE YOU WHOLE
YOU'RE NEVER ALONE, YOU'VE NOTHING TO FEAR
JUST CALL OUT MY NAME, I'M ALWAYS HERE

I LOVE YOU, I LOVE YOU

I felt the rush of His Love sweeping through the place as the altar filled to overflowing.

How I love Him.

"Remember ME" was born November 3, 2001 without one piece of jewelry. I was cradled in His love, nestled perfectly content in the center of His will. I thought I was ready to introduce "Remember ME" to the world.

Remember ME's Birthday with the framed poetry prints.

 **"The Word"**

a blade so sharp It does divide

through flesh and spirit

none can hide

living, breathing, eternal force

power flowing from It's Source

evil must flee in retreat

run and cower in defeat

so speak aloud, let It be heard

yield your sword, It is The Word

IT WAS THE BEST OF TIMES and the best of times. There was no such thing as *worst*. The intense suffering was pushed back into the recesses of my memory, only brought forward when I was asked to speak, which was becoming more and more frequently. And even then, it was victorious. From up on the mountaintop, even the valley looks beautiful. It is simply another view of His grace.

I was alive. Brilliantly, triumphantly alive. Immersed in purpose, I overflowed, imparting His love and hope into every heart in my path. After the November 3rd birthing of "Remember ME," Jewelry so many women emerged from their own closets of pain. God's use of my transparency opened the floodgates of honesty and sparked hunger for more of Him. Thus, a weekly "Wit's End" gathering began at my house, and it was precious. We learned to listen and wait on His presence and then sat under a rainfall of His love. I shared the following word given to me many months earlier, and it became the ongoing theme of study.

"Do not despise your neediness.
Your desperate need is drawing you closer to Me—
your Source, your Savior.
Here in My Arms you shall learn My Love.
Your hunger and thirst is a necessary good.
I shall satisfy your longing soul.
Time and again you will discover My Faithfulness,
and then you shall Trust.
Your need shall be transformed—
from your need to be loved, filled, and healed
into a desperate need to love Me—to be filled
to Love others into wholeness.
Then you shall call Me Lord and it is true.
Then you will know My Father's Heart, go forward
and possess the Land, feeding on My Faithfulness.
Then you will know Me,
then you will… "Remember ME."

"Remember ME" was taking baby steps forward; we had our first couple of pieces of jewelry available in January 2002. My friend Launa asked me to showcase the jewelry at her upcoming art event, and I excitedly accepted the gracious opportunity. She's a world-class artist known for her one-of-a-kind POETRY ART by Launa (www.poetryart.net). I felt supremely honored to have been invited. It was another hallmark altar-building moment for me. Sitting beside a wonderful glass display case crafted by Michele and filled with these treasured, silver pieces of life, I tasted, as if for the first time, His pure, undiluted love.

So humble were our beginnings—from the framed prints, home printed brochures, and catalogs to our very first three pieces. "I Will Praise" and "I Know" symbols sat proudly beside a solitary "Remember ME" ring. All the riches of the world could not compare to the value of these three

Me, Michele, and Mom and Launa's Art event.

pieces. They meant everything to me. They were an outward manifestation of the inner transformation, and there was nothing more precious.

As if life could get any better, Gigi's friend Kathy told us about her daughter Meg's recent dramatic conversion. Shortly thereafter, we met. I was awed by the rapture of "first love"— fully yielded, humble, and willing to be used by God. To my great joy and surprise, Meg felt that doing so meant living with us to nanny the children and help in any way she could. Many other people came forward to volunteer their time, talent, and energy to participate in His glorious wonder called, "Remember ME." I was overwhelmed with gratitude.

I was running so well that when I inevitably tripped, it was almost unexpected and especially hard. I hit some tough relational bumps. "Up on the mountain top," I imagined that I was above the petty troubles of those who dwelt below. The marital gash was still there; it was still raw; it was still crippling. I willed it to be gone; I acted like it was gone … but it was not gone. I thought I had reached the summit of absolute surrender. If only I could transfer that same trust I had toward "Remember ME" and apply it to my relationship with Paul.

I just couldn't seem to apply "acceptance with joy" when it came to Paul. I knew I wasn't a "leper of love" anymore, yet when confronted with the reality of our lack of intimacy, I still felt as if I were. This contradiction tempted me to inwardly blame him for my turbulent dives and crashes, and point to him as the reason I couldn't fly free. The most troublesome aspects of my relationship woes were his recent interest and involvement in "Remember ME."

If there was one thing I wanted to keep separate and sacred in my life, it was "Remember ME." I was intensely protective, making sure that no one would harm her in any way. Between Paul and me, there were conflicts, misunderstandings, and issues deeply embedded in our relationship. I did not want any of those "fleshly," "unspiritual" things to contaminate the purity of "Remember ME." I didn't realize how self-righteous and pompous that appeared to Paul. He felt he was a part of "Remember ME," because he was a part of our marriage.

"Flesh of my flesh" is beautiful imagery for "covenant love," but stinging hypocrisy for "covenant dislike." In other words, I'm bound to you because I have to be, not because I want to be, and since we're bound, everything yours is mine, and everything mine is yours. Oh, I didn't appreciate that whatsoever. There wasn't much love flowing between us in any genuine sense. We both went through the motions of love, but our hearts were still very much disconnected.

Paul was in a perfect situation to take the reins of "Remember ME," so that she could begin walking as a legitimate company. The only problem was my death grip on those reins, which proved to be an enormous problem indeed. Paul had quit his job as Volkswagen manager and was trying to finish the few classes needed for his bachelor's degree so that he could obtain more meaningful employment. He was available; he was interested; he was qualified. There seemed to be no reason that he shouldn't help "Remember ME" along ... no reason whatsoever, except the tiny fact that the mere thought of it made me want to break out in a freakish case of hives! The couple that couldn't agree on anything was going to somehow peacefully co-control a company? I couldn't comprehend it. Most of all, I was convinced that it was not God's idea, and I was therefore justified in resisting it. Resist as I might, it began happening. And much to my chagrin, Paul was growing it beautifully. He was great with people, finances, and managing the numerous details down to the last thread.

Everything should have been peachy, but instead, resentment began building as I blamed him for tinkering with something that didn't belong to him, and for turning something holy into something common. I wanted him to run "Remember ME" like a ministry and consult God on every last detail the way I did. Anything short of that was criminal in my mind. He was running a business, and I blamed him for running it like a business. The tension between us was ridiculous. Can you even imagine the complicated mess this became? It was like we had this huge white elephant sitting in our living room, but neither one of us was going to acknowledge or discuss it. We just walked around it or over it, or pushed with all our might to budge it to the side. Whoever pushed the hardest won in that particular moment.

Oh, the absurd games we play in order to avoid looking deeply into the mirror. I wanted "Remember ME" to be a God thing, yet I wasn't going to let God do a "thing" between Paul and me that was real because ...yes, it was *too painful.* I was finally on the mountaintop after all those years of suffering, and I wasn't about to go willingly back down into the tearful valley to deal with a "thorn in my flesh." If only I could have embraced the pain of imperfect love the way I had embraced the pain of childbirth, these miles in the journey could have been much less treacherous. Instead, I stubbornly walked ahead, hand-in-hand with God, leaving Paul behind in the dust.

The fall of 2002 approached, and pastor Mary Kay asked me to follow up from the previous year with another event sponsored by the women's ministry. I was thrilled! After an entire year of wholeness, my focus had shifted from my personal battle to the battle at large. I desperately wanted to equip other women with the necessary tools to overcome.

The title was "Demolishing Strongholds," and having years of journal notes from walking through the process firsthand, I felt "armed and dangerous." I contacted a local brick company and they graciously donated mini bricks for each woman to take as a reminder of God's work in her life. Life is messy, and we are all under construction. All that He tears down is for our necessary rebuilding. The brick company also donated a truck full of regular sized bricks for me to construct a life-sized "wall of pain."

I carefully and prayerfully stacked a 5 x 5 foot wall and painted it white. On the face of my white wall, I painted words in large block, black letters. Each larger-than-life word represented an enemy that had nearly destroyed me in battle. There was nothing caught in my throat this time around as I stared at these enemies: FEAR, SHAME, TORMENT, PAIN, INSOMNIA, SELF HATRED, DEPRESSION, DESPAIR, and UNSOUND MIND. They had all been defeated. The consuming fear was nowhere to be found. Instead, I held a righteous anger tightly to my breast, ready to wield the Sword of Truth and set the captives free. It was sobering to stand there when all "spiritually grown up," preparing to enter into battle, not my battle, but a spiritual battle being waged in the heavenlies for souls.

For every second of suffering, I asked for a single soul. Calculating all the years of torment and dividing them into months, then weeks, then days, then hours, then minutes, and then seconds added up to ... well, more souls in exchange for time suffered than I could possibly count. There were hilly fields of wheat swaying in the wind, but instead of wheat grains, I saw pairs of eyes—all different shapes, colors, and sizes of eyes were peering at me on the swaying stalks of grain. I stood my ground and raised my hands to heaven and declared the harvest.

Everything was coming together so wonderfully. The only hitch was deciding what I was going to wear. I know, I know. It was a trivial problem, but it was nonetheless a problem. I went to my fashion-ista sister Gigi to scour her ample, overflowing closet. Though the selection was better than most high fashion department stores, nothing felt right. Last year's "Remember ME" birthing was so special in every way, right down to the monogrammed silver buttons on my dark grey suit. But now, my search was fruitless, store after store, dressing room after dressing room ... nothing. I ended up doing a complete fashion no-no and wore the exact same dark grey suit as the year before. Frankly I didn't care. I didn't want this year to be about me. So much of my testimony was "my struggle," and I wanted the focus to be entirely on God and how awesome He is in deliverance.

The morning was different than last year, but equally as sweet as I looked in the mirror in the tiny room off the sanctuary, gazing at the lovely transformation before me. God's goodness was passing right before my eyes as I studied my face and remembered the blood-shot, tormented eyes that had peered back at me in the middle of a raging episode twenty months before. Now, clear, bright, hopeful eyes with purpose stared back, and I thanked Him with all my heart that it was well with my soul.

My dear friend Rebecca stood up and introduced me. I wasn't prepared for the beauty or shining validation that she so eloquently espoused. I couldn't keep my eyes from welling. A year later, she gave me the handwritten copy of her exact words if I ever wanted to use them in my book. As I share her words now, I am as humbled and honored as I was when I heard them for the first time that morning. By God's grace, may I leave such a legacy.

"Legacy"

Each of us leaves behind a legacy. If we are thoughtful and careful, it will be a lasting one that will reflect eternal values. Michelle's legacy is not really about jewelry. Her legacy reflects the richest, most beautiful, and challenging inheritance of all times: the "Word Made Flesh." Michelle has a unique way of presenting the "Word Made Flesh." It is tangible, powerful, and commanding. That is because she realizes that The Word is a demanding reality that is a Holy Spirit inspired tool for change. She puts her entire spirit, soul, and body into living and reflecting the "Word Made Flesh"—whether through speaking, writing, composing, or being a wife, mother, sister, or designing jewelry. (There is no shortage of blood, sweat, and tears in this sometimes-excruciating process!)

I will verify that each word of every poem and song and jewelry symbol has been lived and experienced. Most importantly, the legacy of "Remember ME" Jewelry was created not to point us to Michelle Meade, but to direct us to Jesus Christ, to our "Abba Father," to the Word of God, the "Word Made Flesh."

As we read in Matthew 12, it is from the abundance of the heart that the mouth speaks. It is from the overflow of Michelle's heart that she creates "Remember ME" Jewelry. I know that every challenge that Michelle Meade presents to us is a challenge that she too has successfully faced by being intricately intertwined with His Word.

Just as it has been exciting to see each new piece of jewelry emerge from her tender and vulnerable heart, I am excited to hear what abundance is overflowing in these words that will further point us to the power of His Word, His Presence in our lives.

A different girl walked up on that stage this year. She was no longer a needy mess, and though she wore the same outfit, everything on the inside was completely restored. She was bursting with all the knowledge and revelation that had been poured in and was ready to unload a heaping portion of "The Word" on every heart. Those who had "ears to hear" would be transformed.

I shared for over an hour about what a stronghold is, how it develops slowly over time, and ultimately how to demolish it so that God's love may have full entrance into our hearts. In closing I brought our attention to the "Wall of Pain." I asked each woman to look at those words and identify which enemy of her soul was walled up around her heart, keeping the Truth Himself from having full entrance to bring freedom.

The response that day was evident as each woman came up to the altar and reached for a mini brick. The little brick represented both the demolition of the individual walls of pain surrounding hearts and the new construction that He is faithful to complete.

Tears of healing were shed as humble, willing hearts met Him that day at the "Wall of Pain." Ministry continued for some time afterward. And though I was exhausted, my heart rejoiced as the sun set on another hallmark, altar-building moment in my life.

How I love Him.

CHAPTER 17

Let The Wind Blow

LET THE WIND BLOW
SHAKING THE LIMBS OF DESPAIR
LEAVES OF THE PAST FALLING AWAY
AS IF TO SAY GOODBYE

LET THE RIVER FLOW
LAUGHING STREAMS WASH MY SOUL
MOVING CURRANTS IN REFRAIN
UNDO THE PAIN OF LIFE'S REGRETS

LET THE WIND BLOW
VIOLENTLY YOU ROAR
RELEASING SEED OF NEW TOMORROWS
FROM MANY SORROWS—LIVE

LET THE RIVER FLOW
LIVING WATERS RUSH BELOW
TREAD THIS HEART WITH SHARPENING STONE
CARVE A HOME TO DWELL

LET THE WIND BLOW
BREATHE AND SHATTER WHAT I KNOW
BORN AGAIN FROM CRIMSON STAINS
WHAT REMAINS BUT THE AIR I BREATHE

ONLY WEEKS BEFORE CHRISTMAS I had plenty of "expecteds" lying neglected. All the lists, shopping, decorating, and cookie baking were demanding my attention, but I was lost in a constant whirlwind of ministry. I couldn't say no to a need, so I made up for lost time by working at night. As much as I savored the ministry and work, it began taking its toll.

One afternoon a woman to whom I had previously ministered visited me. We'll call her "Kate." Kate felt stuck, unable to move forward spiritually. I sensed a stronghold preventing her from accepting God's love for her. She was very sweet, already engaged in full-time ministry at church, but desperately, privately in need. We talked and prayed, and when it was time for her to respond, she remained completely silent. She simply looked at me, glazed over. Later Kate told me that she had never experienced anything like it in her life. She couldn't open her mouth or respond to my invitation to receive God's love. It was as if she were mute. I suspected that the underworld was not very happy about my preaching deliverance and prophesying hope. Souls were being claimed, and they were not going to relinquish holds without some resistance. However, it was Christmas with little time to devote to reflection or prayer. Spiritually undernourished by my hyperactivity, it was an opportune time for trouble.

On our drive to Wisconsin to visit family, I began feeling weird, but dismissed the uneasiness as stress. Midway through the week, I could no longer ignore the wide range of disconcerting symptoms. Most of them were familiar old foes, but I was not ready to accept their intrusions as anything more than temporary distractions. I was relieved to return home, hoping that my frazzled nerves would soon settle.

We hadn't even unpacked our bags when a situation arose that caused us to jump right back into the car and drive another twenty-six hours with the kids to minister to someone dear to our hearts. Upon our return, I began unraveling like a ball of yarn tossed into the air only to fall and roll in a tangled whim.

Once again, I found myself frustrated and lying in bed hour after sleepless hour, wrestling with my unquiet mind. Forget all that stuff about not despising my neediness. I refused to go back to that hell. I would not go.

Paul had a dream that seemed to be prophetic. In his dream, there was someone pounding at our front door. Paul looked through the window and saw the largest man he had ever seen. It was as if he were superhuman with bulging veins that emerged from enormous muscles. In the next scene, Paul saw me let this strongman in. Once inside, his face contorted, and he became vicious as he lunged to devour me. Then Paul awoke.

I knew the strongman was fear. I was totally freaked out that I had allowed him back in the door! I was entangling myself again in a yoke of bondage! What started as genuine repentance for my self-reliance and naiveté turned into a repenting circus of compulsive behavior driven by fear.

I can't possibly let this happen! No! What did I do to lose my freedom? I must go back and fix it!

It didn't matter what I did, what I said, or what I tried. I was held hostage again.

I blamed myself for my captivity.

Although I did not willfully walk back into the darkness, I felt as if I were accountable to a higher standard. I had allowed it to happen through neglect. I let God down. I ruined the testimony He gave me and made a mockery of everything I believed and taught all those women. Every Scripture was turned inward as an arrow of condemnation.

I became a wide-open target for the mocking accusations; words that had literally come from my own mouth only a month and a half prior were now used to convict and sentence me to suffering. My heart was collapsing with each piercing stab.

As hard as I tried to combat it through every natural and supernatural means within my grasp, I was being swallowed alive by this monster once more. My heart knew His love, but the tormenting thoughts terrifyingly convinced otherwise. I felt as if I had betrayed my Lord. Like Peter, I wept bitterly.

The damning accusations ricocheted in my head, and I compulsively handed the devil a truckload of bricks to wall me in. This was a sneaky and successful strategy to center the obsessive, disturbing thoughts around the dearest thing to my heart: my relationship with God. I swung precariously from a thread day after day, night after sleepless night, struggling to make it until dawn. I willed myself to get out of bed and be a mother, even though a freakish, scattered, muttering one. In my other episodes, I knew I would find comfort and relief in His Word. It was my only refuge from the storm. Now I literally trembled with physical symptoms every time I opened the Bible.

I couldn't determine if I was allowed to be "sifted as wheat" by satan or if I was simply going back to "Crazyville."

Slurs reverberated through my troubled mind into the core of my soul: *"BLASPHEMER! BLASHPHEMER! JUDAS, JUDAS, JUDAS! You've rejected His love! UNPARDONABLE SIN! UNPARDONABLE SIN!"*

Then two minutes later I would change my mind, convinced I was being "sifted." I tried harder, that my faith would not fail Him. Around and 'round I spun, confusion competing with fear for dominion.

James talks about refusing double-mindedness. I was such a mess that I felt "quadruple-minded." So why did I bother? Because in spite of it all, I clung to the hope that God loved me and would not abandon me.

I had upcoming speaking engagements, and as tortuous as it was to stand before a bunch of women and proclaim to them what I was incapable of receiving, I felt I had to. The arrows pierced deeply as I shared of His Father's heart, feeling completely unable to partake of it myself. Yet His truth, mercy, and rich, unfailing love penetrated. In spite of me, these women were moved to a heartfelt response. I was asked to be their featured speaker for their fall retreat, yet all I could think was, "I have to get out of here!" as *Whitewashed tomb! Dead men's bones! Hypocrite!* raced and pinged.

I was helplessly spinning out of control. All my spiritual knowledge only succeeded in knotting my shoelaces tighter and tighter, until I was immobilized completely. I knew I could not evaluate truth in light of experience. Rather, experiences had to be evaluated in the light of truth. As much as I prayed, quoted, and repented, my reality violently assaulted my theology. Yet, I couldn't believe that God was capable of being false. So it had to be *me*. Down the hill my snowball rolled.

Then one day, my troubled, broken heart simply yielded for the first time since this whole episode began. Ever so weary, I lay quietly with my head in my hands, asking as a child, "Lord, what I should do?"

I was struggling to "do," anything. I couldn't talk to my husband or kids, be still, play the guitar, or read anything … especially the Bible because of the symptomatic physical backlash that accompanied every attempt. His answer was the most precious release I have ever known in my entire life. Gently and softly He came.

"Be, My love. Just Be. Be still and know that I AM God. I will hide you in My Secret Place. This is your warfare strategy: rest, laugh, live, love—just "be" in Me. I will battle for you. No more praying, reading, quoting—simply rest in My love. Be still and know that I AM God."

I remember journaling His precious instruction and feeling as if the weight of the world had been lifted off my shoulders. It was the confirmation my heart yearned for! He assured me that I was His prized lamb.

How precious was His response! Only He could have known what I needed to "do" to "be" whole. I called my mom and Maria and told them, and they rejoiced with me. My Deliverer had come … all I had to "do" was "be."

How I love Him.

The madness stopped and for the first time in many weeks, my heart beat normally in my chest as I rested in peace. This blessed recuperative stillness lasted about an hour when panic struck my heart.

"That wasn't my Lord at all, but the devil trying to trick me to stop praying and to keep me out of the Word! Jesus is the Word made flesh; He would never tell me to stop reading His life-giving Word!"

Those couple of thoughts might as well have been my death sentence. The confusion and horror that followed are indescribable.

"My sheep know My voice … they will not follow another … if a branch does not remain in me, it is cut off, cast into the fire, and burned."

I'm following another voice; I'm not a sheep, but a goat! As much pain and suffering as I had experienced before, nothing compared to this.

I deteriorated rapidly from that point on in a constant state of helter-skelter. I could only sleep minutes. Literally minutes every *week*. I couldn't eat. I tried. I remember Mom standing over me, praying as every bite went into my mouth, commanding the food to stay in my body because it wanted to come back up automatically.

My precious baby, "Remember ME," became a bitter reminder of my failure. After all God had done, I had forgotten Him, and this was too excruciating for words. I wished she had never been born, or rather, had never been born through *me*.

In this condition, you can imagine my horror as the highlighted calendar dates indicated our much anticipated trip to Maui was only days away. Paul's parents planned this special, kids-free get-away to spend a week with them and his brother and sister-in-law in Paradise. I could not fathom leaving my house, let alone traveling umpteen hours by plane to land in heaven while trapped in hell. It was unthinkable. And yet, it was already paid for. How could I disappoint my family and be faithless? I changed my mind about seventy-five times: "There is no way I can go; I need to be in a hospital." Then, "I have to go. I'll be all right. God will heal me on the way." I finally zipped up the haphazardly packed luggage and left for the airport.

By now I was compelled to listen to the Bible on CD, twenty-four-seven to combat the obsessive thoughts of my damnation. Unable to sit or keep from shaking, I paced the airport, mumbling aloud.

Back and forth, back and forth, and back and forth.

Delayed departure.

Back and forth, back and forth, and back and forth.

Delayed departure once more.

Back and forth, back and forth, and back and forth I paced; I mumbled; I wandered.

Though physically in the airport, I was nowhere to be found. I was so far, far away. I was so inexplicably lost.

My nightmare continued when our connecting flight was delayed, then finally canceled in San Diego. After all the hassle, it was 1:00 a.m. as we shuttled our way to the hotel. It was an exhausting day, and Paul collapsed into a deep sleep while I feared being left to myself. I lay with the Bible on my chest, Paul's hand on my head, and my CDs playing loudly through the headphones as my body shook with fear. The clock mocked me.

1:30, 1:31, 1:32, 1:33, 1:34, 1:35, 1:36, 1:37, 1:38, 1:39, 1:40, 1:41, 1:42, 1:43, 1:44, 1:45, 1:46, 1:47, on and on the seconds ticked until 3:00 a.m. and I couldn't endure one more passing second. I jumped up from the bed and paced rapidly in tiny circles. I grabbed my cell phone to call Mom. I just needed to hear her voice one more time.

"Mom," I whimpered.

"Hunny?"

"Mom," I repeated.

"I'm here, hunny."

"Mom," I whimpered once more, the only word I could get out.

"Michelle, it's me, hunny. Where are you?"

"Mom. Mom. Mom ... I have to come home, Mom," I managed to get out.

She must have known rational conversation was worthless because she began praying immediately.

"Listen to me, Michelle. Is Paul with you?"

"Uh huh."

"You go to him. Okay? Do you hear me? I am going to get off this phone and call everybody I know to pray for you. You are going to be all right, Michelle. Do you hear me?"

"Uh huh."

"I love you, Michelle."

"Hmmm."

I snapped my cell phone shut and filled the tub with water as hot as I could stand. Crying would have been a welcomed release, but the tears would not come, so I moaned while rocking back and forth in the water.

I begged silently for one moment of peace, but all I heard were profane blasphemies. I slipped down lower and lower and lower until my nose was barely above the water. Something beyond my comprehension surfaced from the deepest part of me and stole heaven's heart.

"I'm sorry, Lord. I'm so sorry. All I ever wanted was to be Your girl. I am so sorry for everything ..." and then I purposely slid beneath the water.

The hotel tub was tiny and shallow with a low-fill drainage hole, making it difficult to stay under. An indeterminate amount of time passed when I found myself emerging, crying out, "Jesus, Son of David, have mercy on me! Jesus, Son of David, have mercy on me! Jesus, Son of David, have mercy on me! Jesus, Son of David, have mercy on me! Please, Jesus. Please, Jesus. Please, Jesus. Mercy. Mercy. Mercy."

From the depths of my being, I cried out to Him.

Would He not come?

The mental whirlwind quieted enough for me to step out of the tub and pace the floor until daylight.

The eight-hour flight was simply more torture, different environment. While others reclined, listened to music, or watched movies with their headphones, I wrestled to exist. I couldn't believe it. I could not believe this was happening!

Just prior to the follow-up women's event in December, "Demolishing Strongholds," I remembered brushing my teeth and thanking God for the upcoming Maui trip, relishing the thought of enjoying His paradise this time around, since last time I had been incapacitated with pre-natal sickness. Paul and I needed this break so badly, a chance to just be together without any demands. I had anticipated the peaceful sound of lapping waves upon the shore, stunning creation that would take my breath away, and special stolen moments with Paul that I could tuck away and treasure. Instead, I was now headed for Maui, battling for my life. My head tingled, my limbs twitched and shook involuntarily, and I felt as if I were jumping out of my skin. I could not fathom this plane landing with me in the same, demented condition as I boarded. I had to get well. I had to be delivered. I had eight hours to quote non-stop Scripture, to rebuke countless demons, and to believe myself whole.

I felt compelled to torture myself by listening to Revelation 21:7–8. It clinched my fate with brutal imagery replaying over and over in my head:

*He who overcomes shall inherit all things, and I will be His God and He shall be My son. But the **fearful and the cowardly**,*

*unbelieving, abominable, murderers ... shall have their part in
the lake of fire which burns with fire and brimstone, which is
the second death* (Revelation 21:7,8 NKJV, emphasis mine).

Normally, soaring above the clouds, staring at the endless
highway of blue, was one of my favorite pleasures. Now
the blue only tormented. I hid my face inside my trembling
fingers.

He told me, *"The sky was always blue"*... but why could
I not remember His love and faithfulness? After all we had
been through together! Even the precious reminders that hung
around my neck and encircled my finger (the "Overcomer"
pendant and the "Remember ME" ring) only succeeded in
pushing the arrows of condemnation deeper into my heart.

My mood swings were drastic and varied from utter
despair to frenzied determination; I seamlessly shifted gears
sometimes moment-by-moment. I could not land in Maui
with this unsound mind. If I could only believe, then all things
were possible. Faith comes by hearing the Word of God, so I
dried my eyes and put on my headphones. I was listening to
Revelation, reading Colossians, while mumbling Philippians
out loud.

Do we need any further description of madness?

Then I saw Jesus walk down the airplane aisle and reach
out His hand toward me! Just as I was about to stand up
and fling myself toward Him, I realized it was the flight
attendant handing us napkins as he made his drink run. The
hallucinations continued when I paused my listening, reading,
quoting frenzy long enough to look up and around at my
surroundings.

My eyes scanned the rows of seats for someone, anyone
to save me. It was as if I were thrown a lifeline when I saw a
woman quietly reading a well-known Christian book called
The Purpose Driven Life. I felt compelled to go to her ... oh,
if only I could just curl up into a ball and nestle myself next to

her feet. I felt by virtue of simply being near her, I could cling to her faith, and perhaps I would be okay at least enough to get me through the rest of the flight. I did everything I could to restrain myself from making a scene. I even held my urine as long as possible so that I would not have to pass her on the way to the bathroom for fear of assaulting her. I was a freaking mess.

Against all my demented hopes of being "delivered" mid-flight, I landed in the misty warm air of Maui just as sick as when I boarded. My thoughts still raced in absurdity; I had all my funky compulsive behavior to keep under wraps, and I was physically deteriorating by the minute. I believed my coming to Maui was an "act of faith"—that it showed my determination to believe God above my circumstances. Obviously, it confirmed my insanity, because one minute I was quoting Scripture and then the next minute I wanted to kill myself. Then the next minute I despaired over my lack of faith. Then the next minute I rebuked demons. Then the next minute I was hostile over my inability to function. Then the next minute I refused unbelief and quoted more Scripture. Then the next minute I forgot who I was. And then the next minute …

CHAPTER 18

"Remember ME"

taste and see that I AM God
The First, The Last, The Same
drink and eat, I'll complete
the work for which I came
Living Waters flow
deep within My Vine
fruit of My flesh
your skin's made fresh
to carry My New Wine
everlasting marriage
by My own Blood we're bound
I'll never leave, to My Word cleave
your heart's now Holy Ground.

I CANNOT EXPRESS how intensely heart-wrenching it was to be in Maui, beholding such beauty, yet be absolutely incapable of drinking it in. Deeper and deeper the arrows of condemnation struck at my heart for the crippling effects of fear. The stunning sunset over endless waters simply meant a night of horror ahead. Greeting the dawn as it rose in utter majesty over the hilly terrain merely indicated twelve more hours of torture were on the way.

I wanted so badly to keep my suffering under wraps so everyone else's trip would not be ruined. We all sat on the balcony, watching dolphins cavort effortlessly in and out of the blue wonderland. Relaxed smiles and chatty banter confirmed that I didn't belong there. I was in critical condition, clinging to life one breath at a time, yet somehow I had to act as if I were okay. I suddenly broke the air of happiness with a solemn statement of my un-well being.

"Guys, I'm not doing well. I have been unable to sleep and am struggling to fight off anxiety. I am letting you know so that you won't be offended by any lack of participation. Please, act normally and enjoy this trip to the fullest, despite me. I will only worsen with guilt if I sense that I'm putting a damper on your fun. Please. Thank you for understanding," I said simply and sincerely.

Sympathetic looks and verbal exchanges let me know how much they loved me, offering support to do anything possible to minimize the struggle. The kindness was well meaning, but I felt that no one except God could help me. Paul, my precious Paul, as much as he had done to help me, was left feeling frustrated and helpless.

No matter how much he prayed, it was not long enough, fervent enough, or effective enough. My neediness demanded the impossible from him, yet he continued to try. The depth of his love for me was demonstrated the day I looked out our large-paned bedroom windows and saw him in the bitter cold, reconstructing the "wall of pain." Brick by brick, he built it precisely as it had been on December 3. He pieced it together like a puzzle so the black words of bondage could be sanded away as if they were never there. Day after day, I looked out the window and saw him strenuously erasing the letters off the mortared stone, prayerfully removing the damning words out of my life. Even now, I do not know the darkness against which his loving sacrifice of prayer prevailed. But at the time, I couldn't appreciate it. Unless there were results, my desperation demanded more, more, more.

In Maui, as much as I wanted isolation, I couldn't confine myself to the tiny rear condo bedroom because Paul had become my connection to God. I absolutely couldn't let him out of my sight. As hot as the sun bore down, the trembling, shaking, and tingling sensations that vibrated through my head left me feeling eerily stone cold.

And then there were the nights. Everyone would retire to their rooms to sleep while I resisted suicidal thoughts every second of every hour until the break of dawn. I knew I could not be alone, so I clung to Paul for my life.

On the third day, I paced up and down the sandy beach with a cell phone in my hand, desperately trying to think of a way I could get out of there. The only person I wanted to see or hear was my mom. I dialed.

"Mom."

"Michelle?"

"Mom."

"Hunny, I'm here."

"Mom ..."

"Michelle, it's me, hunny ..."

"Mom, I need to come home, Mom."

"Hunny, listen to me; there are hundreds of people praying for you right now. You are going to be all right."

"Mom."

"Hunny, I'm here." Her voice cracked and I could hear her praying in her heavenly language.

"Mom, I don't know what to do. I don't know what to do."

Every morning I would have these same conversations on the beachy hell with my dear mother.

Halfway through the ten-day trip I was so berserk that I didn't think I could contain myself anymore. I was going on my second consecutive week of absolutely no sleep whatsoever, existing in a continual twenty-four-seven state of terror.

Paul went with the boys to snorkel. Of course, I followed along. Being near him was necessary. Only moments after he had entered the water, he severed his finger on some coral. I watched as he ripped a nearby tee shirt and wound it tightly around the injured finger. He had to use both his hands in order to apply pressure to control the bleeding. This meant I had no choice but to drive him to the nearest hospital. Unable to focus for more than seconds at a time, I veered back and forth between the edges of the treacherously steep and curvy roads.

"Michelle! Watch out!" Paul yelled, yanking the steering wheel toward him and averting a plunge off a cliff. "What are you thinking?"

I couldn't answer. I just tried to force my darting eyes to look at the road and my jittering hands to keep hold of the wheel.

When we reached the clinic and I realized that I was within a medical facility, I nearly forgot the reason we were there. He was the one who was bleeding, needing a surgeon to suture up his hand ... and yet I was the one in greater need. I wanted to shove Paul aside and run up to the desk and beg the receptionist for help. Beg her to find a doctor, a psychiatrist, *anyone* who could prescribe anything to bring relief. I didn't care anymore about my lack of faith or fear of man. I simply needed a reprieve from the madness. Instead, I sat glued to my seat in silence, trembling and mumbling incoherently.

I need to mention that I had not escaped medical help completely during my plight. Paul had forced my hand a year prior. As a loving husband, he had no longer been able to sit on the sidelines and observe my rapid, downward spiral. He had insisted that I see a physician. And while I went along with his attempt to get help for me, I sabotaged the medical intervention. I downplayed my symptoms as mere anxiety and insomnia. The doctor prescribed a medication commonly used to treat anxiety disorders along with a sleeping aid. They might have helped, but we'll never know. I stopped taking them after only a week, convinced they were worsening my condition.

And once again, just prior to our leaving for Maui, Paul had insisted that I see a doctor. I saw Dr. Z, and he was wonderful and sympathetic. But a physician's ability to diagnose is only as good as the information his patient gives him. I told him almost nothing. I asked him to prescribe something to "take the edge off," so I could enjoy Maui. He prescribed different meds for the anxiety and the insomnia. Pitting low doses of these two medications against the *true* level of my illness was preposterous, but Dr. Z had no way of knowing that. Had he known, he might have prescribed other medication or greater doses of the medication he chose. Under-treatment did nothing but shatter my hopes for relief, confirm my prejudice against medicine, and solidify my resolve to seek God, and God alone.

Five days into our trip, Paul called Dr. Z and notified him that I was worsening. Dr. Z tried to help, but Hawaii had restrictions about having prescriptions filled from the mainland. My only option was to try and seek medical help there. I refused. I knew that if I walked through those hospital doors, I would have to be admitted. That, of course, would ruin everybody's trip. I just couldn't do it.

I was slowly driving my poor husband half-crazy. As soon as he drifted off to sleep, I would feel myself slipping away. Bolting upright, I would yell out his name.

"PAUL!" I would scream in panic, jolting him awake.

In a drowsy shock, he would ask, "What is it, hunny?"

Shivering silence.

I couldn't answer. I wanted to. But I couldn't. He'd wrap his arms tightly around me, pull us both back down in bed, pray, and fall back to sleep.

A half hour later, the same thing would happen.

"PAUL! PAUL!" I would scream again in panic, jolting him awake once more.

"What, hunny?"

No answer.

Twenty minutes later a sickening repeat.

This continued for the remainder of the night.

By God's grace and God's grace alone, I made it one day at a time. The mental wrestling was unimaginable. I felt a breath away from being pinned to the mat.

On the eighth night, I suggested that Paul and I go out and sleep under the stars. I hoped that the twinkling night sky and lulling sound of waves as they rolled up onto the beach would calm me enough to let Paul sleep uninterrupted. We took some blankets and pillows out to the resort lounge chairs and snuggled close together.

This proved to be a really bad idea.

As I gazed at the stars, my heart throbbed with a familiar knowing. The longings were never more profound, never more real. Though my mind could not recognize God at all now, *my heart did! My heart knew* His wondrous expression of love. But as I probed to remember, I was overcome with confusion and grief because of the violent, blasphemous thoughts.

It was the most disturbing night of my life. I know Him! I know Him not. I Know Him! I know Him not. My heart and mind would have continued bludgeoning one another to the death with each twinkling star had a security guard not interrupted. Waving his flashlight, he informed us that we were not allowed to be on resort property at this hour.

We obediently retreated to our room where Paul resumed sleeping, and I resumed freaking out. I had completely lost control. I could no longer manage the madness. It was like trying to run a company with a computer that had a virus. You want to pull up an order, but the printer starts spewing out meaningless documents. You try rebooting the computer by shutting it off, but it refuses to restart. The situation is desperate. Frustrating. Useless.

I had to make it stop. I walked in the blackness to the bathroom and fumbled through my bag to locate the bottles of sleeping pills. I paced the tiny room in utter pandemonium. I knew where I was, but I didn't know where I was. I knew I was in pain, but I couldn't help myself. Spilling the both bottles of sleeping pills into my shaking hands, I had no alternative but to end the torment.

Paul either knew subconsciously that the automated screaming intervals had momentarily lapsed, or an angel stirred him awake because at this precise moment, in his own state of exhaustion, he awoke and called out "Michelle, are you in there? What are you doing?"

Upon hearing his voice, the gears shifted and I poured the pills back, returned to bed, clutched Paul in a tight embrace, and shook violently until dawn.

Our final night in Maui was spent at an authentic Luau, where I lay with my head buried into Paul's chest, hoping to melt away into the many mixed drinks I consumed. I had to sleep tonight. There was no other option. I simply had to. If it meant drinking myself unconscious, then so be it. I collapsed into bed and didn't move an inch until 11:00 a.m. the following morning.

Departing that afternoon with a new surge of energy I was determined "to possess" my deliverance before I left the island. Manic behavior catapulted the endless quoting and rebuking sessions once more. As the plane lifted off the runway, I pictured myself lifting up and away from this bondage to fly free.

"Yes, My love, you'll fly again higher and farther than you've ever been above the mist of the past, you'll soar with Me, free at last..."

Instead, I opened my eyes in response to the intensifying tingling that moved through my head and up and down each limb. Unfortunately, it was not the power of the God; my body was reacting to the extreme mental and emotional trauma, sending electrical volts through my body. I was in another world all the way home.

I wanted to love on my darling children after not seeing them for ten days, but I was incapable of anything but pain. They bounded toward us in baggage claim, and my empty arms wrapped around each one in numbed response. I was a walking dead woman. As my dad drove us home, he inquired about our trip, but I was incapable of small talk. Paul spilled out a few generic answers like, "It was really beautiful," and covered for my unresponsiveness.

My Meg was nothing short of an angel from heaven. She took care of Isabella every day, and when Bella napped, Meg would climb into bed next to me and read *God Calling* aloud.

Bella and Meg.

She held my hand and spoke words of life and comfort over me. She had the compassion of someone who *knew*, having witnessed the devastation of her brother's mental illness firsthand. One afternoon, Meg, her mom Kathy, and her brother came and prayed over me in my living room. The fragrance of God was present, and I felt something besides pain for the first time in months.

Kathy called and made an appointment for me with the founder of a local counseling center, and implored me to go. Her discernment and obedience saved my life.

———

I sat agitated in the lobby of the counseling center as Paul and I waited for the receptionist to call me in. I wanted to run out of the office and retreat back to my bedroom to hide.

"Michelle, come in …" Maryann (not her real name) welcomed us with a warm smile and an affirming hug.

"Do you want to tell me what's been going on with you?" she asked when we were seated.

I attempted to explain, but my words got lost in translation from my head to my mouth, so Paul finished.

"First of all, she's been unable to sleep. She'll go days and even weeks at a time without a wink. And then, on top of it, she's been in a constant state of terror."

"Michelle, is this true?"

I nodded silently.

"Michelle, have you had thoughts of hurting yourself or someone else?"

I nodded again.

"Are you taking anything?"

I nodded again and Paul continued.

"She's only taking an antidepressant and a sleeping aid. They have not been effective whatsoever. I think she needs more. But under-dosing isn't the only problem. She doesn't like taking medicine, and she fights me every time."

"Is this true, Michelle?"

"The medicine is not helping me. It's only making me worse. God will help me," I whispered.

Maryann had the most sympathetic look I had ever seen as she pulled out a notebook and began drawing a picture of my brain while explaining in simple terms what was going on.

"Michelle, I love God very much. And I know He loves you even more. He wants you to get better. He uses medicine and doctors and therapists like me to help people get better. This is our calling, what we've been created by Him to do. Now look at these: This is what a normal brain looks like. And this over here is what your brain looks like. See the disorganized texture and ragged boundaries?" she asked, pointing to the "scribbled" area of my frantic mind.

She continued to explain the damage that has been done to my brain over the course of these months of trauma and depletion. She explained the function of the medication and how it allows the neurotransmitters to communicate effectively with one another once again inside my brain.

"Do you want to be well, Michelle?" she asked me directly.

I nodded.

"Then you will agree to take the medicine I'm going to ask Dr. Z to prescribe?"

I nodded again.

"Michelle, I am amazed that you have done so well throughout what sounds like insufferable anguish. I know God has been with you. I know it has been hard, and you have wanted to give up. But listen to me. There is help. Promise me that if you feel like you might hurt yourself, you'll tell Paul and he will call me. I need you to promise me."

"I promise," I whispered.

She spoke with Paul privately for a few moments and we departed.

Maryann called Dr. Z and explained that my situation was much more critical than he had known. With new information, he prescribed different medication.

Medical intervention was finally in place. Even though I had agreed with Maryann to cooperate fully, I don't know why, but I continued to be hostile toward Paul every time I had to take a pill. He patiently, lovingly stood over me and waited until I finally swallowed obediently.

Within days, the electrical tingling shock subsided, as well as the tremors and twitching. Most important of all, I began to have recuperative sleep.

My days were still tremendously difficult as my mind continued to revolt against my will. I can never forget my mother coming, just as she did daily to assist with household chores, and I was pacing rapidly in tiny circles in our living room.

"Michelle ... hunny ... what are you doing?"

"I don't know, Mom. I don't know what to do. I don't know what to do," I sobbed.

She pulled me over to the couch and sat next to me grabbing both of my hands in hers. With her head pressed next to mine, never have I been more moved by His love demonstrated through another human being in my entire life. She prayed with such compassion and tenderness that I felt as if Jesus Himself were pleading with the Father through her words. An endless well ran down her cheeks until we were both drenched in the overflow. I felt His love. My mind continued to revolt, but my heart knew Him.

Endless were the prayers of His saints that lifted up incense to His Throne on my behalf. Pastor Mary Kay came over and sat on my bed. Looking into my terrified eyes with His love and compassion, she assured me that God would be faithful. She brought me a tiny lighthouse to remind me that His flame, His light, and His love were inside me, and nothing I thought or felt or did could ever change that. *No matter how lost, His light within would guide me home.*

A friend at church gave me a note with Hosea 3:14: *"Therefore, behold, I will allure her, I will bring her into the wilderness and speak comfort to her."* Then she added Song of Solomon 8:5: *"Who is this coming up from the wilderness leaning on her beloved?"* She wrote, "He is luring you into a place where He can reveal His great love to you. And you will come out leaning on your beloved, your husband, your Jesus. He loves you, Michelle. Your tender heart belongs to Him. He is always with you."

What hope to dare to believe that Jesus would comfort me in this place and that we'd emerge together as one.

Then there was Deb Cap. If I were in a trench, she'd be the one I'd want beside me. She knows God. Not just knowledge about Him, but knows Him intimately, loving Him with all her heart. She would come and sit with me on my bed and just "be" with me for hours at a time.

Each prayer, each word of encouragement was delivering life. Even if my mind was incapable of receiving it, my spirit was alive and active, growing continually. In fact, I can see now, looking back and reviewing journal entries that the worse my mind was, the sweeter and gentler and more precious were the comforts of my God. His love reached me. Though locked in confusion and forgotten moments later, His love was constantly pursuing and feeding my spirit life. The greater the struggle, the more He fed. Never could I exhaust His provision and grace. Never.

"Remember ME" Jewelry was still alive thanks to my husband Paul. He kept things going when I could not. For almost a year, I couldn't bear to go into our office. I couldn't look at the symbols or rings and purposely ostracized myself from all contact. I was so ashamed for forgetting Him, blaming myself for my tumultuous descent, that I felt completely unworthy to be associated with such divine beauty and revelation.

You need to understand this consuming grief and how I had amputated myself from His gift to me, so that the preciousness of "Remember ME," the cup of the New Covenant can be fully realized. In the very middle of unparalleled insanity, after Maui, but before I went to see Maryann, Paul came into our bedroom and asked me to write. He explained that the Symbol "Remember ME," the cup, was completed and that it needed a writing. I couldn't think one coherent thought, let alone write a stream of thoughts on paper. I knew all the "Remember ME" poetry was divinely inspired. I knew the revelations were from Him, but also realized He worked through me. How could He work through me now? It would be like trying to fill a shattered vessel with water to quench the thirsty. How could the vessel contain it, let alone pour it back out? My greater reason for refusal, however, had to do with the scar tissue around my heart. He gave me everything, yet in spite of every precious reminder, I had forgotten Him. There was no failure, no sorrow, no regret to compare.

Paul's request was impossible. The writing for this symbol would have to come from someone else. I apologized, admitting I just couldn't do it. He gently asked that I would "just try," and shut the door behind him.

The following was the most direct encounter with God I had ever had, proving communion with Him flows from our innermost being, enabling spirit-to-Spirit relationship.

"As the deer pants for the water, so my soul longs after thee."

I had no words. Absolutely none. But my heart pined for Him. As I opened my mouth, a foreign language spilled out in rich, fluid, Asian sounding syllables. This was unlike anything I had ever heard. I continued to hear this amazing language being uttered from my own lips in awe. As this beautiful unknown language continued to flow, my upper body jutted forward violently, yet I was completely unafraid. Though my mind was incapacitated, my spirit bore witness to the fact that He was accomplishing something in a realm I could not see.

"The Kingdom of Heaven suffers violence, and the violent take it by force."

This continued on for some time, and I knew that my God was fighting for me and that my participation was simply to yield to His Spirit. My intellect was completely bypassed, producing the purest and most passionate connection I have ever had with God. I knew we were completely intertwined with a singular purpose, and the outcome was breathtaking.

I grabbed my pencil and nearby notepad and scribbled down revelation directly from His Father's Heart. I cannot effectively communicate what this message meant to me then and means to me now, for it is the crux of who I am and why I am. A touching detail moved me yet again when the poetic words formed the shape of a challis.

How I love Him.

TASTE AND SEE THAT I AM GOD
THE FIRST, THE LAST, THE SAME
DRINK AND EAT, I'LL COMPLETE
THE WORK FOR WHICH I CAME
LIVING WATERS FLOW
DEEP WITHIN MY VINE
FRUIT OF MY FLESH
YOUR SKIN'S MADE FRESH
TO CARRY MY NEW WINE
EVERLASTING MARRIAGE
BY MY OWN BLOOD WE'RE BOUND
I'LL NEVER LEAVE, TO MY WORD CLEAVE
YOUR HEART'S NOW HOLY GROUND.

God was absolutely breaking into my pain. He intercepted this moment in time to demonstrate His love very personally to me. Although I couldn't comprehend and seize our connection, He showed me in an unmistakable way that we were more vitally connected than I ever imagined possible.

I was still His girl.

CHAPTER 19

"Intimacy"

O My love in We abide, intimately unified

you'll bear fruit if you stay

entwined in We in every way

make provision, spare the room

for the increase as I prune

then ask of We, it shall be done

when you and I remain as One

I NO LONGER WISH to skip the chapters of the pain, only highlighting my "victories" because what I discovered has forever changed the *quality* of my eternal life. I **know** Him. Not merely intellectual knowledge, but rather, from the deepest part of me, I **know** Him. I know the way He sounds when He is grieved or joyful. I know His favorite pleasures and what brings delight to His Heart. I know I am His and He is mine, and that He has gone away to prepare a special place for me. I know He will come again to return me to Himself to be with Him forever. I know He lives in my heart and His desire is for us to be one, even as He and The Father are one. I know.

All my prayers were coming true ... *that I might know.*

I pray that I would live a life worthy of You Lord, fully pleasing You... that I would be rooted and grounded in You, **that I might know** *by experience the deepest depths of God's Love. The full expanse ... the highest height, the widest width, the longest length, and the deepest depth ... to be filled with the fullness of God* (Colossians 1:9, Ephesians 3:16-20, paraphrased).

From affliction to unparallel intimacy and beauty, I drink deeply from His well of life. Through my difficult journey I have discovered *God's purpose.* It's not doing a certain thing a certain way for a certain end; *God's Purpose* **is** *the process!* The process is defined by the day-in-day-out experiences shared: the laughter, joy, and tears of the mundane, valley lows, steep climbs, treacherous falls, mountaintops, and rescues. Nothing pleases Him more than when we invite Him to be intricately involved in our lives. Oh, His joy when He is received!

God's highest plan and purpose for your life
is for you to commune intimately with Him
throughout the journey.

Embracing this truth allows hope and meaning to seep into the threads of both the trivial and the traumatic. Because of this knowledge, I can share the continuation of my story without an ounce of shame or regret.

One day, still spinning in continuous madness, I walked over to my mom's house and heard a thumping sound in her attic and went up to see what it was. Standing in the dark and dormant space, I was stung with pity for a helpless bird trapped inside. In her desperate efforts to free herself, she kept crashing full speed into the window. She fell sharply to the ground, only to thrash about, get up, and repeat the futile process. It was the most sorrowful sight. I had to help her! I walked slowly toward her, talking gently, but with every step she became more fearful and agitated, which worsened her panicked thrashing. Helpless to help her, I stepped away when I heard His voice:

"Open the window on the opposite end of the room."

I walked over massive heating equipment to the tiny corner window at the front of the house and banged and pulled until the aged, caulked frame finally released. I stepped down the stairs and in a few moments returned to discover that she had found the open window and flown herself to freedom. Something inside me surged knowingly, and His voice explained,

"My love. You are just like that bird. You have been trying to free yourself and with each attempt, you have been crashing into the windowpane. You have resisted My help because of the automated fears. But do not worry, My little lamb. I have opened another window for you. Your heart knows Me; and as you follow Me, you will find the entrance to life and fly though to freedom."

Tears fell freely for the first time in months.

This was a turning point for me. Though He had been continually pursuing me with precious pearls of love and guidance, I had not been able to retain them. As soon as revelation came, it was immediately stolen in response to the pinging fears. This time was different because my heart received and my mind wrapped itself around the picture of the flailing bird.

The reality, however, of my mental collapse continued to be devastating. The effects were deep, wide, and debilitating. I couldn't sit still, read, write, cook a meal, or drive to the store. Even accomplishing the simplest thing was impossible without forgetting my surroundings and panicking. In the laundry room, all that should have been absurdly obvious was lost in confusion, and I'd find myself pacing around piles of dirty clothes. I couldn't connect with other people, and my inability to be present hurt the most when trying to interact with my beloved children. When my girls asked me to sit down and read to them, I couldn't focus long enough to pronounce consecutive words without excruciatingly long pauses. Often during the pauses, my thoughts would terrorize and confuse. Walking away mid-sentence, I'd abandon my precious, wondering children to finish the book on their own.

The most harrowing were the blasphemies and convictions of my damnation. The disturbing thoughts ping-ponged back and forth, back and forth, demanding compulsive responses. On and on I spun. This insanity drove me into my husband's lap one afternoon, where I buried my head in defeat.

"Paully, make it stop; make it stop. Please make it stop," I begged.

He held me tightly, sifting his fingers through my hair as he attempted to comfort me.

However, the continued noise demanded my own response to end the terror.

"I have to make it stop. I have to make it stop. I have to make it stop. I'm sorry, Paully. I have to," I apologized.

"Michelle? What are you thinking? Are you going to end things?" He probed.

I nodded.

"We promised to call Maryann," he said, moving my body off his lap and quickly heading toward the telephone.

Upon his return, he informed me, "Hunny, she is in the middle of a session. She said to drive you to the nearest crisis center."

"Uh-uh." I shook my head in refusal.

"We have to, Michelle."

"No."

Holding my arms, he looked into my lost eyes and repeated firmly, "We have to, Michelle. Get ready to go."

I sat beside Paul in the intake office of the crisis center. A nice older woman at a computer asked question after question. I didn't answer, so Paul politely interjected my essentials: name, birth date, address, Social Security number, and so on.

With every question, I wanted to haul back and punch her right in the face. I wanted to pummel this kind-faced lady, immobilizing her in her own blood so that she could not look up from her silver-framed reading glasses to ask one more damned question. I was consumed with fury that I was here. This woman was the enemy. Violence continued to surge within, as I sat stoically silent and motionless.

Most of the conversation existed between the two of them as she tried to evaluate my condition. She said the psychiatrist would be available to meet with me tomorrow and that she needed permission to admit me to their facility.

"Michelle, we have to. Hunny, I'm sorry."

"No," I insisted resolutely with edgy anger.

"Maybe I should let you two discuss this privately," the woman suggested, pushing herself up from her chair.

I stood up and walked out the front door with Paul following close behind.

"Michelle, I don't know what else to do. I have to do something. I can't leave you alone. Do you understand? I can't let you do this to yourself ..." he tried to reason with me, but I could not be reached.

I was hostile and uncooperative.

"Okay, there is one other option," he sighed. "Michele has been trying to reach me. She sensed that she is supposed to be involved and has offered to drive up here to stay with you. Perhaps you should go and stay with her instead."

"Yes," I quickly agreed.

Anything to get in the car and away from the evil woman with the silver-framed glasses.

As much as I adored Michele, I did not want to go with her. I was in a heightened state of paranoia, believing that my closest loved ones were plotting my harm. But considering the alternative, I obediently crawled into the front seat with her, buckled up, and counted the seconds.

She put on soothing music and tried to engage me in conversation, but I often left one-word answers dangling in the air, as I rubbed my favorite pillow in small circles. I was so agitated that the temptation to open the door and throw myself onto the highway at full speed continued on and off throughout the ninety-minute drive to her new "Wit's End," now located in rural part of Mansfield, Ohio. Without warning, my disposition leapt from panic to irritation and then back to weepy babble. I could do nothing but react.

Michele's house was as cozy and comfortable as her welcoming embrace. I walked from room to room, slowly looking around, trying to notice updates and remodels since my last visit. Michele is a rare wonder, turning a lot of bargain nothings into an exquisite eclectic expression of her soul, and I loved just being surrounded by her comforts. Soft pale vintage linens in enveloping pinks and greens, mixed among endless florals, beckoned me in all of my restlessness to sit and stay.

Her Paul walked into the room and greeted me with a hug and some dry sarcastic humor.

"You look good for a crazy person," he said with a laugh.

"Thanks," I smiled.

"You are welcome here for as long as you'd like, Shelly. You know that, don't you?" he said with uncharacteristic mushy warmth.

"I know," I replied

"Make yourself at home."

And I did.

I dumped my bag onto the floor of the upstairs bedroom with the eastern view of the garden. Sitting Indian style on the bed, I wondered what on earth I would do here for who-knew-how-long. Staying overly busy with menial things was a favorite coping mechanism; facing the unknown with nothing to do was extremely distressing.

The room was cozy, but muggy, so I got up and unlocked and opened the window. As the cool breeze wafted through the lacey sheers, I remembered the trapped bird.

*"My love. You are just like that bird. You have been trying to free yourself and with each attempt, you have been crashing into the windowpane. You have resisted My help because of the automated fears. But do not worry, My little lamb. **I have opened another window for you.** Your heart knows Me; and as you follow Me, you will find the entrance to life and fly though to freedom."*

I knew. Deep within, I knew Michele's "Wit's End" was His opened window. Here He would enable me to find my way to fly free once more. But I had no idea how.

Michele was under strict orders from my Paul to see that I took all my medication, and strict orders from God to "let me be." Michele could talk almost as long and hard as my sister Maria; however, to my surprise, she retreated alone to the dingy basement nearly every day. It was all a part of His plan.

For the first time I could remember, I was completely without access to my piles of Bibles and books. I was allowed to pack only one Bible and one journal. That's it. Nothing else. Contrary to conventional spiritual wisdom, only God knew what would bring me to wholeness ... and it was to stay completely *out* of my Bible.

This was impossible on my own. Though I shook in fear as I read, I couldn't resist. My compulsion demanded that I read, and my unsound mind twisted each verse into a pronouncement of damnation. I tried harder, switched books, and scanned chapters and verses for something that wouldn't condemn me, but it was a pitiful exercise in futility. Sitting on the bed, I reached for my Bible and heard a quiet, but persistent:

"No, My love."

"Lord?" I questioned frantically.

"No, My love," He repeated to hush my troubled heart. *"I AM in you. My Word is hidden in your heart. Just be."*

Paradoxically indeed, I needed supernatural strength to resist the temptation to read His Word. Every time I was tempted to open it, He gently spoke and lovingly reassured me that He was indeed leading me:

"No, My love. I AM in you. My Word is hidden in your heart. Just be."

Day after day, *I followed Him*. I left my room, my Bible, and my compulsive behavior, and simply went wherever He led. I walked barefoot through the tender green grass, splashed my feet through the cool pond water, lay out under open skies, and traced the graceful movements of a black horse across the pasture as she displayed her majesty. Connecting as a simple child to my Father, I was slowly coming back to life.

Resurrection's glory was revealed in simplistic grandeur as blade after marvelous blade mesmerized my senses with an unknown pleasure; grass had a smell! It was fresh and brilliantly alive. He was somehow accomplishing the impossible in me as I followed Him moment by moment by moment.

When the disturbing thoughts would come, before I could automatically respond in fear, my Love held me, literally containing me like He contains the seas within their shores. Then tenderly He'd whisper repeatedly to my heart,

"Let it go, My love. Let it go..."

It was like riding ocean waves. At first it was like riding surges in a raging storm with repeated billows minute after minute. But as the days passed, the size and frequency of the waves decreased to a manageable handful per day. With each cresting wave, I had an overwhelming urge to avoid being crushed beneath the madness. But before I could react, I was miraculously held as He whispered quietly to my soul,

"Let it go, My love, let it go..."

Instead of being toppled, I suddenly found myself on top of the wave, riding safely into shore. This was the intensive care treatment I received moment-by-moment by the One who made me.

How I love Him.

A psalm of David. The LORD is my shepherd; I have everything I need. He lets me rest in green meadows; he leads me beside peaceful streams. He renews my strength. He guides me along right paths, bringing honor to his name. Even when I walk through the dark valley of death, I will not be afraid, for you are close beside me. Your rod and your staff protect and comfort me. You prepare a feast for me in the presence of my enemies. You welcome me as a guest, anointing my head with oil. My cup overflows with blessings. Surely your goodness and unfailing love will pursue me all the days of my life, and I will live in the house of the LORD forever (Psalm 23, NLT).

I could not search for my Love, so my Love searched for me. Yes, goodness and unfailing love pursued me until I was found. However, I was found "cast," and I needed to be restored to live again.

A "cast" sheep is an overly distressed sheep that becomes completely immobilized on its back with all four legs in the air. In this position, it is nearly impossible for it to get up again, and after a few hours on its back, gas begins to collect in its stomach until the sheep suffocates. The rescue effort begins when the sheep is found, but continues until the sheep is restored. This takes time. First the shepherd must massage the legs to restore circulation. Then while calmly reassuring the sheep with his voice and soothing its fears, he gently turns the sheep over. His hand braces the sheep under its belly until it can stand on its own.

This is a perfect metaphor for what my Good Shepherd did for me.

The rescue was only the beginning of my restoration. Being carried on His shoulders with my face nestled right up against His was the culmination of all I had ever dreamed; my Prince had come for His beloved. Because I was incapable of doing anything more than listening, my ability to listen was finely tuned until I could discern His most gentle whisper, even His faintest sigh.

Repairing the destruction from the damning thoughts, He reassured me continually, sometimes moment-by-moment as the need arose with this same whisper of His Heart, *"I AM in you. Rest in My love."*

The following are just a few of the journal entries from my weeks at Michele's "Wit's End." They relay just a glimpse of how His Love reached me.

M: Lord, I want to cry on Your chest. I want to lie in Your Grace. I want to forget the past now and feel Your embrace. My sin is forgiven, but its effects still remind that things still remain twisted up in my mind …

Please. Please, please bring me out of this place soon. I am a scared child … Hold my heart in Your hands … remind me who You are and who I am. I am your frightened girl. Remember me.

AΩ: *I will not fail you, Michelle. My Word is My Promise. Trust me with your ravaged heart. Rest in My Arms of Love. Each day as you rest, I AM healing you. Do not fear, daughter of Zion, lift up your eyes … for behold your Messiah comes.*

M: Lord, make me *know* that I am Yours with every fiber of my being.

AΩ: *Michelle, you are My rare rose, a special delight to My heart. Your fragrance moves Me.*

M: *All* through the night, in my sleep I heard, *"Truth is alive."* When I awoke I heard,

AΩ: *My Spirit of Truth is alive in you, leading you. I led you here … resist those thoughts to weep more, hurt more, read more, quote more, pray more. I say to you, It is Finished. All you must do is Receive.*

AΩ: *Let not your heart be troubled, neither let it be afraid for I AM alive in you. The Words, I speak, are Spirit and Life.*

I AM revealing the depths of My love, the depths of My grace, the depths of who I AM. Is this not proof of how real I AM?

AΩ: *I AM breaking habits, fears, and mind-sets off of you as you rest in My Love. I know you expect more pain, more anguish, more discipline—but I tell you—Expect Freedom. Expect Laughter. Expect Joy. Expect Peace. Ah, I know you, My love ... do not concentrate and force these things ... for you say to yourself, "I must laugh. I must be joyful. I must have peace. I must Trust," and only fret. I am teaching you how "to be." Be like a child. Become as a little one and enter My Kingdom.*

AΩ: *I have been aching and crying with you. Trust in My love. I hear every whispered and unspoken cry of your heart.*

AΩ: *I AM provision for you. Oh, be not seized with fear, little Lamb. It is Your Father's delight to give you the Kingdom!*

M: The Lord is opening the prison of my soul to feel again. Like a child, I have been looking, smelling, touching, and feeling everything around me. Blades of grass, dandelions, water ... He is setting my mind in agreement with my heart as I simply "be." Relationships nurture the soul.

AΩ: *Your love, your trust, your praise, your time, your worship ... your heart ... bring much delight to The Father. Partake ... enjoy this unhindered relationship. As you take and eat of from My hand, you become more like the One you love.*

M: It's all about Relationship.

AΩ: *I do not make mistakes, Michelle. I chose you. You shall bear luscious fruit that will remain. You shall be mighty for My Kingdom. Your heart is in the process of healing. Let Me mend. Let Me revive your heart according to My Word.*

M: Lord, why was John referred to as the "One whom You loved?

AΩ: *Ah, freely I give, but not all freely receive. John knew My Love because he received unabashedly. When you come and recline at the table on Me as he did, you become very comfortable in My Love. John simply stated what his heart knew.*

M: I opened the windows and watched the lace curtains dance happily in the wind.

AΩ: *Don't complicate or rush this healing process. The curtain was incapable of taking itself off the rod to shake the dust off. It isn't trying or resisting; it is merely responding to My breeze. Just open the window of your heart to receive these simple, humble instructions. Gently My Spirit is blowing through you, My love. Have ears to hear.*

M: I thank You for all you've done and all You are going to do in me.

AΩ: *I've been delighting in you and our conversations. I adore you, Michelle. You'll always be Mine. Rest in My Love. Rest in My forgiveness. Rest in My Grace.*

AΩ: *It is Finished.*

AΩ: *Nothing is wasted with Me, My love. Watch how I'll use all this for good, as My purpose unfolds.*

AΩ: *Let the pain go now.*

AΩ: *It's okay to cry.*

*Sing O daughter of Zion! Be glad and rejoice with all your heart, O daughter of Jerusalem! The Lord has taken away your judgments; He has cast out your enemy. The King of Israel, the Lord, Is in your midst; You shall see disaster no more … Do not fear, let not your hands be weak. The Lord God in your midst, the Mighty One, will save; He will rejoice over you with gladness, **He will quiet you in His love.** He will rejoice over you with singing* (Zephaniah 3:14-17, New King James, emphasis mine).

I was being held, cradled by the arms of The Living God and literally "hushed" in His love. My Comforter, my Counselor, my Breath of Life nourished and restored my soul. No human hands could have pulled those arrows out of my heart. Only Him. Although I returned home still desperately needy, I was well enough to be receptive to His Love.

I had cancelled all my speaking engagements during this time for obvious reasons, but there was one I couldn't cancel. I knew I was supposed to go, even though I had been home only two weeks and was still very much in recovery. Raw and not even "allowed" to read my Bible yet, I stood before a crowd of women and shared *"The Gospel According to Michelle Meade."* The resident priest stared at me as if he had allowed a heretic in his parish, but there was no stopping me as I passionately espoused my experience with The Living Christ, beckoning them to embrace the same opportunity to be intimately unified with their God.

"No more worship from afar, merely feeding weekly on secondhand meals. Instead, you can feast daily on a buffet table of spiritual delights unlike any you have ever dreamed or imagined. Gazing deeply into your soul, feeling as if you are His only love, He proceeds to nourish every part of your being with Himself. He *is* your Bread of Life, your Living Water. The only thing He asks for—the only thing He's ever longed for—is your heart. COME! He will receive your heart just as it is, in whatever condition it may be, and transform it into His glorious dwelling place. Come!"

The Spirit of God moved in a miraculous, tangible way. One-on-one ministry continued for hours afterward and chains of religious strongholds rattled vacant in protest upon the high places.

How I love Him.

As I continued to "take and eat" from His hand, He was faithful to complete the process of healing and restoration. One-by-one, He tenderly removed the embedded arrows of shame and condemnation and within six months, I was able to open my Bible once more. Slowly and sweetly, I savored every morsel on every page as He opened my eyes to new delights.

Fear ye not, stand still, and see the salvation of the Lord ... The Lord will fight for you and you shall hold your peace (Exodus 14:13-14).

The "wall of pain" was demolished; each and every wicked word was erased from my soul, but not by my might or power. Not a single ounce of "great faith" can be heralded. My precious "Friend," my intimate "Lover," my supreme "Everything" destroyed them for me. His perfect, complete, intimate, extravagant love suffocated my every fear. And the gentle, continual hush of His reassuring voice of comfort quieted me.

CHAPTER 20

"I AM Enough"

do not doubt or be dismayed

your provision has been made

be content and do not fear

for your God I AM is here

though circumstances may be tough

lift up your eyes - I AM enough

for HE himself has said,

"I will never leave you nor forsake you."

ACCEPTING GOD'S FATHERHOOD was a crucial monument marker on my journey of trust. It was here in my helplessness that I learned what it meant to be His girl. Away went all my grown-up packaged theologies, fears, and doubts as I held the hand of the One who holds time and eternity.

Hand-in-hand with my Father, I learned obedience. By "obedience," I don't mean following a bunch of rules. It had been reduced to very simple terms: follow Him. Follow Jesus, just as He followed His Father, doing and saying what He had seen and heard. I am to simply follow His whispers, gentle nudges, and quiet requests—the leading of my Good Shepherd.

After six months of intensive care upon His shoulders, He gently released me to walk again. Slowly, day-by-day, I regained my equilibrium until I could fully participate in life once more. Before long, I was able to enjoy my children, happily fulfill all my responsibilities as homemaker, and find pleasure in living again. I began weaning myself off the medications at this point, albeit very, very slowly. After another six more months, I was completely off the meds and I felt fantastic. It was well with my soul.

At least I thought so. Unbeknownst to me, my Love was aware of some unfinished business in my heart, and He had a very specific plan of action. Part of His plan was to move our family and business to a remote part of northwestern Wisconsin. I didn't want to leave Canton, Ohio, my friends, or my family—especially my mother, sister, and Michele, but I couldn't dismiss His gentle whisper.

"Go, my love."

Indeed, it was very good. We went from a huge money pit house in the ghetto with no yard or garage to thirteen rolling acres, a newly built log home with a heated garage, a gigantic pole building with a heated office for "Remember ME"

Jewelry, and best of all for my kids, the lake. It was a taste of heaven on earth for the six of us. The children made a smooth transition with great new friends and wonderful teachers, and notched out spots for their individual sports. Life was good.

It was as if we were immediately rewarded for our obedience to move. With boxes still stacked everywhere, we received a most curious phone call one day. A businessman from California called and said he felt like we were to go with him to be a part of the upcoming annual Dove Awards in Nashville, Tennessee. This man's company supplied gifts to artists backstage at such big events as the Grammy Awards, and now this year he was going to try his first "Christian event" and wanted us to accompany him to the Dove Awards.

Us? Why us? "Remember ME" Jewelry was still small beans. How did he even hear about us? His answer uncovered another answer that trumped every other question. He said he kept having repeated dreams about a company named "Remember ME" giving away jewelry at the Dove Awards so he finally acquiesced, discovered who we were on-line, and called with the invitation. I happen to know the "Dream-Maker," which obviously led to our answer. We are so there!

So there we were backstage for two consecutive years at the Dove Awards, gifting jewelry to famous artists like Smokey Robinson, Amy Grant, Wynonna Judd, Mercy Me, Jars of Clay, Jeremy Camp, Steven Curtis Chapman, Natalie Grant, Nicole C. Mullen, Cece Winans, and many, many others. It was as if in a dream, talking with these incredibly down-to-earth, but insanely famous people, we shared The Father's Heart of Love through "Remember ME" Jewelry. It was another hallmark, altar-building moment ... this time not for me, but for *us* as a couple.

Yes, God took what I thought He had given to me, and lovingly placed it within *both* of our hands at this event. However, at the time I "didn't get it." I didn't realize the significance of our working *together* for Him through

Paul and me with Amy Grant and Vince Gill at Dove Awards 2004.

Paul, me, and the legendary Smokey Robinson.

Mercy Me at Dove Awards 2004.

A very pregnant me and Darlene Zschech, Hillsong.

We brought Josh with us to the 2005 Dove Awards for his thirteenth birthday. Here he is with Wynonna Judd.

Paul and Peter Furler of the Newsboys.

"Remember ME." Nor did I grasp His specific reasoning for our move to a solitary place without any friends or family; He wanted Paul and me to learn to "leave and cleave," that He might make us "one flesh." Though we had been married fifteen years, we had failed to forsake all other relationships in order to place ours in its rightful priority. I was accustomed to running to Mom, Maria, or Michele when things got tough. And though outside relationships have their rightful place, mine were used as replacements for Paul. I allowed these other relationships to fill gaps that should be only filled by him; therefore I refused God the opportunity to make us "one flesh."

I love solitude, so many aspects of our move were easy to swallow. However, when marital conflicts arose, I had no one else to run to. Being forced to face large piles of yuck and the huge white elephant in our living room was no easy task.

Rather than run away in denial (as was customary for me), I flew directly into the arms of my God, where He lavishly poured His love and grace into my emptiness. All I had to do was receive. When I was sufficiently filled, He nudged me to venture into the realm of the unknown with Paul—heart-to-heart relationship for the first time.

The whole "cleaving" thing was going fine until we had to make some decisions for "Remember ME," and then things got a bit ugly. Even though I had removed myself from the day-to-day business activities, I couldn't remove myself from the steering wheel. And now that I was well and able to contribute, I wanted my voice heard.

I was actually a year into writing this book when God began to connect the dots for me. Things that might be obvious to you, as you have been reading my story, were all stunning revelations and epiphanies to me. I was blindsided when I saw it all laid out in chapters.

Thinking of Him Daisy Journal

The book is almost completed. Through writing it I see myself—the mental illness and how it affected others, particularly Paul. He has borne the brunt of all the ugliness. He has been blamed for way more than his share. And through it all, He never threatened to leave or run (so unlike me). It was never an option or slight consideration. All the depression, all the severe ups and downs. All the junk. He's stayed. I need to value these most prized qualities of a very good man.

—*m*—

I had no idea of the damaging effects of mental illness on my loved ones. I didn't see Paul's love and forbearance all these years, nor did I acknowledge his huge sacrifices along the way, especially his hard work in growing "Remember ME" Jewelry. Well, to be honest, I didn't even accept that I had a "mental illness." I still packaged all of my suffering in spiritual terms, refusing to look at it honestly. As you might imagine, I had a wake-up call.

Along came another episode, which began just as surprisingly and unexpectedly as all the others. Out of nowhere, the crazy thoughts, insomnia, pendulum mood swings, and obsessive behavior roared back into my life. But this time, I "rode the waves." Just as they crested, when I felt surely they would crash on me if I didn't compulsively respond, my Lord comforted and counseled me through.

"Let it go, My love. Let it go. It'll pass. Just hold Me tightly. It'll pass. Let it go."

As I clung to Him, the disturbing thoughts would ping a couple times and then melt into the water and dissipate as we gently rode to shore.

The insomnia was not so easy to manage. It was what it was; I accepted it and used the nighttime hours productively. Like my previous episodes, the fears were raging, but unlike my previous episodes, they were not controlling. This was acceptable to me—exhausting at times, but acceptable. However, it was not acceptable to Paul.

"Michelle, you shouldn't have to fight through it. You should be able to sleep like everybody else; you shouldn't have to accept that this is the way it is. You should go to the doctor and get back on medication, and you should *stay* on the medication. It helped. Michelle, why would you wean yourself off if it helped?"

Oh, I didn't like that question whatsoever. And I hated that he might be right. Going back meant admitting I truly had a mental problem. I hated the idea of putting chemicals in my body to regulate myself "normal." The thought of being on medications the rest of my life was not an option I wanted to consider, but neither was refusing medical help and spinning out of control in the name of faith.

I asked God to guide me. To my chagrin, He gently, persistently urged me to go back on medication. I couldn't resist dishing out all my spiritual and intellectual arguments to Paul, but when God said, *"Go, My love,"* I could do nothing but obey.

All the years of resistance and resignation fell away in the wake of God's approval. Just because medicine is not perceived as a "supernatural" remedy, doesn't mean it is not a tool in His hand for our good. I heard the following said, and it struck my heart as truth: If you have dealt with everything in the natural realm and still have a problem, then it is a spiritual problem. If you have dealt with everything in the spiritual realm and still have a problem, then it is a problem that must be addressed in the natural.

When I had done everything I knew to do spiritually and was still struggling, I should have gone straight away to seek medical help. Yet I refused. God in His mercy never let me drown in my stupidity as the man in the fable waiting for His divine rescue when all along God had made continual attempts with a *natural* rescue by sending three different boats. I was finally willing to stop treading water needlessly. I was finally willing to lay down my pride. I was finally teachable enough to learn wisdom. With the courage of God's approval, I could go to the doctor, *be honest*, and face whatever disclosure surfaced.

I ended up with a wonderful, caring, female physician who was easy to talk to. After discussing my symptoms at length, I actually asked for a psychiatrist referral, which was nothing short of miraculous. Sounds like I was in effect asking for a shrink with a side of drugs?!?

I booked my own appointment, drove myself the hour-long drive, and knew that I was on the road of no return. I had done some research online to familiarize myself with different mental illnesses and their symptoms and treatments, so I walked into this psychiatrist's office with my eyes wide open for the first time in over fifteen years of suffering.

Many of my symptoms crossed over into several different areas, so it wasn't obvious which of the disorders were mine to deal with, except for one.

This was a certainty.

The following description of OCD is courtesy of www.mentalhealth.samhsa.gov:

Obsessive-Compulsive Disorder (OCD)

Obsessions are recurrent, intrusive thoughts, impulses, or images that are perceived as inappropriate, grotesque, or forbidden (DSM-IV). The obsessions, which elicit anxiety and marked distress, are termed "ego-alien" or "ego-dystonic" because their content is quite unlike the thoughts that the person usually has.

Obsessions are perceived as uncontrollable, and the sufferer often fears that he or she will lose control and act upon such thoughts or impulses. Common themes include contamination with germs or body fluids, doubts (i.e., the worry that something important has been overlooked or that the sufferer has unknowingly inflicted harm on someone), order or symmetry, or loss of control of violent or sexual impulses.

Compulsions are repetitive behaviors or mental acts that reduce the anxiety that accompanies an obsession or "prevent" some dreaded event from happening (DSM-IV). Compulsions include both overt behaviors, such as hand washing or checking, and mental acts including counting or praying. Not uncommonly, compulsive rituals take up long periods of time, even hours, to complete.

I finally knew the name of the beast that tormented me most. That was *me*—not just medical jargon, but a personal self-portrait written in black and white. The terrifying thoughts of abusing my children, the disturbing sexual images, my damnation and separation of God ... for the first time the nonsensical made sense.

This new discovery was truly bittersweet. I was completely overcome with relief to know that I was not alone or destined for a straightjacket, yet I grieved for all the lost time and endless suffering. My soul longed for more answers than could be given by a Web site.

A million troubling questions were instantly put to rest when My Comforter came along side and assured me that it was indeed all a part of His plan. Absolutely nothing is wasted with God because ...

His purpose is the process!

How I love Him.

With the warm blanket of divine love and purpose covering my insecurities and doubt, I could go forward without regret.

—————

Beyond OCD, I was uncertain of what the psychiatrist might diagnose. A very pleasant Middle Eastern woman introduced herself and began the extensive, exhaustive examination and evaluation. After two visits, she was ready to give me her medical opinion:

"Michelle, you most definitely suffer with Obsessive-Compulsive Disorder, along with a variety of other interrelated anxiety disorders. However, they are not the primary pathology. I am confident that your primary disorder is Bi-Polar Disorder, also known as Manic Depression."

I listened intently as she explained her reasoning behind the diagnosis. There was no way any intelligent person could refute the evidence. If I were she, I would have said the same thing. However, I was on the other side of the professional desk, and I didn't want to believe it.

The following description of Bi-Polar Disorder is courtesy of www.mentalhealth.samhsa.gov:

Bi-Polar Disorder

Bipolar Disorder causes dramatic mood swings—from overly "high" and/or irritable to sad and hopeless, and then back again, often with periods of normal mood in between. Severe changes in energy and behavior go along with these changes in mood. The periods of highs and lows are called **episodes** of mania and depression.

Signs and symptoms of *mania* (or a *manic episode*) include: Increased energy, activity, and restlessness, excessively "high," overly good, euphoric mood, extreme irritability, racing thoughts, poor concentration, little sleep needed, poor judgement, a lasting period of behavior that is different from usual, increased sexual drive, provacative, intrusive, or aggressive behavior, and denial that anything is wrong.

Signs and symptoms of *depression* (or a *depressive episode*) include: Lasting sad, anxious, or empty mood, feelings of hopelessness, feelings of guilt, worthlessness, or helplessness, loss of interest or pleasure in activities once enjoyed, difficulty concentrating, remembering, making decisions, restlessness, irritability, sleeping too much or can't sleep, change in appetite and/or unintended weight loss or gain, thoughts of death or suicide.

She also explained the "psychotic" spurts: the paranoia, and hearing and seeing things that were not real. She believed that they were a tragic consequence of the prolonged lack of treatment and sleeplessness. Her considered opinion was that they were not defining symptoms in and of themselves. Unfortunately, many people that experience these symptoms like I did are often misdiagnosed with schizophrenia.

I told Paul what the doctor had said, but I still found myself resisting, as if taking these medications indicated personal failure. Paul explained otherwise, and he made sense. I don't berate myself if I need some Advil for a headache. Why do I berate myself when I need something to help regulate my malfunctioning brain? No matter what rationale I dished out, the reality remained: I refused to believe that *I* needed that kind of prescription intervention. Maybe *other* people with Bi-Polar Disorder needed it, but I refused to consider the possibility that *I* might need it as well.

I researched extensively on-line and gleaned every bit of information I could on Bi-Polar Disorder and treatments including alternative medicine. Knowing the recovering extremist I am, you probably know which route I preferred (not that alternative medicine is "extreme" in and of itself, but it can be if you refuse any other medical care if needed). However, Paul was not budging. I didn't know how I could squirm around his resolute insistence that I put myself into the care of a medically trained and board certified psychiatrist. I talked with a psychiatric nurse, continued to research, and finally came to a conclusion.

"Paul, I am not hostile about medications anymore. I'm not. And I am willing to go on the mood stabilizers. But, please allow me to continue with just the uptake inhibitor and some natural stuff, including vitamin supplements and a revised diet to try to manage this disorder. Please? Now, before you protest, I need to tell you that I'm giving you the right to determine if and when I need mood stabilizers. If you see me struggling and think I need them, then I'll agree."

I sighed in relief as he agreed, but he added that he would not waste one second in getting me to the psychiatrist and on those medications if he saw me suffering even a little.

I determined that my lifestyle would have to change to encourage wellness. I worked out several times a week to increase endorphins, rested more, and eliminated refined sugars. I also began to load my diet with natural foods, especially those loaded with fatty acids and B vitamins, along with a few supplements. Through this combined effort, I actually felt a substantial difference in my well-being.

My self-prescribed wellness program was working so great that I figured I no longer needed any medications, and I prepared to wean off once again. (Constantly wanting to wean off meds is a common symptom of Bi-Polar Disorder. When you are manic, you feel invincible and think the meds are unnecessary inhibitors). Before Paul had an opportunity to protest or I had an opportunity to flounder, I made a surprising discovery that would trump every other consideration.

I was pregnant.

Although my doctor said that there was "no conclusive evidence" that my medicine was harmful to the baby, I couldn't accept the possibility and went off immediately.

The pregnancy took its toll from physical sickness to the hormonal surges that aggravated my tendency toward extremes. Through it all, I can tell you I was supernaturally contained. When I felt as if I were on the precipice, I could feel His Divine Presence holding me, stabilizing me, and anchoring me until precious Gabriel Antonio Thomas Meade was born.

Gabriel 10 months old, another boy, another joy.

This was by no means a glorious home birth. It would be like comparing five-star dining to fast food. Paul was in full "event mode," consumed with the craziness of traveling all over the country, selling "Remember ME" Jewelry at Christian music festivals. He booked himself to run back-to-back-to-back events all surrounding my due date. In order for Paul to be present, I was forced to induce labor and ended up having a horrendous experience because of it.

Gabriel had scarcely taken his first breath when Paul was out the door and on a plane to New Hampshire. There are no words to describe how angry and hurt I was over his poor decision-making and skewed priorities.

Because he was gone for two weeks, I had sufficient time to stew in my wrath. Sore, infected breasts and sleep deprivation didn't help at all. I unleashed my fury over the phone. I told him not to bother coming back. Of course, I was emotional. Of course, I was weary and battling post-partum blues. Of course, I didn't really mean it. Or did I?

We were back to *this* again. I couldn't take it, any of it. Once again I felt completely overwhelmed with my life. The huge white elephant (our conflicting philosophies on how "Remember ME" should be run) was consuming enough to deal with, but my continued invisibility? Nope. I shook my head in refusal.

NO MORE.

The next few days were atrocious. Unwillingness to forgive Paul was eating me up alive. I ignored God as He prodded several times:

"Love never fails, My love."

"Forgive Paul, he knows not what he's doing."

I was being called to practice what He had taught me firsthand: the *One Thing*.

I finally said Yes to God and released the emotional anguish in His Presence. I stayed to receive a filling supply of divine Love—the only thing that truly satisfies a longing soul. Once gratified by His perfect love, I could re-enter the topsy-turvy circle of imperfect love without being toppled in the process.

I know that explanation may sound too simplistic and trite (especially when facing earth-shattering disappointments) so I'll give you a few examples of what this soul care looked and sounded like, for you to fully lay hold of this truth.

We often crave a quick 1-2-3-step process to apply to every situation. Yet, since *God's purpose is the process*, His desire is for us to go *inside our relationship* for the specific answer ... to a specific need ... at a specific time. It's not a "one-size-fits-all" solution. *It's a relational process!* God will slay you in sweet abandon as you discover just how intensely personal and affectionate His responses are to your heart's cry.

One dark night, while soaking fresh relational wounds, I asked God why Paul was so unaffected by my pain; his casual disinterest was tearing me apart inside. I felt helplessly incapable of a Godly response and was left floundering in my hurt. As I sought Him, He answered, and it was exactly what He knew I needed at that precise moment.

He enveloped me in a sweet, warm embrace that completely anchored my soul: mind quieted, heart stilled, emotions captured and restrained, immediate comfort, immediate hope, and immediate peace.

There are no human arms that can compare.

His extravagant Love continued to sooth and repair.

*"I'm affected by your pain. Remember, **I know** ..."*

"I know *You* know, my Love, but Paul doesn't seem to care ... at all," I said, reflecting on his consistent lack of response and the subsequent heartache I have unsuccessfully tried to manage for over eighteen years. I was totally taken aback by the Lord's response.

"What if I care enough for the both of us?"

Wow.

He was saying that His supply would be sufficient enough to meet my needs, while covering Paul in grace for his failure.

Wow.

How I love Him.

"What if I care enough for the both of us?"

How do you respond to something so beautiful? With all of my heart.

I retrieved my "Agape" ring that I had flung across the floor only days earlier, along with my several-stacked "I Have Decided" rings. As I purposefully slipped each one over my knuckle, I quietly recited the writings.

"Agape"

help me Lord to be true
to Your command to love like You
to forgive, selfless and free
surrendering all thoughts of me
to bear the arrows of offense
reflecting grace as recompense
to keep perspective from above
for i am nothing without Love

"I Have Decided"

this is it, i've made my choice
to walk with You and heed Your voice
to mortify my flesh within
to separate myself from sin
to love in all i say and do
for i've decided to follow You

The first hurdle had been cleared when I decided that I was willing to forgive; now several others loomed before me. My second hurdle was to finally address the white elephant in the living room. Was "Remember ME" Jewelry truly God's to control or mine? I would release my control and cast my burden away, only to reel it back into my own hands time and again, especially when Paul made a decision I didn't like. Would I trust God with Paul? Was He able to handle all management, including mismanagement, whether through my own hand, Paul's, or anyone else's?

Writing this book began uncovering so much previously hidden from my view. I had accused Paul of having ears, but not hearing, and eyes, but not seeing, but *I* was guilty of those very things. Wholeness is directly related to our *willingness* to be transparent. No more denial, masking, or pretending. The Oscar-worthy drama queen had to choose whether or not to surrender her crown and place it in the vault to stay.

I did it. After a lifetime of resistance, I finally came willing to give 100 percent of me. Wholly turned, face-to-face and heart-to-heart, His Love beckoned a true response. *Now I was in a position to receive, to take from His hand.*

In a place of total abandon, I let God wash my feet. It was here, with the brush of His servant's towel wiping away my stains, I finally *believed* with *all* my heart, God wanted *me.* Yes, even me, Zazoo Pits.

Throughout these past two years of receiving in "The Secret Place," I was being filled with His majestic, wondrous Love, but I was also being "un-peeled." Layer after layer of self-deception was being exposed, that I might honestly address "The State of Our Union." Not what I wanted it to be, confessed it to be, but what it was.

It wasn't pretty, but with His arms lovingly around me, I could face this "problem" with Him. Whether I called it a weakness, a sickness, or a disorder, I had to acknowledge that it was real and had significantly contributed to and intensified conflicts all these years. I had wronged Paul by unfairly blaming him for my misery, justifying myself over his indifference and neglect. I had super-spiritualized everything from my sickness to "Remember ME," to our marital conflicts.

There was nowhere to run, nowhere to hide. I ultimately bowed my knee in surrender. I fully released "Remember ME" into God's hands without any personal preference clauses attached.

Repentance began in my heart and ended on the cold cement floor of our office as I knelt at Paul's feet. Genuine heartache and fresh tears accompanied my apology. Repentance has to be much more than mere words, and this was truly a deliberate turn of heart. There was a beautiful shalom in our tearful embrace. Gigi had given me a magnet that says, "A successful marriage is the union between two great forgivers." I testify, it's true! As we forgave, mercifully pardoning one another fully for all past hurts, we were both released to start loving and living as one flesh.

Bar none, the following is my *most cherished* Thinking of Him Daisy Journal entry: a rare letter from Paul offering an even rarer glimpse into my husband's heart. The significance of this letter can scarcely be expressed. It was an answer to the countless desperate prayers for a drop of Paul's love. Flood warnings are officially being posted: *the long awaited rains have fallen!*

Dear Michelle,

I consider myself so fortunate to be a part of your life. Though these years have been anything but easy, I have more and more often been touched by what I see in you as a person, a wife, and as a mother. I see a glimmer of hope that I want to breathe life into.

I want us to be together forever, growing old together, knowing I'm with the one God chose for me. I want to make the most of every day and our experiences together. I think we are both learning a lot about our family, our purpose, and ourselves.

I've really appreciated how much patience you've granted me over these years. I know I haven't deserved it, much the opposite. I hope to someday be the man I was intended to be—for you, our family, myself, and most importantly, for God. You are making me better. I hope in some way to do the same for you. Bear with me.

I'm blessed, thanks to you. Our kids are blessed, thanks to you. All those who have come into contact with your presence or stumbled upon what you birthed through "Remember ME" are blessed. Thanks to who you are and Who you represent.

With God's help I'll make these tough years, missed anniversary and birthday celebrations up to you. There will come a day. As for now, I want you to know, you're my heart's desire, now and always will be.

Love you, Michelle,

Paul

How I love Him.

The third hurdle was my on-again, off-again acceptance, then refusal of my medical condition. I could accept the fact that I had a problem, but that's usually as far as it went. I didn't want to really deal with the issue of *treatment*, so I avoided altogether any conversation about medications ... until I became desperate.

Postpartum blues sent me spiraling downward, and I decided to get back on the anti-depressant. I also decided to stop my belligerence. Instead of skirting the issue by meeting with my general practitioner only, I made the conscious decision to fully heed the advice of my psychiatrist. This meant monthly visits and full accountability. I couldn't continue to stop taking whatever I wanted, whenever I wanted, just because I wanted. I was finally addressing my disorder with the necessary mood-stabilizing medications specifically prescribed for the treatment of Bi-Polar.

I have since learned that finding the right medicine in the proper dosage can be like dancing the two-step with one foot; it's not easy. But if you are patient and cooperative with your medical professional, it is very much worth the trial-and-error process.

I've finally abandoned myself to God's care. Doing so means a willingness to receive *all provision* from His hand, not just supernatural provision. Knowing God as my Source, receiving whatever natural re*source* He might choose to use in my life for good is just as much of an act of faith as receiving whatever supernatural resource He bestows.

I'm finally learning to apply wisdom; I can be content in any situation because God will never leave me, and He is always *enough*.

Please note: If you or someone you love needs help please read the following quote from the book *Blue Genes. (Blue Genes:* breaking free from the chemical imbalances that affect your moods, your mind, your life, and your loved ones. Paul Meier, MD; Todd Clements, MD, Jean-Luc Bertrand, DMD; and David Mandt Sr., MA).

"If any of the conditions described in this chapter (Mood Swing Blue Genes) sounds like you, please see an M.D. (Psychiatrist), and at least get an evaluation. If you realize your mate, child, sibling, parent, or friend is suffering from a bipolar spectrum disorder, please love that person enough to do what you can to persuade him or her to get help. With or without treatment bipolar people have a one in five chance of committing suicide. Without treatment, it is much higher. That is a sad fact families have to deal with everyday.

Having psychological problems such as depression, bi-polar, anxiety, or addictions does not mean these problems are a result of moral weakness or lack of will power ... but all these can have genetic components as well. And bi-polar is nearly totally genetic, regardless of spirituality."

CHAPTER 21

"Mustard Seed Faith"

plant your tiny seed of faith

deep inside of Me

bring your little fish and loaves

and I will meet the need

watch in wonder as I work

Our Father's will demands

the tiny seed to spring forth life

when placed within My Hands

WHAT FREEDOM IT IS to release the pain of my past and all my unanswered questions into God's sovereign hand. Before, I used to get theologically hung up over details and explanations I could never fully understand. All my whens, whys, and why-nots have fallen peacefully before my Who; The great I AM who is All in All. Releasing my questions and embracing the truth that *all I really need to know is Him* is like standing under a waterfall of grace. I am healed. I am whole. Maybe not the way I would have liked, but that's completely immaterial. I dance in the wild beauty of God's purpose for my life.

God's purpose is the process: building our relationship day-by-day.

Jesus made a way for our complete provision, here and eternally. And the beauty of this mystery? *He IS our Provision.* He Himself is our Daily Bread and our Living Water. He is more than enough. Intimately knowing The Healer brought my healing, not vice versa.

When I realized that all provision springs forth from faith in a Person, the focus shifted from my lack to His sufficiency. *It's not about faith in "my faith" to acquire. It is about faith in my God to supply.* As my relationship grows with Him, so does my child-like ability to trust implicitly that my Father will provide absolutely everything I need. All I need to do is receive.

It doesn't matter anymore whether He chooses to calm the storm or calm me (preserve me) in the storm. My security and peace rise out of the truth that He Himself dwells in me. Therefore the storm becomes absolutely irrelevant! It can't frighten me, control me, or harm me because I am completely anchored in the One who made the clouds … hidden in "The Secret Place."

Today, I marvel at my Wonderful, my Faithful and True, my Love. Daily He helps me, strengthens me, and upholds me with His righteous right hand as I lovingly give Him mine. He continues to grow "Remember ME" Jewelry as He steadily imparts His Heart to those seeking, one by one by one. I am excited to tell you that He Himself is fulfilling the prophetic words He gave concerning "Remember ME." His Father's Heart of Love has already begun to leave our U.S. borders and reach the global community. Not because of a slick marketing strategy, or a brilliant business plan, or through lofty contacts, but simply by "Following Him."

Step-by-step He leads. He's not in a hurry; He doesn't wear a watch. He functions outside the realm of time. He sometimes likes to stop in places we'd rather not. He likes to pause and smell flowers, watch sunsets, look into eyes of children, and most of all, encounter "nobodies" like the woman at the well, and turn them into glorious "somebodies" through Him.

We earnestly prayed for years for God to lead us to another manufacturer to pour our pieces. I was praying so specifically for a godly company with our same singular purpose and vision in mind that when the answer came, we totally dismissed it.

A man from Singapore approached us at a wholesalers' marketplace, gave us his card, and said that he would like the opportunity to make our jewelry.

"Yeah, sure," we thought. "You would like the opportunity to make and distribute our jewelry … behind our backs!" Unfair or not, we totally bought into the fearful rumors that Asian companies notoriously steal original ideas and designs and then duplicate them on the other side of the planet, never to be discovered.

However, this man we'll call Peter relentlessly pursued us with phone calls and e-mails like you would not believe. In our busyness, we disregarded them all … until one day Paul finally fielded Peter's call.

When Paul recounted his conversation with Peter, my spirit immediately bore witness that he was, in fact, the very source for which I had been praying all along, and that we should trust him and move boldly forward. We later discovered just how precise an answer Peter is to our very specific prayer. Peter loves God with all his precious heart and seeks nothing more than His purposes for His pleasure. I was awestruck once again by God's unsearchable ways. Does it get even better than this?

Yes, in fact, it does. Recently Peter shared "Remember ME" with a prominent Asian distributor. She fell in love with our product and is now currently preparing to market and sell it to the massive Asian market. I can see those Asian sets of eyes on the grains of harvest wheat swaying in His wind. I believe there was no coincidence that remarkable day God reached me, when from my own lips a *"foreign language spilled out in rich, fluid, Asian sounding syllables."*

How I Love Him.

On and on, He leads. On and on, we follow.

Our product was already sold in one particular bookstore, so participating in an "Artist and Author" open house could have seemed insignificant and meaningless "business." But in fact, it was a beautiful part of His plan. There I spoke one-on-one with dozens of interested people. I prayed over several as the Lord led and imparted His Heart through prayer and gifted jewelry pieces. I went home and never thought twice about that day.

About two years later I received a most amazing email:

I am sure you get tons of emails ... We met two years ago at the River House in Delafield. You prayed with me and prophesied to me, before I knew what that was. ☺ You spoke healing to me and were a vehicle the

Lord used to reveal His extravagant love. You gave me five symbols ... each one with profound prophetic revelation of His Love. Prompted by the Spirit, I write to tell you that I am fluent in Spanish and if you ever consider translating your writings, please consider me.

You told me two years ago I was pregnant with purpose. Since we talked that day in the bookstore, the Lord has healed my heart, which was broken by years of emotional, physical, and sexual abuse. I have been filled with the Holy Spirit, my husband is now saved, and I am ministering to pregnant teens and enrolled in ministry school (having completed high school in seven weeks after not having been in school for ten years)! I have forgiven my mom and my stepfather (the perpetrator of the abuse). I am living in the overflow of God's love, grace, and mercy with a determined purpose to know Him and make Him known!

In His love,

Jess

How I love Him!

Through our correspondence and phone calls, it was apparent that she was sent for "such a time as this." She is her Father's daughter; her heart is so full of His that it bursts forth out of every syllable and pore of her being. I released her to translate all our poetry into Spanish. This is her response along with the first translation, "Remember ME," the cup of the New Covenant:

Bueno, the Lord has given me such a passion for your writings that as soon as I got your gift from Him (The Cup), The Spirit moved, and this was birthed:

Recuérda ME

ESTE SÍMBOLO REPRESENTA
LA COPA DEL NUEVO TESTAMENTO
LA COPA DE UNA RELACIÓN RESTAURADA
"HAZ ESTO EN MEMORIA DE MI"
PRUEBEN Y VEAN QUE YO SOY DIOS
EL PRIMERO, EL ÚLTIMO, Y EL MISMO
BEBAN Y COMAN, YO TERMINARÉ
LA OBRA QUE VINE A COMPLETAR
AGUA VIVA CORRE
DESDE LO PROFUNDO DE MI VID
FRUTO DE MI CARNE,
CUENCO TRANSFORMADO
LISTO PARA LLEVAR MI VINO NUEVO
MATRIMONIO ETERNO
POR MI PROPIA SANGRE ESTAMOS UNIDOS
NUNCA TE DEJARE, A MI PALABRA AFÉRRATE
TU CORAZÓN AHORA ES TIERRA SAGRADA

Upon the painful disclosure of her abuse to her mother, Jess was asked to leave their home in the United States to live in a remote part of Uruguay at only thirteen years old. The only English spoken was through a woman named Rachel, the lone missionary who occasionally came through. Jessica had to learn everything the hard way, including speaking and understanding Spanish. But God was at work, even then.

Many years later, He used me in my brokenness (via "Remember ME" Jewelry) to minister and impart life and hope into her brokenness. And now He is using what Jessica thought was a "wasted place" in Uruguay to impart hope and healing into millions of Spanish-speaking seekers. I need to mention a touching detail. God brought her turbulent relationship with her mother and stepdad full circle. Once ostracized, Jessica and her newfound relationship with God have been fully embraced by *both* of her parents. Lasting, sweet evidence of God's redeeming love will linger on each and every one of the Spanish translations of "Remember ME"; Jessica's mother's heart could not refuse her daughter's request that they collaborate together on the translations. This endeavor bound their hearts together with His as healing balm, covering all past wounds. Together, the both of them have beautifully translated every single one of our ring and symbol writings for our first Spanish catalog! I can already see those South American eyes on the grains of harvest wheat, swaying in His wind.

How I love Him.

Finally, I have to tell you about how my Love provided the last missing component in "Remember ME." Jewelry. We struggled for over six years with how to package our product. We knew we wanted to emphasize the message more than the shiny pieces of art themselves, for the life is in the seed. However, this created a dilemma when it came to packaging the jewelry in a creative way. We prayed; we brainstormed; we made prototypes of several different options, but none of them was right. Then one day the answer came.

It was a Saturday morning, and Paul was still in bed at an unusually late hour. In the hustle of the morning with feeding the kids and cleaning the never-ending bowls and cups, I found myself frustrated that I had no help. I went into to our bedroom and asked politely, yet with enough sass to let him know I meant business, "Hunny, can you please get your bungee up and out of that bed?"

"I can't," Paul replied with his head buried in his pillow.

"What do you mean you can't? It's after ten o' clock!" I prodded.

"Not yet. Give me a minute, okay?" he grunted beneath the fluff.

I sighed in irritation and continued in a flurry about the house. I was feeling manic and not a piece of furniture was left unmoved. I felt the need to rearrange and redecorate the entire house. My frenzy was unstoppable until I hit a road bump. I was trying to remove a very heavy bathroom cabinet that was filled with vintage glass bottles. Carefully removing the precious antique bottles was easy, but trying to hold the monstrosity of a cabinet with one hand and manipulate the drill with the other had me stumped.

Drill in hand, I bounded into the bedroom and spun it loudly several times to urge the sleeping wonder awake.

"Paul! I need you. I need you now! I can't hold this cabinet myself and I'm trying to ..."

Rolling over, eyes wide open, and fully awake, he interrupted my rant.

"I'm praying and I can't get up yet."

"Ahhhhhh! All right," I conceded and left the room.

Then later, just as I was about to hunt down my sleeping saint (I hadn't fully bought into the Saturday morning pillow prayer warrior thing yet), Paul came bounding through our bedroom doors and into our home office excitedly. We nearly collided against the desk when he said through a broad smile, "I got it!"

"You got what?" I asked, thinking, "... besides *bedhead*."

"I got it!" he said again with both wonder and satisfaction.

"You got what?" I repeated for the second time.

"I got ..." Just as he was about to answer, he leaned down toward the desk and grabbed the vintage bottles I had removed from my bathroom cabinet and held them right under his nose to examine closely. (He's nearly blind without his glasses).

"Where did you get these?" he demanded.

"What? What does that have to do with ..."

"Where did you get these...? Oh, this is amazing! You won't believe this ..." his words trailed off.

"Okay, you have to explain to me what in the world you are talking about before I ..."

"I was in bed this morning and sensed I was to pray and wait. I can't explain it. I just felt like the Lord was going to tell me how we are supposed to package everything. I knew it was coming, so I couldn't get up until I heard. And then it came. Bottles! Glass bottles! He told me to package the jewelry in small glass bottles! *Message in a bottle.* Then I come out of the bedroom and see all these small glass bottles all over the desk! This is just so amazing ..." he said.

"Wow." It was all I could say. I thought my husband was spiritually asleep, and how wrong I was. God chose to reveal this powerful concept to him. Not me. Him. I was looking at outward expressions of Paul's love for God, and all God was looking at was Paul's heart. And it was lovely: willing, tender, and waiting to receive.

Once I acknowledged my own misjudgments, and the beauty behind the Giver and receiver, I was blown over by the concept itself. It was brilliant. Utterly brilliant! The jewelry was protected while being showcased as the treasure it is. We had already planned for the poetry to be printed on hand-pressed, hand-torn bookmarks, and now these scrolled bookmarks would be tightly rolled up and placed inside the bottle with the jewelry.

His Message in a bottle.

The jewelry hangs beautifully from the cork and dangles playfully from inside the precious bottled gift in front of the scroll. It was perfect, and how could we have expected anything less from Him.

Our first wholesale show presenting "Remember ME" Jewelry with our new packaging to the marketplace was in July 2007 in Atlanta, and we were overwhelmed by the response. We won an Impact Award for our product display and drew the admiration, compliments, and business of those who ventured near our booth. The increased awareness and demand have been wonderful, but my pleasure is found in knowing that untold souls who may never enter church doors will experience a real God right where they are. There is nothing more wonderful.

How I love Him.

Me with Impact Award.

"The Secret Place"

more of You, more of You
ever so much less of me
open eyes, open eyes
that in the Spirit i might see
ears to hear, O to hear
what it is that Your heart shares
unify our hearts as One
in the Secret Place of Prayer

NO LONGER SIMPLY LIVING TO EXIST, today I'm *living in love*—fully and freely in Him. Joy used to trickle a drip here and there on the parched ground of my severely hardened heart. Now I giggle at the overflow.

"The Secret Place" is the place where I live, move, and have my being. The revelation of "The Secret Place" came as a result of prayer. About two years ago I was preparing to speak at a women's retreat, and in prayer I asked what I should share. He poured His heart into mine once more.

I loved the beautiful imagery of Psalm 91 about being completely sheltered and protected from harm when dwelling in "the secret place of the Most High." However I had no idea where this elusive place was. I figured it was so secret that no one really knew.

Psalm 27:4-6 answered my questions:

*One [thing] have I desired of the LORD, that will I seek after; that I may dwell in the house of the LORD all the days of my life, to behold the beauty of the LORD, and to inquire in his temple. For in the time of trouble he will hide me in his pavilion: in **the secret place** of his tabernacle will he hide me; he will set me up upon a rock. And now shall my head be lifted above my enemies around me: therefore will I offer in his tabernacle sacrifices of joy; I will sing, yes, I will sing praises to the LORD* (Psalm 27:4-6, NKJV, emphasis mine).

These verses hit my heart full force with excitement and awe. David was saying that it didn't matter what enemy or fear assailed him because his focus was to dwell with the Lord and behold His beauty. (His focus was on the *Who*!) He knew that he was hidden in safety from harm in *the secret place* of God's tabernacle. And in this tabernacle, he offered sacrifices of praise.

It all made spiritual sense. My heart is His home, and we dwell together in this "secret place" of intimate communion.

Literal dwelling places can be penetrated and inhabited by evil, but access is denied in this "secret place" of impenetrable, inseparable union. By living, daily abiding inside this "secret place" of communion in the most intimate part of our being, our real "self" is hidden, protected, and nurtured in God's loving care.

This point again hit home when Jesus taught His disciples how to pray in Matthew 6. He admonished them to not stand on street corners, spouting long and impressive discourses, but rather, He said to pray in secret, and His Father who *is in the secret place* will reward openly. The Father doesn't dwell on the street corner, or in a man made temple, but in "The Secret Place" of the human heart.

It's not about our words, the location, the audience, or the dialect we speak; the Lord Himself lives in our hearts and speaks the language thereof.

God speaks the language of every individual heart!

He looks past our words and deeds, and peers deeply into the heart of man.

Being carried those many critical months, I learned that the secret of "The Secret Place" was simply *being "in Him"* and *receiving* from Him. Early on, all my prayers were either lengthy lists of needs or "prescription faith prayers," trying to get what I thought I needed. Over the course of this journey, I have learned to come and allow God to fill me with all that He knows I need most. The following example leaves me ruined to this day.

I have got into the habit of coming into His Presence and asking, "My Love, tell me what's on Your heart?" Many times He'll put people and situations on my heart that I might intercede for them. But this particular time, the answer was the last thing I expected, but the one thing He knew I needed to hear.

Clearly and sweetly, He said, *"You."*

I was on His heart.

My whole life had been spent searching for significance, longing for approval, attention, and affection. All was satisfied in that singular moment. God wants me. His longing for me saturated every fiber of need within.

I shall satisfy your longing soul and fill your hungry soul with goodness (Psalm 107:9).

I am ever so grateful to be off the terminal Ferris wheel of performance. However, I'm not immune to the snares. Once in a while I'll find myself going 'round once or twice before I realize it. One such ride was completing this book.

I wanted to please Him so desperately that I had nearly burned two years worth of work and two hundred plus pages in the fireplace, to start over with a more "worthy" copy. Even though I prayed before I began, ultimately I was very unsatisfied with the result of my work. *I felt* it needed to be better, express His Heart more profoundly, and leave no trace of my humanity in the process. I was convinced that I needed to start all over again.

I waited until I could not stare at an unmarked screen one more day. I was blank, getting nothing, and frustrated. All I wanted to do was please Him, yet I got caught up in performance, feeling as if my efforts weren't good enough. My dissatisfaction and demand for perfection somehow got thrown onto God. Later, I found He wasn't thinking like I was at all.

Weeks of wrestling ended sweetly, quickly, and painlessly when my Love whispered His thoughts about this book. Driving into town, talking to Him about my frustrating re-write attempts one day, He stilled my heart with His once more.

"My love, your desire to please Me, pleases Me."

The sinking weight was immediately lifted. I could have drawn stick figures as illustrations and penned a couple of simple pages of testimony, and He would be most pleased and proud of His girl.

It is not the product in which He is interested. It's the process!

My desire to please Him, pleases Him! Is there anything more wonderful?

How I love Him.

Living, moving, and having my being in the "Secret Place" are as amazing as they are "dangerous"—amazing because of the beauty of intimacy, dangerous because God beckons me leave the safety of "predictable," and follow Him. Often this means being launched way out of my comfort zone, doing and saying things I never would have dared considered.

We often pass an opportunity to be His hands and feet; we leave it for someone more "qualified" simply because of pride and prejudice. Fear of man (what will people think?) equals pride, and predisposed notions of our presumed unworthiness equals prejudice (God couldn't possibly use me). But the reality is, it's not about us. It's about Him. We need only to get ourselves out of the way … and His Spirit will do the work.

After Maui and my subsequent recovery, I walked cautiously forward when it came to public ministry. I stepped out only on the very rare occasion and frankly, with much more fear and trembling than before. I now knew the high cost and accountability involved, and to tell you the truth, I wasn't so eager to do it. I'd much rather stay right where I was, nestled ever so comfortably inside His ample arms of Love.

But what about the purpose in the pain?

"I pour Myself into your pain so that you can pour into theirs."

Ouch.

Revelation *always* requires a response. I was about to have my chance.

My heart was utterly seized with compassion the day I heard the plight of a local family. A young woman named Maggie (not her real name) had been admitted as an inpatient in the "Behavior Health" floor of the hospital for drinking toilet bowl cleaner. Maggie wasn't a candidate for something like this. Oh, no! She was a beautiful wife and mother of four lovely children. She was well respected, well loved, and never showed any signs of struggle, let alone something so ... unspeakable.

It sounded too hauntingly familiar. She had a different name, maybe a different diagnosis, but inside—it was the very same consuming pain and shame. Oh, she was me all right. When I heard, my heart was pierced through. However, after saying I would pray for her, I walked away from the situation.

Maybe I didn't want to go near it because it would be such a direct confrontation with my past. Maybe I didn't want to go near it because I would have to ruffle some feathers simply to see her. (Because her loving husband was determined to protect her well-being and her dignity, only a few trusted souls knew what had happened, where she was, and why.) Maybe I really wasn't needed. After all, there are pastors and deacons for visits like this. All of my refusals cleanly wrapped in "maybes" were torn to bits in the wake of God's request.

"Go, My love."

Even with all my trepidation, I simply could not say no.

I quickly made arrangements to meet with her husband and another close friend of theirs. We talked at length; I shared some of my story and began imparting hope. Someone on the inside of me rose up, and looking this heartbroken husband in the eye, very boldly said, "She will recover. Do you hear me? I'm not saying *maybe*, I'm not saying *if*. I am saying *she will*. You will have your wife back. Your kids will have their mother back. And you both will be forever changed by the power of God's love."

He agreed to allow me to visit, but Maggie still had the right to refuse visitors. He said I could go, but he couldn't promise me she'd even see me. I hastily packed my bags and called my sister-in-law, who lived within twenty minutes of the hospital, to arrange to stay with her.

It was one of the longest two-hour drives of my life.

What if I get all the way there and chicken out?

What if I go and she won't see me?

What if I look into her vacant, bloodshot eyes and lose it?

What if what I told her husband was not God, but my wishful thinking?

What if ...

I quietly prayed, hoping to release my fears in His presence. Yet, I was stricken. Like **raging** floodwaters, all my haunting memories **rushed** to the surface. My hands trembled and silent pain dropped one-by-one onto the steering wheel.

LET THE WIND BLOW
SHAKING THE LIMBS OF DESPAIR
LEAVES OF THE PAST FALLING AWAY
AS IF TO SAY GOODBYE

He took all my "what ifs" captive by His knowing gaze.

LET THE RIVER FLOW
LAUGHING STREAMS WASH MY SOUL
MOVING CURRANTS IN REFRAIN
UNDO THE PAIN OF LIFE'S REGRETS

Capturing my tears, He held my face and said, *"I Know."*

LET THE WIND BLOW
VIOLENTLY YOU ROAR
RELEASING SEED OF NEW TOMORROWS
FROM MANY SORROWS — LIVE

His sweeping presence filled our SUV with glory.

And then, very distinctly and in a commanding tone, which was different than I was accustomed to, He spoke again.

"Michelle, You are not going alone. You are encamped about by a mighty host of angels. Do not be afraid."

Revived with courage and sustained with strength. I was ready to *"Let The Wind Blow,"* and leave the outcome in His capable hands.

It was now approaching dusk, and I knew I'd have to try to find my way to the hospital in the dark, so I called on my cell phone to confirm directions and visiting hours. A kind young man at the behavior health desk answered and we chatted. He not only gave me directions; he stayed on the phone for ten minutes, guiding me street-by-street until I wound my way there.

Just as I was leaving home, the Lord prompted me to go back into the house and get my guitar. I hesitated because I was uncomfortable about playing in front of other people. It was something for my private worship time only. Even though my precious friend Mary had taught me well, I was still a beginner, often fumbling with my fingers to find the right chords. Yet His request was unmistakable, so I retrieved it. Now in the parking lot, I reached for my guitar, my Bible, and my purse ... and slammed the door shut.

When I reached the desk, a nurse greeted me and said she would first check with Maggie to see if she wanted to see me. Maggie agreed, so the nurse walked me through protocol, which was to remove all jewelry, belts, and personal items, and leave everything in a locker.

"Okay, I'm ready," I announced waiting for her to buzz me through the door.

"Sorry, I can't let you take that in," she said, pointing to the guitar.

"Oh, please ..." I began to plead my case when someone over her shoulder interjected.

"Hi, Michelle!" he said with a wink.

"Oh, she'll be fine. I know her. She can take the guitar in," the male nurse added.

I recognized his voice! He was the one who answered the phone and escorted me all the way to the hospital parking lot! The two of them had a brief interchange, and the female nurse walked off, exasperated, as he buzzed me through.

I walked slowly toward her numbered door, trying to disregard the stale, unpleasant smell. Patients were walking blindly around, barely seeing me through vacant stares. Yet, I knew I was not alone, and I remained undaunted.

Maggie was lying down when I walked in. She made a motion as if to get up, but was too weak to accomplish the simple task. I could quickly tell there would be very little conversation tonight. I sat next to her and held her. I gently stroked her hair and quietly began speaking life over her. She remained unresponsive, but I kept on. After a while I grabbed my guitar and began playing worship songs. I keenly recall one especially. I sang Chris Tomlin's "How Great is Our God" and as I repeated, "You're the name above all names.

You are worthy of all praise, and my heart will sing, how great is our God," Maggie sat up. Her eyes opened and she was able to focus. I kept singing, and as I did, I noticed a small crowd of patients, who had been blindly walking the halls, come near the door to listen.

I could feel His presence. I knew He was there, but what was even more precious, *they knew He was there.*

Visiting hours were over and I was ushered out, but not until I held Maggie again long and tightly as she wept on my shoulder. I assured her that I would be back tomorrow. She stood up and whispered, "Thank you."

That entire night I listened for instructions, and they were very specific. Fill a journal with all the personal words He had given me when I was incapacitated and give them to her. Sing her "I Know"—the song He wrote to me in the aftermath of Maui while in recovery. And, then, I was to go and buy the softest blanket I could find. (Those rooms leave much to be desired when it comes to comfort: plastic sheets and plastic-covered pillows.)

While at the store, picking out her gifts, I proceeded to have a very private moment in a very public place. Leaning up against the pillow aisle in bedding, He gently asked me to give something I didn't think I could. Over the years He has asked me to part with some treasured possessions, like original pieces of "Remember ME" that had never left my finger before. And I willingly did so. But this … it just seemed different, so ultra personal. I winced at His request.

*"Give her **your** pillow, My love."*

Tears fell slowly and quietly down my cheeks.

I had that pillow since I was twelve years old. It was a down feather pillow, so used and worn that the feathers were crushed to a velvety softness. I was as attached to that pillow as an adult as I had been to that black velvet cat as a child. It was irreplaceable! All the sleepless nights. All the tears I had cried into that very thing!

"That's why," He whispered. *"It has been anointed with your tears."*

I hardly recognized her when I walked in the next day. She was dressed, wide-eyed and waiting for me. I looked at her longer and harder this time … she looked familiar, like I knew her from somewhere else, but I couldn't place it. She later told me that she was at that women's retreat I spoke at a year or so prior—the very one where I shared the message of "The Secret Place." She reminded me that at the bonfire, she had approached me and asked for prayer for her brother who was losing his battle with Bi-Polar Disorder. She said the only reason she had let me in to see her was because of that retreat. She *remembered* me. Wow.

We spent a lot of time sharing. I found myself prophesying hope over her. Then I encouraged her to talk to me. She cried as she tried to get out bits and pieces of her pain in broken sentences. I just listened and held her. Later I gave her the gifts (which were again, amazingly approved by my special boy "friend" at the front desk), and I told her *Who* they were from, how much she was loved, and assured her that she would be fine again.

I then got out my guitar and sang "I Know." I'm not sure which one of us was more moved, because even though the words were unmistakably resounding from my own lips, His heart was piercing mine so completely. I didn't think it was possible to fall more in love; I was proved wrong once again.

VERSE 1
I KNOW YOUR NAME
I KNOW YOUR FEARS
I DIVE INTO YOUR SOUL
WHEN CAPTURING ALL YOUR TEARS
I HEAR YOUR CRIES
I TASTE YOUR PAIN
MY RENT HEART TEARS THE SKIES
MY TEARS FALL IN THE RAIN

CHORUS
WHEN THERE ARE NO WORDS LEFT TO SAY
AND THE PAIN WON'T GO AWAY
AND YOU'RE FEELING LIKE YOU CAN'T GO ON
I KNOW
WHEN THERE ARE NO TEARS LEFT TO CRY
ONLY ENDLESS QUESTIONS WHY
AND YOU FEEL LIKE YOU CAN'T TRY NO MORE
I KNOW—OOOOH—I KNOW

VERSE 2
I KNOW YOUR EYES
I SEE YOUR HEART
I PUT YOU BACK TOGETHER
WHEN THE PIECES FELL APART
I UNDERSTAND, I WEAR YOUR SHOES
YET I KNOW YOU'RE HANGING ON
THAT YOU MIGHT HEAR GOOD NEWS

Chorus 2
Tomorrow's gonna come
Your race is almost won
This battle overcome
I Know
It's nearly over now
So don't throw in the towel
Just hold me tighter now
I Know—ooooh—I Know

By our third day, I knew it was going to be my last. And
with her rapid improvement I sensed she wasn't very many
days behind me. I was privileged to witness a powerful
transformation in only three days. And since then Maggie has
made a joyous and complete recovery!

How I love Him.

Those three days marked my life in a profound way.
Through that experience, I knew He had brought me full
circle. I knew that I was no longer lying in wait for the next
episode to shatter my world. I knew I was no longer captive to
the chains of my past. I knew in the deepest part of my heart
… I am free.

"I Am Free"

those old chains that used to bind me
they fell off, now they remind me
i am free
those old habits, ways, and deeds
no longer have a hold on me
i am free
those old feelings fear and shame
have lost their home i'm not the same
i am free

Tonight I'll rest my head on the pillow of another. My precious sister Maria later mailed me a priceless gift when she found out about my pillow's new owner. She responded to His nudge and released her own very prized pillow she had slept with religiously for over thirty years, *anointed with her tears.*

On her pillow I dream of the day my sister will run again (she's been diagnosed with an inoperable spinal cord tumor), picturing her waist-long hair blowing in the wind. On her pillow I dream of the many thousands of harvested wheat grains, representing lost and wounded souls who have found their way into God's loving arms through "Remember ME." And on her pillow I dream of the day I will once again walk those sandy shores of Maui.

With clear eyes and a full heart I'll watch as the horror of the past forever melts into the receding waters, drifting far into the deep of the ocean floor. I'll run in the waves and bask in the sun as I lift up my eyes to behold the beautiful artistry of the changing sky. Dark clouds may threaten, salty rain may pour down my face, yet hand-in-hand with the One I love, I'll rest within the safety of His care. The fullness of living in love; *It's All In The Knowing ...*

How He loves me.

The sky is always blue.

CHAPTER 23

"Believe"

do not doubt, extend your hand
touch My own, you'll understand
I've been here, lovingly real
despite the questions that you feel
like a child, Trust in Me
to lead and guide continually
I'll never go, I'll never leave
all you need is to "Believe"

I KNOW YOU'RE THINKING, "There's *more*? What's this? I thought the book was over!"

You're right, *my* part is.

This chapter is *all about you.*

Remember, *revelation always requires a response.* And now it's your turn to respond.

There are no "accidents" or "coincidences" with God. This book came into your hands by divine providence. You were either given this book by a loved one or He drew you to it. Either way, He knew it beforehand and ordained it from the beginning of time as a means to reveal Himself personally to *you.*

From cover-to-cover, you have witnessed His power, mercy, and grace. Every chapter unfolded another mystery of His immutable character, confirming the unbelievable.

The sky *is* always blue.

You have heard God's voice of love beckon me, pursue me, and ultimately capture my heart. But haven't you also heard His voice of love beckon and pursue you? The question remains, will you let Him capture *your* heart?

Whatever doubts and fears have kept you from fully embracing a real love-relationship with God—they fall like lightning from the sky next to the weight of His Love.

Don't put the book down and walk away.

Don't rush yourself right out of the most crucial decision of your life ... and death.

Don't be afraid. Only believe.

Jesus is God's very manifestation of His love for you.

He made a way for you to have unhindered, 24/7 access to Him.

He loves you deeply.

He longs for you passionately.

How do you respond to such Love?

With all your heart.

Simply acknowledge your need for Him. (We all have a need for a Savior—no one is exempt. Judgment for sin must fall. It will either fall on you or on Jesus Christ).

Open up your heart to God and receive His amazing gift of Grace. His Grace covers the ugly sin of your past, enables you to give Him the fears of your present, and grants you the glorious hope of your future—in this life and the one to come.

Ask Him to be the very center of your life. Ask Him to cover all your failures and sins by His blood. Ask Him to be your "Everything."

In return He'll give you the blessed assurance of your salvation by the indwelling of His Spirit. His Holy Spirit will lead and guide you in all Truth as you begin your never-ending journey with God.

You're Washed.

Forgiven.

Made New.

Eternally His.

i never found, i never knew

forgiveness until i met You

You took this wretched, dirty, mess

and clothed me in Your Righteousness

now i'm clean, just as though

i've always been as white as snow

Epilogue

YOU HAVE BORNE MY HEARTACHE right along with me as you read these pages, and I bless you for it. I pray that you heard His voice of encouragement cheer you to *"Overcome"*—that in whatever fierce storm you face, you sensed His anchoring Presence as "Everything" you need. And most of all, I pray that you felt His divine comfort as He leaned tenderly toward you to hold your face and say, "I Know."

You have seen what God has done with my nothingness … just imagine what your destiny holds! There is absolutely *nothing* impossible for you! Dare to believe!

I want you to know that it truly is well with my soul. As for my marriage, because I'm anchored, fully secure in my love-relationship with God, I am better equipped to weather the storms that come with imperfect love.

My children … ah, the constant delight of my heart! Joshua, still the perfect angel he has always been. Kaylin, by far, gets most improved honors! She has surpassed my every expectation to become a lovely young woman after God's own heart. Elianna is my tenderhearted, cute-faced cherub. Isabella is my adorable princess. (She seems to possess some of Kaylin's genes, but let's just save that bit of fun for Zazoo Pits.) Gabriel is my irresistible darling. I remember the days I wondered how I would survive motherhood. Now I wonder how I could have survived at all without them.

How I love *them*.

This is the end of this book, but only the beginning of the story as His plans and purposes gently unfold through our daily union. If "Remember ME" has forged a special place in your heart, stay tuned for more: individual books based on each one of the symbols and ring writings perfect for devotionals or group study, and a book on becoming one flesh have already begun. As He leads, I still make myself available for public speaking.

Zazoo Pits continues to write about the chaos of managing a marriage, five children, two pets, and a business. Laughter is so much better than tears! Log on to receive your prescription dose of hilarious encouragement and to read my daily blogs at www.myspace.com/theskyisalwaysbluealways.

Remain in His Love.

It's all in the knowing ... how He loves y-o-u.

All my love,
m. meade

www.remembermejewelry.com.
www.michellemeade.net

Recommended Resources – Take and Eat!

Blue Genes
> From Tyndale House Publishers, breaking free from the chemical imbalances that affect your moods, your mind, your life, and your loved ones.
> Paul Meier, MD; Todd Clements, MD, Jean-Luc Bertrand, DMD; and David Mandt, Sr., MA

NAMI - National Alliance of Mental Illness
> www.nami.org

United States Department of Health and Human Services
> Substance Abuse and Mental Health Services Administration
> www.mentalhealth.samhsa.gov

God Calling
> The power of love and joy that restores faith and serenity in our troubled world.
> A.J. Russell, ed.

Come Away My Beloved
> The intimate devotional classic.
> Frances J. Roberts

Word-By-Mail
> Verse-by-verse teachings.
> Pastor Dave Shepardson
> www.calvarynuevo.org

(I feel completely undernourished if I don't get the opportunity to listen to one of Pastor Dave's teaching CDs every morning. Take advantage of this amazing resource.)

GOD TV (Check your local cable and satellite provider. It's a must-have!)
TVO the live conferences and the daily devotionals from Mike Bickle's IHOP (International House of Prayer).

Hinds' Feet on High Places
An allegory dramatizing the journey each of us must take before we can live in "high places."
Hannah Hurnard

Battlefield of the Mind
Winning the Battle in Your Mind.
Joyce Meyer

Breaking Free
Making Liberty In Christ A Reality in Life
Beth Moore

LaVergne, TN USA
18 February 2011
216975LV00001B/4/P